TWO CERAMIC HORSES
ON A CRACKED BASE

TWO CERAMIC HORSES

ON A CRACKED BASE

A Treasury of Family Milestones

HENRY MICHAEL STRAGE

ISBN 978-0-9856595-9-2
LCCN 2014904448

To my wife, Alberta,
and our children, David, Geoffrey, Susan, and Jennifer,
and our eleven grandchildren,
Sonya, Katya, Michele, Eva, Juliette, Miranda, Maksim,
Allegra, Aleksander, Taylor, and Spencer,
and their children, who someday might want to know
how their ancestors lived.

CONTENTS

RAISON D'ETRE

The world is made up of two types of people—the Savers and the Throw-Awayers. I am a severely addicted Saver. This obsession initially prompted me to assemble my memories into a series of snapshots, or vignettes, rather than the more conventional approach of producing a long sequential recitation of events in one's life. In topless shoeboxes, ancient file folders, yellowing photo albums and old derelict suitcases, and, in fact, in any other available storage container from all over our Addison Road home, I found an extraordinary treasure trove of family memorabilia—letters, photos, travel documents, passports, and much more. Most people would call it simply "junk."

I never bothered or found enough time to organize these papers, photographs, newspaper clippings, letters, and souvenirs into anything remotely resembling some logically classified order, either by dates, locations, individuals, or specific events. I also never hired a professional archivist to make order out of the mayhem. Additionally, there was unlikely to be any material of great historic significance or interest to anyone except our immediate family and friends.

In one of my all-too-frequent and totally unsuccessful campaigns to tidy up, I collected a few items and decided to compose a short explanation of how and why those particular pictures, letters, and media clippings played a unique role in my life or the life of the family. The physical process of actually

Disorganized mess or priceless family archive?

writing my recollections based on those items brought back many forgotten memories that had probably been stored deep in my subconscious. It never occurred to me to put my various ramblings into any order or even attempt to develop some common theme or approach to these unstructured meanderings through papers and photographs, which I whimsically labeled, simply, "Archives."

As I was collecting and writing these mini-sagas, I decided to share some of them with my family and a few close friends. They in turn passed them to their friends and acquaintances who, they thought, might find them of interest, sometimes because they were connected to the events described. To my surprise, family and friends were fascinated and asked me to continue writing. Perhaps they were being polite or wanted to humor me. In those episodes in which they had been involved , however, or thought they had profound insights, they were not shy to comment, correct, edit, or even rewrite my recollections. And as the list of interested parties grew, so did my reflections. I was amazed at how many people wrote back thanking me for jogging their own memory banks of adventures which, while not identical to my own, were reasonably similar.

Alberta enthusiastically urged me to collate all of my short stories and make them into something more permanent than my desktop computer was capable of. Essentially, this was going to be an enduring record of family milestones, together with my feelings in connection with them. A great deal has been left out or mentioned in passing. And some is still hidden, waiting to be unlocked, in the deep recesses of my memory.

Perhaps there will be a second volume. In the meantime, at least some of the family stories, folklore, and myths will be available to future generations who might ask, "What were Baba and Pampa really like?"

All of the material and anecdotes in this volume are, to the best of my recollection, based on real events in real situations involving real people. Where I have not been directly involved, by an accident of birth or other excusable absence, I have done my best to be as accurate as possible. However, I have taken the liberty in certain stories to add dialogue without the benefit of actually having been present to hear the words spoken. In these situations, I have tried to recreate conversation based on my knowledge of the people involved, and my knowledge of how they might have reacted and what they might have chosen to say. While I was fortunate to have a rich cornucopia of original family documentation in the form of photos and personal papers, I found it necessary to fall back on Internet sources for some supporting evidence about dates and specific locations.

Despite an extensive amount of information in these pages, I recognize that there are many gaps. Ideally, it would have been invaluable to have interviewed even a few of the original and supporting players who are no longer with us. We are all "too late smart." Also, there is conflicting information about some events and dates. While it is said that photographs do not lie, in fact they sometimes effectively mask the truth. Interestingly, my own children, relatives, and friends sometimes disagree about details of events in which they were personally involved. Our ancestors were as forgetful as we are today when it comes to documenting dates, people, and locations on photographs. Fortunately digital photography is able to preserve actual dates and locations with amazing accuracy.

Will there be a Volume Two? Perhaps. Hopefully, its gestation period will be shorter than its predecessor's.

Alberta is threatening to write her own version of our life together and memories of our children's and grandchildren's lives. The race is on!

WHAT'S IN A NAME?

If there were such a thing as a Strage family heraldic crest or shield, it would certainly incorporate an image of two crackle-glazed ceramic horses. I cannot with any certainty provide details of how, or even when, these horses became part of our family history. However, they appear in photographs of our apartment in Brussels and I clearly remember them sitting on our mantelpiece in Cleveland, as well as in our apartment in New York City in front of the large mirror above the pseudo-fireplace.

At some point after we were married and living in New York City, my mother decided Alberta and I should have the horses. In our Riverside Drive apartment they sat in a prominent place on one of our book shelves. I think it was then that I first noticed the cracked base. Their next home was in London, in our first flat, on Cheyne Walk. Finally, after several stops in other temporary lodgings we lived in, they arrived at their present permanent location in Addison Road.

The glazing on the horses is characteristic of common Chinese pottery and so one might assume that they were bought in Manchuria. Of course, there are no markings to confirm this. In fact, the horses are the work of a famous Spanish artist, Isaac Diaz Pardo, whose name appears on the base. I believe the horses were most likely bought by my father in Belgium. When did the base break? Who repaired it? I can remember repairing the broken base once several years ago. By then, it seemed to me that there had already been several attempts to restore the base, but I cannot recall who was responsible for any of the earlier efforts. They certainly were not done professionally.

One of the horses is always looking far ahead, seeking new adventures, looking for new challenges and preparing the path for those that will follow. The other horse is staring at the road immediately ahead. He seems more concerned with the present, ensuring that the path is clear of obstacles, focusing on investigating the opportunities around him and savoring the environment in which he is moving.

The restored cracks suggest that life has not always been without pitfalls, disappointments, and unforeseen tragedies. And one such devastating event in particular Alberta and I think of every day of our lives.

WHO'S WHO

Many of my relatives have more than one name, such as a birth name, a nickname, and a name after immigration. To make it easier to figure out who is who, here is a list of them.

In the Strascheffky family
Laser = Leo
Lyubov = Luba
Mariana = Mara
Mark = Marcus
Michel = Misha = Michael Strage
Nissan = Nison
Schmuel = Salmen = Samuel
Voldemar = Wulf

In the Halperin family
Gita = Gitel

In the Dinaburg family
Anna = Anya
Batsheeva = Faigie
Benjamin = Benny
Ephraim = Fima
Genry = Riri= Henri = Hank = Henry
Gitel = Gita
Israel = Isa = Jack
Michel = Michael
Michele = Misha
Sophia = Sonya = Sophie
Tatiana = Tanya

THE STRASCHEFFSKY, FREUDENFIELD, BREWNER, HALPERIN FAMILIES

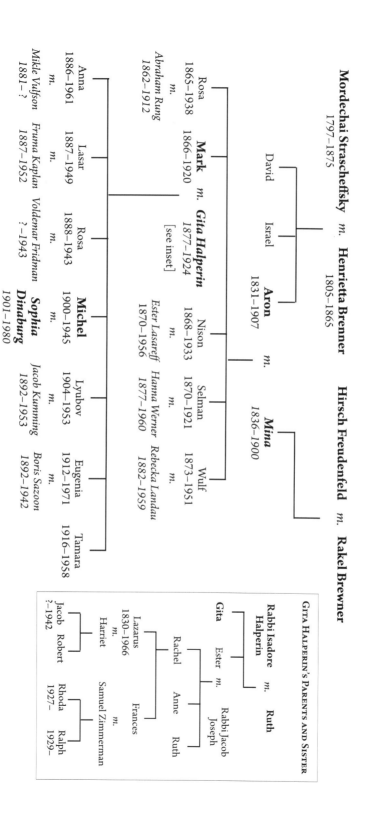

The Dinaburg Family

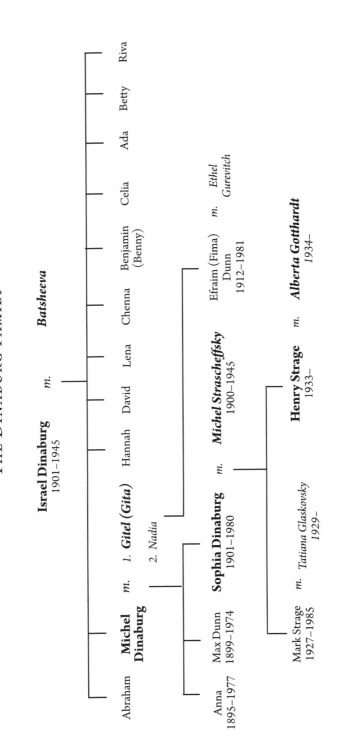

THE DESCENDANTS OF MICHEL STRASCHEFFSKY AND SOPHIA DINABURG

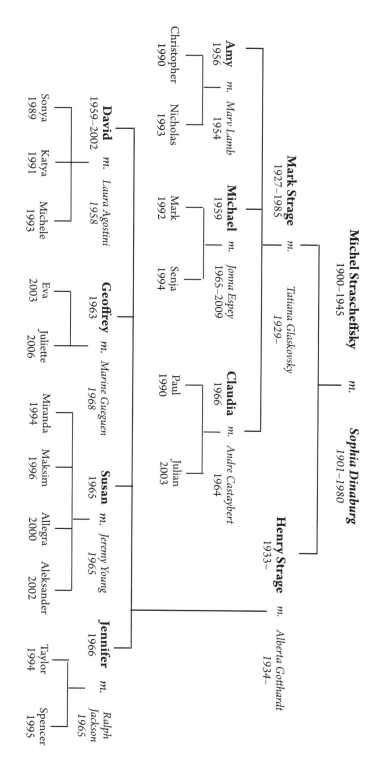

Michel Strascheffsky
1900–1945

m.

Sophia Dinaburg
1901–1980

Mark Strage
1927–1985

m.

Tatiana Glaskovsky
1929–

Henry Strage
1933–

m.

Alberta Gotthardt
1934–

Amy
1956

m. *Marv Lamb*
1954

Christopher
1990

Nicholas
1993

Michael
1959

m. *Jonna Espey*
1965–2009

Mark
1992

Senja
1994

Claudia
1966

m. *Andre Castaybert*
1964

Paul
1990

Julian
2003

David
1959–2002

m. *Laura Agostini*
1958

Sonya
1989

Katya
1991

Michele
1993

Geoffrey
1963

m. *Marine Gueguen*
1968

Eva
2003

Juliette
2006

Susan
1965

m. *Jeremy Young*
1965

Miranda
1994

Maksim
1996

Allegra
2000

Aleksander
2002

Jennifer
1966

m. *Ralph Jackson*
1965

Taylor
1994

Spencer
1995

TWO CERAMIC HORSES
ON A CRACKED BASE

PART I
ROOTS

Family visit in July 2009 to my grandfather Mark Strascheffsky's gravesite in St. Petersburg, Russia. My grandmother's and grand-uncle's graves were nearby. Front row: Henry, Leggy, Eva, Geoffrey. Second row: Sonya, Katya, Juliette, Misha, Lexi. Third row: Spencer, Taylor, Max.

Introduction
Putting the Pieces Together

Trying to trace one's Russian-Chinese roots is both incredibly rewarding and desperately frustrating. It is rewarding because as I began to find documents and verify information about my ancestors, what seemed at first to be vaguely related pieces of information, data and photos began gradually to fall into place and make sense. Slowly the complex puzzle that is my family history took shape. Pictures came into better focus and questions began to get answered. Frustration arises when you realize that information you would dearly like to have was never documented or over time has vanished.

Both the maternal and paternal sides of my family lived, as did most Russian Jews during the nineteenth century, in the vast Pale of Settlement. In fact, my two families in this narrative, the Dinaburgs and the Strascheffskys, who surely did not know each other, lived barely six hundred kilometers apart, Father's family in the Ukraine and Mother's in Belarus.

The saga of my great-grandfather Aron Strascheffsky's career in the Imperial Russian Army from the time he was abducted when he was eight years old is surprisingly well documented. Similarly well documented are the details of the various rabbis who seem to be liberally sprinkled throughout my paternal family tree. The emigration to the United States of Mother's uncles and aunts from China is available in well-maintained American records, including census data, burial records, and ships' manifests. Nevertheless, the family mosaic is far from complete and there is still much to be discovered. I leave this to my children and grandchildren.

1

The Eight-Year-Old Soldier

When he was eight years old, my great-grandfather Aron Strascheffsky was kidnapped and forced into the Russian army. In 1839, he and several other youngsters from Vinnitsya, Podolia, in the Ukraine, were forcibly separated from their families and sent to a Cantonist army school thousands of miles away from home. Aron never saw his father, Mordechai Strascheffsky, or any other members of his family again.

The Cantonist system had been originated by Tsar Peter the Great in the eighteenth century, but was not rigorously enforced until the reign of Tsar Nicholas I in the nineteenth century. For Tsar Nicholas, it was a means to increase the size of his army and at the same time coerce young Jewish boys into denouncing their religion, being baptized, and becoming active members of the Russian Orthodox church. In 1827 he introduced compulsory military service for a period of a minimum of twenty-five years after the recruit reached age eighteen. By the time these men were released— at age forty-three if they had not died from disease, malnourishment, and other harsh conditions, and had not been killed in war—they had certainly forgotten their families and early upbringing as Jews. Every region of Russia was assigned a quota for military conscripts. For every thousand Jews, ten males had to be recruited into the tsar's army annually; for every thousand non-Jews, only seven had to be recruited over the course of two years. Communities that could not reach their quota were harshly penalized with burdensome taxes, and more recruits were required than their original quota stipulated.

The severe, often brutal military conditions and the prospect of their boys being cut off from them until middle age meant that families did everything they could to avoid the conscription of their eligible sons. The tsar made local leaders, known as "kahals," personally responsible for meeting the community's quota. To avoid punishment for failing to meet it, the kahals in turn appointed and paid "khappers" to seize and abduct children who were twelve years of age or younger in order to reach the quota. Most, but not all of the khappers were local Christian peasants. Unfortunately, the easiest way to fill the quota was to kidnap children from the poorest homes with the largest families, where presumably they would be less missed. The khappers were paid a fee for each child and were not particularly careful to adhere to the minimum age requirement—children as young as eight were regularly pressed into the Imperial Russian Army. Although the Cantonist legislation only lasted twenty-nine years and the data is incomplete, it is known that at least 50,000 Jewish boys were forcibly conscripted during this period.

Aron was one of them, kidnapped and conscripted into the Russian army at age eight. The youngest of eight children of Mordechai David Stracheffsky, a poor subsistence farmer, Aron would have been an obvious candidate for the khappers. Like all Jewish boys in Vinnitsya, he began school when he was three years old, probably attending a typical cheder, with four or five students who met with a melamed, or tutor, in a local home. Each student's parents would contribute to the melamed's wages, which were usually so small that most of them had to have a second source of income.

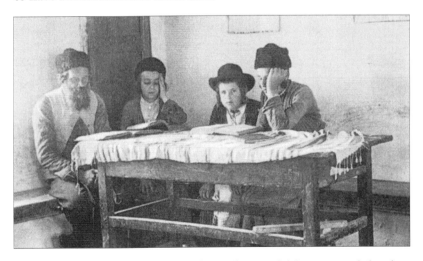

Children would often spend a whole day studying and debating a single line from the Bible with their teacher.

Aron Strascheffsky, far right, with some of his fellow commandos who, after serving twenty-five years in the tsar's army, chose to settle in Helsinki.

At home and with friends, Aron's family spoke Yiddish. Although he spoke Russian, Aron did not learn to read and write fluently in Russian until he was over forty years old. His education began with learning the Hebrew alphabet. At the age of five, he began to study the Five Books of Moses, known as the Torah. By the time he was seven, he had begun to learn the Mishnah, oral teachings that had been organized and written down, and was introduced to the Talmudic commentaries in the Mishnah. The usual form of learning consisted of students reading out loud to each other, memorizing the most important passages as designated by the melamed, and engaging in detailed discussion and debate in Yiddish about the meaning and possible interpretations of every line being studied, permanently embedding the text into the young students' minds. Aron's Jewish education came to an abrupt end in 1839, the year he was abducted and sent to live in a government-sponsored Cantonist school thousands of miles from his home. There, conscripts' tzitzit, tefillin, and prayer shawls were forcibly confiscated and names were changed to Russian names. So Aron became Ioron, a common Russian name, until he was finally able to leave the army thirty-two years later, in 1871.

There are only a few written accounts of life in the Cantonist system. *The Cantonists: The Jewish Children's Army of the Tsar* by Larry Domnitch provides a chilling snapshot of one aspect of the life of a recruit named Itzkovitch:

> ... From Petersburg, Itzkovitch and his detachment were forcibly marched to the distant Siberian city of Archangelsk. The march lasted from March 1853 to June 1854. En route, the children were beaten and harassed, and so many perished that the road was littered with their corpses. Finally, the surviving children reached the "Promised Land," Archangelsk, and were taken to a building shared by other Cantonist children. For Itzkovitch and his unit, day-to-day life was one of extreme hardship full of suffering and torture. The children were beaten daily and pressured to convert to Christianity and be baptized. Even after Itzkovitch contracted an eye disease, a non-commissioned officer beat him with his fists.

When he was eighteen, Ioron was officially designated a commando in the tsar's army and was stationed on the Finnish island of Sveaborg, just outside the city of Helsinki, which had a stone-walled defense fortress called Suomenlinna. The fortress still stands today and has become a popular tourist attraction.

Jewish soldiers who had served their twenty-five years in the tsar's army were given the right to settle anywhere in the Russian empire. However, in the Grand Duchy of Finland, which was part of the empire, they were given a special citizen classification that made their lives exceptionally difficult. The only trade they were allowed to practice was the sale of second-hand clothing, and they could not without permission travel to other parts of the country. Nevertheless, Aron, like many other former Russian soldiers who had been stationed in the Grand Duchy, decided to stay and settle in Helsinki, fearing that returning to his place of birth would almost certainly be challenging and probably far less attractive.

On September 22, 1865, at the age of thirty-four, Aron formally registered himself as a member of the Jewish community in Helsinki. How was it that after twenty-five years of being almost totally isolated from any facet of Jewish culture or religion, Aron decided to return enthusiastically to the religion of his parents?

In the 1840s, Russian Jewish conscripts, referred to as "Nicolai's soldiers" by historians, established the first stiebel, a small prayer room for conducting services, in Finland. Given the prevailing attitudes towards Jews, these prayer rooms were clandestine and typically without the benefit of proper texts or even a sefer Torah.

Ioron was probably pleasantly surprised when he arrived for active duty in Sveaborg, at the age of eighteen, to find a functioning prayer room. Despite the tsar's strident efforts to convert systematically the Jewish soldiers to the Russian Orthodox Church, it is astonishing that the influence of early religious training had made a deeply embedded impression on many of them that lasted even after so many years. Although the soldiers came from different parts of Russia, they shared a common military experience and a bond of friendship that they maintained even after their release.

Once he "left" the army, although officially he was still in it, Aron took the only occupation permitted to Jews, applying in 1870 for a license to operate a second-hand clothing stall at Number 14 in Narinkka market, the central market in Helsinki. Later, he began to import clothing from St. Petersburg that the authorities designated as second-hand and thus within trading regulations for Jewish merchants. On March 29, 1889, he was finally granted permission to stay in Helsinki, based upon his active service in the Russian Imperial Army.

Narinkka market in 1870. Today it is one of the largest shopping malls in Helsinki.

The majority of the small Jewish population in Helsinki, fewer than one thousand, were former Russian soldiers, and Aron was made to feel most welcome. Without a formal place of worship, the community met and prayed in private homes and managed to operate an amazing array of Jewish communal services involving issues of health, welfare, education, and even the provision of kosher food. Jewish holidays were celebrated, Jewish marriages were performed, and a Jewish cemetery was built.

The Chevra Kadisha, created in 1864 to prepare the deceased for burial, was the oldest of the community's organizations. Another, the Bikur Cholim, helped members of the community who were sick, poor, homeless, isolated, or in need of assistance in some other way. About half of the total male Jewish population in Helsinki was actively involved in Jewish community groups.

The Bikur Cholim. Two of Aron's sons were active members. Third row, extreme right, is Schmuel, and in the same row, four beyond, is Nissan.

Aron's impetus to register formally with the Jewish community in 1865 was motivated by his decision to marry Mina Freudenfeldt, who was from Tikums, a town in Latvia, near Riga. Mina was twenty-nine years old when they met and married. How did the two find each other?

In established Jewish neighborhoods, arranged marriages were common practice, a tradition still practiced today in many religious communities around the world. Although it is possible that one of Aron's army friends wrote to his family seeking to make a match for Aron, a more likely approach for a soldier like Aron who wanted to marry and raise a family was what later came to be known as a "mail-order bride." Carriages transported eligible young women from relatively nearby Jewish communities, mainly in Latvia and Lithuania, to Finland. This practice gave rise to the expression, "She was not taken down from the carriage," referring to women who were strictly local women, not mail-order brides.

Aron soon realized that his knowledge of the responsibilities of the head of a Jewish family was extremely limited. In 1868 (while he was still effectively in the army), he took the highly risky step of enlisting the help of a local rabbi and teacher to learn as much as he could about Jewish religious practices and customs. He was anxious to make up for the many years he had been forced to live a non-Jewish life.

I always felt I had a special relationship with Aron because I have the honor and privilege of sharing his name. Aron is my Hebrew name.

A local army veterans group helped soldiers return to normal civilian life.

2

Mighty Oaks from Little Acorns Grow

Aron and Mina's first child, Rosa, was born in Helsinki on 14 February 1865. In America, the Civil War was about to reach a conclusion as General George Sherman began his triumphant march towards Atlanta, Georgia.

The couple had four more children in the next eight years. My grandfather Marcus Strascheffsky, their second child, was born on 25 November 1866. Nison, Selman, and Wulf followed in the next five years. The Strascheffsky family turned out to be very prolific, and by 1910 there were thirty-two grandchildren, all living in Helsinki. As in most emerging Jewish communities, providing the highest quality of education was always a top priority, and the Jewish School Council took its responsibility most seriously.

Aron maintained his stall in the market until 12 June 1896, when he retired at the age of sixty-six and passed the responsibilities for operating his business to his oldest son, Marcus, my grandfather. By that time, the business had grown to the point where it had opened a store in St. Petersburg; Strascheffskys was to become a busy and popular shop for a broad range of linens, woolen goods, and fashionable clothing.

After Marcus married Gita Halperin in 1887 and the St. Petersburg store began to grow and prosper, he decided to move to St. Petersburg. Their family grew quickly and by 1916 they had seven children. My father, Michel, was the fourth child, born on 14 May 1900. Jewish families, while allowed under special circumstances to live in St. Petersburg, were forbidden legally to give birth to children there. So for "administrative reasons," my father's official birthplace was Terjoki, a seaside resort in Finland less than fifty-five kilometers from St. Petersburg.

Marcus, Gita, and their seven children lived in two connecting apartments in St. Petersburg, not far from the store. Private tutors were engaged to augment their children's education. All of the children were expected to learn German, which in my father's case was very useful, as German was a prerequisite for admission to an engineering university. Not as successful as German was the decision to teach the children Hebrew. My first cousin Mara (Mariana) Bykhovskaya recalls clearly

My paternal grandfather, Marcus, 1866–1920

that whenever the Hebrew tutor would arrive, there was a sudden epidemic of stomach ailments. In addition to foreign languages, musical education was a prerequisite. In fact, each apartment had its own piano. At least one of the children, Uncle Laser, was a serious student and later became a recognized professional pianist.

As a youngster, my father was fairly adventurous and would wander off on his own to explore his neighborhood. On one occasion when he was six or seven, he could not find his way home. He bravely hailed a passing horse-drawn taxi and with great confidence asked to be driven to his father's store, Strascheffskys. When asked by the coachman if he had enough money to pay for the transport, Father confidently announced, "When we arrive at the store, you will be well taken care of!"

My grandfather's older sister, Aunt Rosa, was born in 1888 in St. Petersburg and married Wulf (not to be confused with her brother Wulf), also known as Voldemar Fridman. A textile merchant in Poland, he provided Marcus with a supply of textiles for the shop. Rosa and Wulf lived in Poland and had two children, Aida and Mark Fridman. In 1943, the whole family was transported by the Nazis to Auschwitz-Birkenau and exterminated.

Lubov Markovna was my father's younger sister. For most of her life she lived in Leningrad, where she had a distinguished career as a teacher of foreign languages, eventually becoming the director general of the foreign language department in the city's Ministry of Education. She introduced her own unique method of teaching foreign languages, which she later tried out on me (with, frankly, marginal success).

Luba's husband, Jacob Kumming, was a well-known portrait artist. (When we visited Luba later in Detroit, Michigan, his portrait of her was a centerpiece in the living room.) Unfortunately, Jacob was not only Jewish but had all the necessary credentials to be described by the Russian government as "a useless intellectual leech." For him, it was not jail, torture, or execution, but deportation to Tashkent, which became a favorite place to send those who were either permanently disabled or had no productive role in the order of useful citizens in Stalin's new Russia. It has been estimated that Stalin was directly responsible for the deaths of thirty million of his own citizens.

Luba was able to write to Jacob, but never saw him again. Without warning, his letters stopped coming and her letters were returned. She was never able to trace what happened to him or learn where his remains might be interred.

Another victim of Stalin's brutal, inhuman regime was Luba's brother, my Uncle Laser Strascheffsky, an accomplished concert pianist and highly respected professor of piano master classes. Unfortunately, he, too, fit perfectly into Stalin's definition of a useless intellectual, being a professional musician and Jewish. Unwilling to give up his musical career and get a real job as defined by the regime, he was arrested while returning from a performing engagement in Pinsk, and faced what surely were trumped-up charges of corruption and smuggling. When he refused to recant or confess, and insisted on pleading his innocence, he was sent to Lubyanka prison to rethink his crime and confess. Months later, he was able to return to his family in Leningrad. But he never played the piano again. His captors had made certain that at least he would never play the piano again. They had systematically broken all of the fingers in both of his hands.

In the mid-1970s, during one of the infrequent lulls in the Cold War, emigration restrictions were briefly relaxed, and Aunt Luba, along with her son Sam, his wife, and their two children, came to America. Sadly, Sam became ill shortly after they arrived and passed away. Because her son was employed in a top security branch of the Soviet defense industry, Aunt Luba had been forbidden to communicate with my father or any member of the family in the United States. Thus, her arrival with her immediate family came as a surprise. No one had heard from her for about twenty years.

In 1978, Aunt Luba was the guest of honor at our daughter Jennifer's bat mitzvah celebration in London, and she captivated the audience with a memorable speech that began in Russian, which I was obliged to translate. I must have translated for three or four minutes when Aunt Luba interrupted my painful and obviously inadequate translation, and in English, with only a slight hint of a Russian accent, announced to a cheering audience, "That is not, my darling Genri, what I said," and completed her remarks in near-perfect English.

When she settled in a suburb of Detroit, she was disappointed to learn that although there was a small Russian community, there were no Russian cultural activities, and Russian children were growing up without Chekhov, Gogol, Marshak, Gorky, or Turgenev. She decided to remedy the situation. At this stage in her life, while not a young woman but with massive energy and passion, she created the first Russian Children's Theatre Company in Detroit, and was able to produce several plays per year, as well as numerous poetry- and prose-reading events. In her spare time, well into her eighties, she began to translate Russian texts into Yiddish, which she told me she regarded as the language of her ancestors.

Luba died in Detroit in 1992, when she was eighty-seven years old.

Whenever I met Luba, I took the opportunity to collect and document as many details of our family history as possible. My talks with her were long, detailed, and extraordinarily depressing insofar as the family history was concerned. I learned all about her and my

Aunt Luba, standing at left, *at her Russian children's drama school.*

other aunts and uncles, with the exception of the last sibling, Tamara. Luba uncharacteristically refused to talk about Tamara at first, but I persuaded her that I wanted to know about the whole family and about Tamara and her life. No one in the family had ever mentioned her name to me before.

By Luba's account, Tamara was not only the youngest of the siblings but very popular, beautiful, and independent, a bit wild. Sometime in the 1930s, she had an affair with a Cossack, a term Luba used carefully. Cossacks, who were not seen as part of the normal military forces, were generally regarded to be anti-Semitic and a law unto themselves. In fact, during World War II, some Cossack forces served with the Germans.

The romance with this Cossack, let us call him "Igor," met with considerable disapproval and resentment by the family. Before they had a chance to get married, Tamara had a child and Igor disappeared into the bowels of the Cossack army; he spent the rest of the World War II years somewhere on the western front. Miraculously, Tamara and her child survived Germany's deadly three-year siege of Leningrad.

When the war was over, Igor reappeared, wounded but apparently anxious to see Tamara and their son. From here on, the story becomes more legendary than factual because none of the family members who survived the war stayed in touch with Tamara. Apparently, however, they did get married and had two more children. It is likely that the children, who would be my first cousins, are still living in Russia, perhaps in St. Petersburg. It is unlikely that we will ever be able to trace them.

Meanwhile, Aron died on April 15, 1907. His great-great-grandson Geoffrey Ian Strage was born on the same day fifty-six years later.

The official school photograph of the first Jewish School Council in Helsinki was taken in 1895. Aron sits in the first row, seven in from the left.

3

A Gaggle of Rabbis in the Family

During one of my family history tutorials with Aunt Luba, she told me that I should not be surprised, when piecing together the family history, to find an amazing number of rabbis throughout our family tree.

RABBI JACOB JOSEPH, MY GRAND-UNCLE

Perhaps the best known and most important was my grand-uncle Rabbi Jacob Joseph. He was married to Ester, my grandmother Gita's sister.

When the great Jewish migration from Eastern Europe to the

United States in the 1880s gathered momentum, more than two hundred major new congregations were established in the country. Less than twenty of these were Orthodox. The vast majority, a virtual monopoly, were those organized by the Reform movement, which had been brought to America primarily by German-Jewish immigrants.

Within the Orthodox congregations, factionalism, petty jealousies, and differing interpretations of Jewish laws and rituals led to bitter arguments and schisms. The problems were exacerbated not only by the shortage of qualified rabbis but by a fundamental change from the traditional jurisdictional role assumed by rabbis in the Old World to the system established in America, where virtually all matters related to the law, such as marriage, divorce, inheritance, and adoption, were strictly reserved for the state. Affairs came to a head in New York City, specifically over the laws of kashrut, the dietary code.

In 1886 the situation had deteriorated so badly that a special association was created to import a rabbi from Europe who would be given the title of "Chief Rabbi" and who would be responsible for rulings on all matters of rituals and belief, and this, it was thought, would bring order to the warring congregations. Two years later, in 1888, the search committee identified and invited Rabbi Jacob Joseph to take up the newly established post. A highly respected rabbinic scholar from Kovno, Lithuania, Rabbi Joseph was, at the time of his appointment, the maggid, or popular "preacher" of the great Jewish community of Vilna. The decision to appoint him chief rabbi was not met in America with universal approval and, in fact, led to heated

Rabbi Jacob Joseph, the first and last chief rabbi of New York City. His lack of familiarity with American culture and practice made him initially unpopular, despite his erudition.

controversy. While learned and respected, he spoke little English, had no significant contacts with the United States Jewish community, and was unfamiliar with American customs, laws, and regulations.

While the notion of a chief rabbi had a long history in European countries, it had not existed before in the United States. Rabbi Joseph concentrated his attention on kashrut once he discovered that more than half of the meat sold in the U.S. as kosher was, in fact, non-kosher. Lucrative deals were being made between the butchers and the abattoirs, or slaughterhouses. He attacked this abuse, which was rational but fragmented the community even further. Housewives saw it as a form of price fixing. Butchers saw it as invasion of their freedom. And those phony shochetim (slaughterers) felt that the new chief rabbi was depriving them of an "honest" living.

In the meantime, Galician and Hungarian congregations, who were unwilling to submit to a Litvak (Lithuanian) rabbi, decided to look for their own chief rabbi, and several were, in fact, appointed concurrently. As the number of chief rabbis increased, so did the unsightly competition over who could and who could not supervise the ritual slaughter. Eventually, the special association withdrew from the hiring agreement and Rabbi Joseph concentrated on what he did best—teaching.

Despite the turmoil, Rabbi Joseph left a significant legacy. He founded several yeshivas in New York City and was a prime mover in the establishment of the Henry Street Settlement. Today, a college in Staten Island and a high school in Plainfield, New Jersey, bear his name. After his death, it was decided that the position of chief rabbi

be abandoned permanently, given its controversial nature. Nevertheless more than 100,000 people lined the streets of the Lower East
Side at his funeral to pay their respects.

The rabbi's oldest son, Raphael, married in New York and had
three children, Lazarus, Frances, and Max.

RABBI ABRAHAM ABA WERNER, THE FATHER OF MY
GRAND-AUNT HANNA WERNER STRASCHEFFSKY

Rabbi Werner, my great-grand-uncle,
was chief rabbi of Finland and came
to England to establish the Great
Spitalfields synagogue.

In the absence of professional wedding photographers at the turn of the century, it was considered almost mandatory that newlyweds, after the formal wedding ceremony, would nip on down to the local photographer's studio for an official portrait photo. Only in rare cases did the couple pose in their wedding attire; rather, it was usual for the photographer to provide them with clothing befitting their social status and financial means. On 14 September 1897, Hanna Werner and her husband, Selman Strascheffsky, posed for their wedding portrait. This was no ordinary wedding, for Hanna's father, Abraham Aba Werner, had been the chief rabbi of Finland, and her great-grandfather Leibel Lipschitz was also a rabbi from Kovno. As their synagogue was still under construction, the wedding ceremony was performed in a privately owned social hall reserved for such occasions.

Rabbi Werner later immigrated to England from Finland and founded the Machzike Hadath Community Synagogue, also known as the Spitalfields Great Synagogue. Twenty-five thousand mourners attended his funeral on 23 December 1912. He was buried in the Federation Cemetery in Edmonton, not far from our home in London.

RABBI ISODORE HALPERIN,
MY PATERNAL GREAT-GRANDFATHER

Rabbi Isodore Halperin was my great-grandfather. He had two daughters. Gita, the eldest, was my grandmother. Gita's sister, Ester, married Rabbi Jacob Joseph.

Isodore Halperin, my paternal great-grandfather and another of the rabbis Aunt Luba said I would discover, had two daughters: Gita (my grandmother), who married Michel (Mark), and Ester, who married Rabbi Jacob Joseph. Apart from the fact that Isodore was from Kovno and lived in the middle of the nineteenth century, little is known about him, however.

*   *   *

When we arrived in America, Father was determined to find his only direct relative in the United States, a lawyer whose last name was Joseph. He decided to write personal letters to every lawyer named Joseph in the telephone directory in New York City, introducing himself and explaining that he was seeking his cousin, whose grandparents were from Russia. (The responses to these letters are still in our family archives.) Eventually Father was successful.

Finding Lazarus Joseph, his wife, Henrietta, and his sister, Frances, was an exciting experience for us all, especially Father, who had not seen anyone from his family for more than twenty years. While we saw them primarily on holidays and special occasions, Lazarus took responsibility for all of the details of the probate of my father's will and helped Mother clear up many difficult matters. Mother forged a close bond with Frances. In fact, Frances was the only representative from Father's side of the family at my wedding in 1958.

Lazarus's oldest son, Jacob, was a captain in the U. S. Marine Corps and was killed in action at the Battle of Guadalcanal in October 1942. At the time, he was the youngest Marine Corps officer to be killed. Lazarus's children were older than me, so we never had an opportunity for close social contact.

Frances's children—Rhoda, who was the same age as my brother, Mark, and Ralph, who was just a few years older than me—became our friends, despite the fact that they lived in the Bronx, which seemed to be a different world from where we lived in Manhattan.

We eventually found Samuel Halperin—he was related to my paternal grandmother—living close to us on the Upper West Side. He owned a small textile shop on Broadway and West 82nd Street. He and his wife, Ruth, did not have any children, but visited our apartment from time to time to celebrate family events and religious holidays.

While we now know that there were many other family members in the United States, none of them were identified until, thanks to various genealogical search sites on the Internet, we discovered several other branches that descended from Aron Strascheffsky.

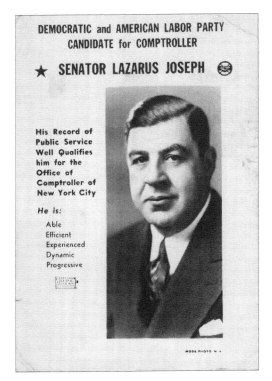

Cousin Lazarus Joseph, grandson of Jacob Joseph, was chief financial Officer of New York City.

My grandfather's tombstone in St. Petersburg became our own family Rosetta stone that unlocked the mystery of our original family name.

4

The Missing "scheff"

A significant finding in my search for my paternal family roots came when our daughter Jennifer discovered the true spelling of our family name.

All of the original documents, passports, citizenship papers, and travel documents indicate our family name as "Strajevsky." This is the name on my United States citizenship papers, passport, and birth certificate. Shortly after we came to America in 1940, however, Father decided it would be less complicated if, like so many immigrants, he officially changed our name so that it would be easier to pronounce and spell. This was the genesis of the name "Strage."

In the process of researching the family roots, references to our family name—Strajevsky—seemed surprisingly limited. Then Jennifer tracked down an Internet site that included more than one thousand photographs of tombstones in the largest Jewish cemetery in St. Petersburg, and there were several photos of our family tombstones, including that of my grandfather Mark. When we studied the inscription carefully, we were astonished to find our name spelled in a way we had never seen before—Strascheffsky. Somewhere along our family history, "scheff" seems to have disappeared and been replaced by "jev."

I believe the "scheff" disappeared when Father was escaping from the Russian police in St. Petersburg and probably modified the name, albeit slightly, to avoid detection, as he hoped to escape the authorities' grasp. It was done cleverly, since the replacement of six letters apparently did little or nothing to change the pronunciation. Although it may seem trivial today, he obviously thought it was enough to provide him with some measure of protection.

Equipped with a new spelling of our name, we once again interrogated the established genealogical databases, and were taken by surprise when we uncovered a veritable treasure chest of family members about whom we had vaguely heard but had been unable to find out, as there was no supporting documentation. And when we entered our new information, we were suddenly deluged with emails from people all over the world declaring themselves to be relatives—some direct, others by marriage. Overnight our family grew to include over six hundred names.

That is a lot of birthday cards to send!

5

The Manzhouli Connection

Catherine the Great, in 1791, created the Pale of Settlement—which was mainly Russia but included parts of Poland, Latvia, Lithuania, Ukraine, Crimea, and Belorussia—as the territory in which Jews were forced to live. Her objective was to create a Jewish-free Moscow, and thus eliminate the alleged unfair business competition and "evil" influence of Jews on the rest of the population.

Although the Pale represented only 4 percent of Imperial Russia's land area, at its height it was the home of 5.6 million Russian Jews, the largest concentration of diaspora Jews in the world. Most of them lived in villages, or shtetls, in the Pale, where strict laws limited the number of Jews allowed in secondary schools to 10 percent of the school population. Jews there were not allowed to own land, immigrate into Russia proper without special permission, or hire Christian servants. They had limited voting rights in municipal elections.

The first systematic wave of large-scale anti-Semitic pogroms began in the Ukraine in 1881, after the Jews were unfairly blamed for the assassination of Alexander II. Hundreds of Ukrainian towns and shtetls suffered from pogroms and thousands of Jewish homes were destroyed, properties confiscated, and inhabitants killed. Pogroms, as well as boycotts of Jewish businesses and other official as well as unofficial anti-Semitic attacks, led to the mass immigration of Jews to Europe, the United States, and beyond.

*   *   *

"All the children would leave this place if they could," Israel sadly concluded.

Batsheeva responded, "But Rogachev is their home. They were born here, they've grown up here, and we still live here."

Looking around the room and pausing at the open window, Israel lamented, "They can hardly make a decent wage here. There is no future for them here. Pogroms will soon become more frequent and more violent."

"Where will they go? Who will give them money for travel?"

Israel and Batsheeva Dinaburg, my maternal great-grandparents, knew that there was a good possibility that most of their eleven children would leave Rogachev, which was in the Ukraine, if they could. The prospects for the younger generation were extraordinarily

*Israel Dinaburg sadly saw all of his eleven children
permanently leave their home in Russia.*

depressing, with opportunities for education and professional careers limited by national decree. Breaking out of the poverty trap, in which their family and neighbors were all prisoners, was almost unthinkable. Ongoing and public anti-Semitic policies affected practically every aspect of their day-to-day lives.

Despite nearly insurmountable challenges, almost two million young Jewish Russians emigrated from the Ukraine between 1881 and 1914, one of the largest movements to date of a mass emigration of a homogeneous population group. The biggest challenge was unquestionably financial. Some were able to scrape together enough for a ticket through a combination of contributions from wealthier relatives, local Jewish welfare groups, and overseas Jewish charities. They usually arrived at their destination with virtually no funds. A search of Ellis Island ship manifests clearly shows that few of them arrived with more than the minimum required $5.

It was not uncommon for the oldest son of the family to leave home first, explore the possibilities for a new life, and if favorable, encourage the remaining brothers and sisters to follow. The oldest Dinaburg son, Abraham, had been conscripted into the Russian army, so it had fallen upon my grandfather Michel (Michael) to explore possible places for the family to relocate. North America was beyond reach for him and his wife, Gita, and their daughter, Anya (Anna), born 1 November 1895. Instead, they looked eastward to a foreign and distant frontier.

The Russian city of Zabaykalsk shares a common border with Manzhouli, a Mongolian city in the province of Manchuria. At the turn of the century, the two cities, one Russian and the other Mongolian, also shared a common railroad station, where the Trans-Siberian Express connected with the Chinese Eastern Railroad. In 1895 the Russians received a concession from the Chinese government to extend the Trans-Siberian railroad about one thousand miles eastward. Russia was so anxious for rapid economic development in the new region, it promised Russian Jews that if they moved there, they would have freedom from the restrictions that made their lives so miserable in the Pale.

For Russian Jews, relocating in Manzhouli was a chance to start a new life without changing their basic lifestyle, language, or religion. Entrepreneurs, such as fur traders and lumber merchants, were the first to establish themselves, followed by professionals, such as doctors, lawyers, and architects. Compared to the immigration of Russian Jews to the United States, the number arriving in China at the turn of the century was insignificant. By 1908, after the Russo-Japanese war, there were still only twenty-five Russian Jewish families in Manzhouli.

Michel was one of the first to arrive, emigrating in 1899. Three years later, having settled and feeling reasonably certain that Manzhouli would provide a suitable and safe home for his family, he made arrangements for his wife, Gita, and two children, Anya and Max, as well as several of his brothers and sisters to join him. Israel and Batsheeva never left Rogachev.

Despite the isolation and weather of Manzhouli and Zabaykalsk, where the arctic climate reached forty degrees below zero

Michel Dinaburg. Sabbath in Manchuria was a day for dressing up, ready to go to the synagogue.

(Centigrade) in winter, the small Jewish community prospered. Its remoteness proved an advantage, as there was a bare minimum of government interference. In 1910, the kehillah (community) opened a kosher kitchen, perhaps the first one in China, and provision for kosher meat and other food. It organized a shul, a school, a mikvah, and a chevrah kadish (burial society). A famous Jewish rabbi, Israel Rifa from New Zagora in Russia, even joined the community as spiritual leader. Michel quickly became a leader in the kehillah, and in the rear of his home, he started a small printing business that later printed a daily Jewish newspaper in Russian and Yiddish.

Then, with the outbreak of World War I in 1914, Jewish refugees from the west poured into Manzhouli, and the city's Jewish population soon expanded to more than 150 families. As there were no hotels, visitors, traveling merchants, and homeless refugees were made welcome in private homes—and when I was growing up in New York City in the 1940s, I vividly recall hearing fulsome stories from a variety of visitors about how warmly and kindly they had been received and given lodging for varying lengths of time in Grandfather Michel's home. By then he had married Nadia, who later lived in New York City, so I got to know her. One of those guests was the stepfather of a friend of mine in New York, a fur trader named Adolphe Schapiro.

Anya, Michel and Gita's oldest of three children, was a brilliant student and after her marriage studied dentistry. Her only son, Fama, contracted polio when he was a teenager, and Anya decided to take him to a world-class specialist clinic near the town of Omsk, in

As new Russian immigrants settled in sleepy Chinese villages, they created their own familiar infrastructure.

Russia, for treatment. Unfortunately, what was to be a visit to cure a terrible illness ended tragically. Fama died shortly after they arrived and Anya never received the necessary authorization to return home to Manzhouli. In 1965, when my wife, Alberta, and I, together with my brother, Mark, and his wife, Tanya, travelled to Russia, Anya came to meet us in St. Petersburg. In 1982, we finally arranged to have her come to live with her sister (Sonya, my mother) in our apartment in New York. A few years later she passed away.

Max, born in 1899, always longed to go to America, and near his twentieth birthday joined some of his uncles in Cleveland, Ohio. There he began what was to be a short-lived career as a professional boxer, eventually joining the family furniture business, albeit for a short time.

Mother practicing the piano in Manchuria

Sonya, my mother, was born in Manzhouli, and lived there with her parents until 1922, when she left to study the piano at the St. Petersburg Conservatory.

Gita died in 1905, and a few years later Michel married Nadia. Their only child, Ephraim (Fima), was born on 26 July 1909.

Over the coming years, the small Jewish community in Manzhouli began to disperse. Some families immigrated to the United States. Others moved east to the fast-growing railroad hub of Harbin, which today has a population of over ten million. As one of the founders and later the gabbi, who essentially ran the Manzhouli synagogue, Grandfather Michel felt an obligation to stay as long as there were Jews in the city. But eventually, in the mid-1930s, he, too, left for Harbin. He was nearly the last Jew to leave.

Alberta and I went to Harbin in 2004 with two friends, Judy and Herb Schwartz, as part of an international seminar and conference for about one hundred former Harbin residents and their families. When we visited my grandfather's grave in the Jewish cemetery there, Alberta and I placed a pebble on his tombstone. A Chinese media team filming the visit asked us why we had done that. We explained that it is the traditional Jewish practice showing respect for a deceased relative or friend, whereupon they went off and soon returned with armfuls of stones, boulders, and even small bricks, which they left on my grandfather's grave to express their personal solidarity and respect. It was a lovely gesture that we will always remember.

My mother and Aunt Anya in a studio photograph, wearing bird hats suggesting the coming of spring

46

Grandfather's dining room in Manzhouli had all the trappings of a middle-class contemporary European home. Left to right, unknown servant, my mother, Nadia (his second wife), and Michael Dinaburg.

Ephraim (Fima), Michael Dinaburg (seated), and Nadia.

Nineteen Strages visited my grandparents' graves in Harbin, China in December 2013, in minus 25 degrees C. In the absence of stones to mark our visit, Lexi created a snow cube.

6

The Manchurian Diaspora,
A Tale of Two Cities

The saga of the dispersion of the Dinaburg family from Rogachev at the beginning of the twentieth century repeated itself in Jewish families throughout the Pale of Settlement for more than a decade. By 1915 more than two million Jews had emigrated and settled in new homes around the world. The majority of those millions had moved westward, ending their journeys in England, Canada, the United States, and various countries in South America. In most cases, they had gone to places that already had a Jewish population. Only a handful of Jews decided to venture eastward, which was much more problematic than going to the west. Not only was it farther away, but there were only a handful of Jews in the Far East.

The first Jews who settled in Manchuria arrived in 1899, when it was a drowsy little station on the Chinese Eastern Railroad, or CER. The 30,000 inhabitants of Manchuria were mainly Chinese and Mongolian peasants eking out a bare existence in a bitter climate. (Today, with a population of over one million, the city is called Manzhouli and is a thriving industrial metropolis.) Despite the climate and isolation, for the next fifteen years a small but dedicated flow of Jewish "pioneers" who were fleeing the aftermath of Tsar Nikolai's cruel anti-Semitism continued to arrive there.

When the Dinaburgs decided to go to Manchuria, they had only general information about the conditions they would find there. They did know, however, that the trip by train from Rogachev to Manchuria would take them almost three weeks.

The exodus of the Dinaburg children did not follow any pre-set plan or pattern. Each sibling took a different route, but by 1913 all eleven had left the home they were born in. For many, Manchuria was only a first step in a journey to their final homes.

The first of the Dinaburg family to join Michel in Manzhouli was his brother Abraham. As the oldest son, born in 1880, he had been conscripted into the Russian army to serve for a period of twenty-five years. The story of his escape or, more accurately, his defection from the Russian Imperial Army is one of the family's treasured legends. As a young recruit, Uncle Abraham served as an orderly to an officer somewhere in the far eastern corner of Russia. One cold night, he was given a five-ruble gold coin and commanded to go and buy vodka for the officer's dining rooms. He saw an opportunity, albeit risky, to escape from the army and decided to take his chances. He dressed warmly, pocketed the coin, and never returned. He had heard that there was a small Jewish community somewhere far off near the border of Manchuria and Russia, and thought his brother Michel might live there or nearby. I believe the story is true. I have personally seen the gold coin that Uncle Abraham gave his grandson, my cousin Mark Lebo. Then, with two Dinaburgs comfortably settled in Manzhouli, it was time to invite the rest of the family to join them.

Uncle David and his family were the next to arrive. David took over most of the purchasing for Michel's now established general store. In the region of Manchuria, camels were the most economic form of long-distance transportation, and it was not unusual for a whole caravan to be found resting near the rear of the store. The need for frequent long trips away from home eventually persuaded David to move his family to the booming metropolis of Harbin. In Harbin, he joined friends in a textile enterprise.

MANZHOULI (AKA MANCHURIA) KEEPS GROWING

While the serenity, security, and comforts of Manzhouli provided a safe haven and relatively secure environment for the Jewish families fleeing pogroms and tsarist restrictions, something important was missing. Opportunities for economic activity were limited to the creation of essentially family-centered activities, typically managed from one's home.

Yet there were 350 Jewish families who, by 1917, were able to support the newly built synagogue with its own dedicated full-time rabbi, Jewish school with 170 students, library, and multi-functional Jewish community center that had permission to issue its own birth, marriage, and death certificates. Then, a trickle of Jewish families began moving away from Manzhouli, to Palestine, Harbin, and far eastern destinations such as Tientsin, Shanghai, and Hong Kong. Eventually the trickle became a torrent, with Jewish communities once again on the move. By 1920, the Manzhouli community was left with only eighty members, including my grandfather.

As the community shrank, the remaining Dinaburgs—my grand-uncles and grand-aunts and their families—also made their way to their next homes. A few managed to arrange passage directly to North America. The others moved to Harbin, the thriving hub and adminis-trative headquarters of the CER.

My grandfather Michel, together with Misha Muiseev, the other leading member of the Jewish community in Manzhouli, had the inevitable task of dismantling the once-vibrant community, overseeing the distribution of all moveable Jewish religious artifacts to suitable locations, and the disposal of other holy items in accordance with the appropriate religious practice.

HARBIN, A FAR EAST BOOM TOWN

In 1896 a major political event occurred that was to change the economic prospects of northern China, including Manchuria. That year, the Chinese government granted Russia a twenty-five year concession to construct an extension of the Trans-Siberian Railroad. The Chinese Eastern Railroad, CER, connected Moscow to Vladivostok, Russia's only warm-water strategic port.

The center for the CER, as well as its principal administrative offices, was to be in a location on the Sungari River that was given the name "Harbin." Until 1900, it was just a cluster of tiny fishing villages and a modest trading center for lumber and fur traders. The construction of the new railroad, however, turned it into a magnet for new industry, with opportunities for a myriad of mercantile services and a good climate for all types of commercial and domestic construction.

The Jews took full advantage of the times and reveled in being able to practice occupations not open to them in Russia or elsewhere. They became teachers, doctors, lawyers, and owners of construction companies, hotels, and other businesses.

As the new crossroads of trade between Asia, Europe, and North America, the region of Manchuria attracted the attention of the world's powers, and a diverse array of enterprises sprang up to support aggressive development of its rich mineral and agricultural resources by Russia, Japan, and the United States.

Harbin provided an unbeatable combination of unique economic and financial opportunities as well as a dynamic environmental umbrella under which to construct, develop, and expand the community and its associated infrastructure, both religious and cultural. Prosperity meant that what was once a few small villages grew into an oasis of opportunity with a wide range of cultural activities. Jewish initiatives were the prime movers in the construction and operation of many of the city's new theatres, concert halls, and music conservatories, which enriched the lifestyles of its residents, as did the new libraries, schools, health facilities, a home for the aged, a soup kitchen, modern hotels, and fine restaurants. Factories owned by Jewish people sprang up practically overnight, producing refined minerals, furniture, basic food commodities, and textiles.

As their affluence grew, two spectacular synagogues sprang up in Harbin. The Main Synagogue opened on January 15, 1909, and the Hasidic Synagogue, known as "the new synagogue" began services on September 25, 1921. At the same time, a wide variety of Jewish support institutions, including several mikvah, a bespoke matzo-making facility, social clubs, youth organizations, as well as an active young Zionist movement, became active community institutions. At its apex, the Jewish population reached more than 20,000 souls in the early 1920s, representing almost twenty percent of the "foreign" population of the city. Russian became the lingua franca, and of the more than twenty Jewish magazines and newspapers published in Harbin, all were in Russian with the exception of one publication that was in Yiddish. The Dinaburg families and others who moved there from Manzhouli were rewarded with a rich lifestyle and commercial opportunities that exceeded their expectations.

But the good life soon began to erode. The end of World War I and the revolution in Russia saw a stream of Bolsheviks settle in Harbin. With them came the first signs of anti-Semitism. In 1931, certain segments of the "White Russian" community established the headquarters of the International White Russian Fascist Party there. In the same year, the Japanese army invaded Manchuria. A year later, it occupied Harbin, which became part of the puppet state of Manchukuo. The Japanese were quick to start a program of expropriating private property owned by Chinese, Russians, and Jews.

For the Dinaburgs, a turning point was the brutal kidnapping of Aunt Ada's son-in-law Lonya Sherrell, a wealthy merchant. His wife, Anta, lives today in Australia. The kidnappers, one of several well-organized gangster cliques, threatened to cut off his ear, or worse. A few months earlier, there had been another kidnapping in which a Jewish youngster, Simeon Kaspe, who was the son of Joseph Kaspe, the owner of Hotel Moderne, had been murdered. After a significant ransom was paid, Lonya Sherell was freed, but the incident was a clear wakeup call that things were changing for the worse.

Three Dinaburg families left Harbin during the next eighteen months. Their first stop was either Tientsin or Shanghai. Eventually, the families settled in either Australia or the United States. Today some of their offspring have moved to the United Kingdom or Israel.

Meanwhile, Michel and his second wife, Nadia, still lived in Manzhouli, as did his unmarried sister Riva Rebecca until 1930, when he decided that despite his leadership role in the community there, he had done all he could do for the shrinking Jewish population, which was now only a dozen families, and it was time to join his brothers and sisters in Harbin. When he finally arrived there, he continued to operate a modest printing enterprise.

The Jewish population of Harbin, like Manzhouli, dwindled. At the end of World War II there were less than two thousand Jews remaining there, including Michel, who had become active as the synagogue's gabbi in the disheartening task of protecting the remaining Jewish buildings, including the synagogue, library, and cemetery. It was while he was in the synagogue one morning, looking after some administrative matters, that he was set upon by hooligans and badly beaten. Sadly, he never recovered from his injuries and died in 1946. The following year, Nadia came to New York and lived with us on Riverside Drive for many years thereafter until her death.

For a period of almost twenty years, Harbin had been for my family a safe haven from the miseries of Jewish life under the bitterly anti-Semitic tsar. It deservedly came to be known as "the Paris of the Orient" and constituted the largest center of Jewish life in the Far East.

Aunt Lena was the first of Israel and Batsheeva's children to come directly to the United States, where her husband, Meyer Teplitz, embarked on a custom-built furniture manufacturing business in Cleveland. Furniture making was, surprisingly, one of the more popular businesses for newly arrived Jewish immigrants in the U.S. It required little start-up capital, simple tools, and few skills—and there were minimal barriers to entry. It was the marriage of his elder daughter, Helen, in 1939 that provided a suitable excuse for our whole family to travel to the United States on a visitors' visa.

With its religious tolerance and economic opportunities, Manzhouli suited Uncle Abraham, but several years after he settled there, he decided to immigrate to North America. Immigrating to the United States was difficult at that time and, hoping that the restrictions would ease up in the future, he settled first in Toronto. He had saved enough funds to buy a pushcart, from which he was able to start a thriving business selling fresh fruit. Having had a taste of army life in Russia, he did not want to be drafted into the Canadian army at the outbreak of World War I and moved to Travis City, Michigan, where he opened a grocery store. After the war, he returned to Toronto and started a wholesale fruit business. For the rest of his life or nearly so, he rose at 4:30 a.m. to get to his "office" in the Toronto fresh fruit and vegetable wholesale market. When he was close to seventy-five years old, his family convinced him that it was time to slow down, which he did. He died two years later.

I remember during one of my visits to Toronto, Uncle Abraham convinced me to join him in the morning and see how the food market really operates. "I'll fix my usual breakfast for us," he proudly exclaimed the night before, "but you must be dressed and downstairs by 4:30 in the morning."

It was an offer I could hardly refuse. The next morning, bleary-eyed and sleepy, I trudged down the stairs, not thinking as much about breakfast as how to stay awake. Indeed the kitchen table was set, but instead of porridge, orange juice, toast, and coffee, to my surprise I saw two enormous juice glasses full almost to the brim with the highly prized, best fifteen-year-old Johnnie Walker Canadian Whiskey, its distinctive pinch or dimple bottle nearby.

He greeted me as if it were ten in the morning and offered me a rousing toast. "L'chayim!" he exclaimed and proceeded to down the entire glass in one great big gulp, as if it were orange juice. Under ordinary circumstances, it probably would have taken me the whole day to finish all the whiskey, which I had hardly ever drunk before. On that morning, I somehow felt my manhood was being tested. I am sure that if I had not been half asleep, I would have found several plausible excuses for giving it a pass.

Somehow, to my everlasting surprise, I bravely returned the "L'chayim!" and grasping the glass as firmly as I could, in one majestic stroke poured it down my throat.

"Wonderful!" a delighted Uncle Abraham remarked. "You are a real Dinaburg!"

Later that day, when the family heard what Uncle Abraham had "prepared" breakfast, he was not very popular. Aunt Mira told him, "You must not teach your little nephew Henry such bad habits!"

Although I don't remember anything about the wholesale fruit market, the breakfast experience is vividly inscribed in my memory.

Benjamin, Uncle Benny, was the next to leave for the New World. Unable to go directly to the United States, he went to Canada, where he married Aunt Jenny, and then joined his sister Lena in Cleveland, Ohio. Uncle Benny decided to sell rather than manufacture furniture.

When we moved to Cleveland in 1940, visiting Uncle Benny's store on a Saturday morning was one of the great treats for a seven-year-old boy. Saturday was always moving day in the store, the day the furniture on display in the front window was changed. Beds, one week; sofas, the next week. Perhaps dining room tables, bureaus, or couches after that. I am sure the changes were not based on carefully analyzed market research data and that it was simply Uncle Benny's belief that if he changed the display every week, people might think the store had new stock to offer. A busy Saturday morning moving furniture was always followed by a visit to his house—and Aunt Jenny's kitchen. Things could not get better.

*   *   *

The Dinaburgs who settled in North America had their first and only family reunion in Toronto in May 1946. I was fortunate to attend. Fittingly, the venue was the home of the oldest child in the family, Uncle Abraham. It was a moving, unforgettable experience for all.

A Dinaburg family reunion in Toronto, Canada in spring 1956, with only four of the eleven children present.
Front row: *Jack Stern, Sophie Stern, Aunt Lena Teplitz, Mother, Aunt Hanna Dunn.*
Second row: *David Dunn, Margaret Lebo, Aunt Mira Dunn, Margaret Dunn, Aunt Jenny, Sam Lebo.*
Third row: *Uncle Abraham, Dorothy Zelles, Sam Zelles, Uncle David Dunn, Uncle Benny Dunn, Uncle Meyer Teplitz*

7

Home, Sweet & Sour Home

Meanwhile, despite the isolation and basic living conditions in Manchuria, Sonya and Michel, my mother and father, were surrounded by close family and friends. They found their new life together comfortable and secure. The little Jewish population rapidly built a thriving and supportive community structure, although by the time Mother and Father left in 1925, there were still only about 150 Russo-Jewish families.

Manzhouli's location made it ideal for trade and finance. A by-product of the resulting prosperity was that families could afford a lifestyle with all the trappings of affluent Europeans.

There is some confusion about the origins of the name

"Manchuria," as well as the region called "Manchuria" and the city known as "Manzhouli." Manchuria is the historic name given to a large geographic region in northeast Asia. In time, people began to distinguish between Inner Manchuria, which was largely Chinese, and Outer Manchuria, which was more closely related to Russia. The major city in the area became known as Manchuria (hence the confusion), but the Russians who came at the turn of the century used the Russian name for the city, Manzhouli.

So by 1925, the city in which Sonya and Michel—the soon-to-be married couple—decided to settle was Manzhouli, a thriving, economically viable entity, with an active Jewish community. Before they were married, Father was able to find well-paid employment that was interesting and used many of his university-acquired engineering skills. As part of its regional development strategy, the Chinese administration had decided to accelerate economic growth by purchasing small manufacturing installations from Germany that would provide basic products and some employment. These so-called "package plants" arrived in Manchuria carefully disassembled and packed in large wooden containers, along with precisely scripted construction and operating instructions in German. What was missing was someone who could translate the instructions and supervise construction. Father's combination of engineering skills and knowledge of German were ideal and soon became an invaluable asset. An unusually rare but attractive fringe benefit of his position was an automobile, which was a highly prized status symbol at the time.

Father drove a smart, open-top automobile, with a custom-made quilt blanket.

While the compensation and other aspects of his work were attractive, the working hours and living conditions were not. Father spent long periods of time away from home and occasionally Mother would go to keep him company. She once described the living conditions there as similar to a tent I lived in at a children's summer sleep-away camp in New Jersey. Nevertheless, the young couple settled into a small but comfortable, single-story bungalow with an active lifestyle, enriching their social network and strengthening their family ties.

In addition to the immediate family, Father developed ties with professional and business colleagues. While perhaps not a typical office gathering, a snapshot of a picnic in the Manchurian desert provides some insights to living conditions.

Despite hardships, the newly married couple seemed very happy together. Father's footwear suggests he had just come home after a long working day in the field. Mother's smart shoes suggest she was home preparing supper.

Three cousins living in Manzhouli—Moulia Vilinsky, Father, and Sam Zelliznicoff (later Zelles)—have no trouble carrying two smartly dressed young ladies. Mother is on the right.

Hardly a "cool" spot for a summer picnic—no tables, benches, or fireplace and a bit short on trees.

One may be excused for thinking it is a stage set for a Turgenev or Dostoyevsky drama or a backdrop for a Borodin or Glinka opera. In fact, it is a photograph of real life, not a stage set. It is summer. The year is 1926. The place is somewhere in northern Manchuria near the route of the Trans-Siberian Express. A group is having an afternoon picnic away from the busy life in the city. No one is eating much, but the kettle is on and the lady on the right is using a rather large knife to spread the moose-liver pate on the pumpernickel bread, which has already been generously covered with yak butter. A few local people are there, too, and they will probably have some buuz (mutton dumplings), booddog (goat stew), or chanasan makn (boiled innards).

"Misha," suggests Odvai. "How can we smile for your photo if we are all still hungry and freezing?"

"You can at least pretend you are having a good time," says Misha.

"Next year we should have the office party IN THE OFFICE," pleads Bayarmaa. "At least then we don't have to wear all these crazy costumes."

"Look," Sonya says sternly. "This is all about bonding. You know, feeling you are really part of the group."

Chuluun does not seem convinced. His fur hat, which Misha made him wear, is most uncomfortable, even though in the -20 degree Centigrade weather, he has to admit that it keeps his ears warm.

"Stop this chat!" cries Kukhbataar. "Pass the MAKN!"

"We only have chopped yak liver today," Sonya explains. "Anyway, all this goat stuff isn't good for you."

The two wicker baskets on the left suggest that the group had planned a feast—boiled mutton for sure. I don't suppose smoked salmon had been invented yet. The only person I recognize is my mother, the lady three in from the left who is lighting up a papirosi (cigarette). What a shame that I never asked her who the other people were and what they were doing in such a desolate place. She seems to be the only one who is hungry, and already has her napkin on her lap, ready for the first course. I think my father was the photographer. My guess is that this was most likely an office day out.

The others in the picnic picture were probably some of my father's colleagues. They don't look like people who would be laying railroad tracks, as the concession to build an extension of the Trans-Siberian Railroad into China was made on condition that only Chinese labor would be used in its construction.

Ten years later, in 1936, a Sunday picnic in Belgium stands in sharp contrast to this picnic in Mongolia.

A Chekov-like pastoral scene after a tasty picnic lunch in the park in Brussels. Front row, left to right, *Isa, Father.* Second row, *Frederica Bernstein, Mrs. Bernstein, Henry, Mark, and Mother.* Third row, barely visible, *unidentified person, Mr. Bernstein.*

8

Embedded in Our DNA: Photography

One is never surprised to find that a gifted musician comes from a family of musicians. The same often is true for actors, writers, and sports celebrities. In our family, what seems to be in the bloodstream is recording family history and special events in photographs.

Because my father was a keen photographer, I have a rich collection of family pictures that have provided invaluable insights into our family's lifestyle, as well as a remarkable permanent gallery of family and friends in different locations and situations. It was not, unfortunately, the custom to annotate photos with dates, places, and names.

As a result, identifying, cataloging, and arranging these treasures sometimes involves both detective work and intelligent conjecture.

There is something rather pleasing and special about holding a photo album in which carefully selected pictures are arranged in some order, and someone has taken the trouble to annotate each photo with factual details and, perhaps even more importantly, impressions or sentiments about the occasion and the cast of characters shown. Digital photographic collections, while they will certainly be more extensive, will lack a thoughtful human input, I fear.

My motivation for recording these thoughts comes from this treasured photo, which I found tucked away among the myriad images in my archives and scanned exactly as I found it—no retouching, no resizing, no adjusting. The back of the photo gives the date as 1928.

P to K4

It is one of my favorite photographs because of the many things it says about my grandfather. He was clearly intrigued with photography and its possibilities. But he also must have enjoyed leaving for posterity his little practical joke. (No doubt Geoffrey must have inherited some of his genes. It also may be where Jennifer gets her curly hair.) You will notice that although each of the three chess players are dressed differently and have different expressions, they are all, in fact, the same person.

Player on the left: "I think this move will really finish him off."

Player on the right is thinking: "This is really too easy. In the next game I must get some more serious competition."

Player in the middle says to himself: "They both would be better off playing checkers."

The photo was taken in Harbin. I do not know how one would take such a photo even today. And I suspect that if it were in digital format, it would survive into the year 2093! By then perhaps our external hard drives will be safely stored on Mars.

I took a course at the Open University in London several years ago on how to write family histories, and my eyes were opened to the treasures and mysteries that are hidden in family photographs. Many family photos will carry secrets that are unlikely ever to be deciphered unless one takes the trouble to scan them, enlarge the original, and study carefully the minute details, which are often hidden in the background.

Mother, right, does not seem very pleased with the message from her gypsy-dressed sister, Anya, after having her future told.

Having photos taken in a professional photographic studio was a popular activity. Most studios would have available an eclectic mixture of props and costumes. While photographs celebrating special events were most common, often people wanted to make a statement or leave a unique message.

In this studio photo, taken in Manchuria in 1919, one can only imagine what message my mother and her older sister were trying to send. Dressed as a gypsy fortune-teller, Anya seems to be reading Mother's palm. Note the high-heeled shoes, which must have been the latest fashion, and the short, curly hairstyle. At Mother's feet is a four-foot rod, or perhaps a walking stick. It was specifically placed there, but for what purpose? Anya has obviously just given Mother some worrying information that she has read from her palm.

"Maybe I shouldn't have told her?" Anya thinks.

Mother clearly is not pleased with her fortune. She looks away from Anya and is wondering if this fortune-telling game was such a good idea.

Sometimes photographs were taken just to provide a permanent record of a person. The photo of Noravhi, who was a loyal Chinese household servant in my grandfather's home, is perhaps an example of this. Fortunately, someone took the trouble to write her name and position in the household on the back of the photo. But studio photographs like this were a luxury at that time. It is most unlikely that Noravhi would have spent her own money for a professional

*Loyal household servant
Noravhi sat for classic
studio portrait.*

portrait, so it must have been my grandfather's idea. But why would Noravhi want to be photographed in Western dress?

The 1942 photographer of a Little League baseball team in Cleveland, Ohio, shows another unique function a photograph can play, that of triggering memories. As I was too young and inexperienced to be on the team as a player, I was thrilled to travel with the team as "bat boy." I suppose I was the only Belgian-born, Russian-speaking bat boy in the 1943 Little League in the Northwest Conference. It was when I found this photo that I was able to recall my critical role on the team and the excitement of helping the team play.

This was probably the only Little League baseball team in America that had a Russian-speaking bat boy who hardly spoke English.

My passion for baseball grew out of my almost certain knowledge that this was the quickest route to become a real American, and explains my unflinching, at times irrational, support for the local Cleveland baseball team and its star pitcher, Bob Feller.

The use of photos in creating this autobiography was an invaluable aide-memoire of persons, places, and events previously forgotten, with far greater accuracy then legends and a cluttered personal memory bank.

9

A Manchurian Odyssey

**A HISTORICAL DRAMA
IN TWO ACTS**

CAST OF CHARACTERS

Michel, a graduate engineering student

Sonya, an aspiring pianist

Boris, virtuoso violin student

Sophia (Sonya)   *Michel (Misha)*

ACT ONE

SCENE ONE

An interrogation room in Trubetskoy prison in St. Petersburg, 1925.
A simple table sits in the center of the room, which is lit by a bare bulb
hanging from the ceiling. There is one chair at the table.

INTERROGATOR: *(sitting)* You've broken the law, Comrade.

MICHEL (MISHA): *(standing)* I've done nothing wrong.

INTERROGATOR: You're not a fool. You must know what the rules are.

MICHEL: I'm just an engineering student. I know nothing of politics.

INTERROGATOR: You Jewish students are all the same. Troublemakers.

MICHEL: I don't want to make trouble for anyone.

INTERROGATOR: It says in this report that you are responsible for stealing your family's silver and jewelry.

MICHEL: Why would I want to steal from my own family?

INTERROGATOR: When the police searched your home they found no silver, no jewelry, nothing of any real value.

MICHEL: I don't know what you are talking about.

INTERROGATOR: The account here *[looking at an open file]* says your mother reported that they had been stolen two days earlier.

MICHEL: How could I have done that? I was at school. That's terrible. Who would do such a thing?

INTERROGATOR: You make a useless liar.

MICHEL: Can I go home now?

INTERROGATOR: You are likely to be here for ten years unless you start telling me the truth.

MICHEL: Why would I steal from my own family?

INTERROGATOR: Jews can't pay wealth taxes on property they don't have.

MICHEL: Everyone pays taxes. Even I know that.

INTERROGATOR: Each according to their ability. Have you ever heard that? The more you have the more taxes you pay. That's the way it is in Russia these days.

MICHEL: Father has a small shop. Trade has been slow. The family earns very little. We aren't a rich family.

INTERROGATOR: We know all about your father. This is not about earnings. It's about family wealth. Redistribution of assets. Everyone knows that all Jews are rich.

MICHEL: The government is taxing success?

INTERROGATOR: Listen, Comrade. We are only taxing those who have an unfair portion of the country's wealth. They don't use the money anyway. They hoard it. And we need it.

MICHEL: I only have ten rubles in my pocket. Does that make me wealthy? Oh yes, I also have my slide rule.

(*Shows slide rule to INTERROGATOR*)

INTERROGATOR: Your smart-aleck answers will be recorded when the time comes to punish you.

MICHEL: I've done nothing.

INTERROGATOR: I'm going to give you one more chance, Comrade.

MICHEL: Chance for what?

INTERROGATOR: Go home, find the jewelry and silver you hid from the GPU, and come back here by eight o'clock in the morning tomorrow.

MICHEL: I have no idea where it could be. How can I find it?

INTERROGATOR: Someone in your family is playing games.

MICHEL: And if I can't find it?

INTERROGATOR: Come back here tomorrow morning and we'll discuss what to do next.

MICHEL: Can we make it Thursday afternoon?

INTERROGATOR: Eight o'clock tomorrow. I also want some information from you about some of your friends in school who haven't been too friendly to the Government lately.

MICHEL: I have no such friends.

INTERROGATOR: You must think we are very stupid here or blind, Comrade. Some of your classmates have been very cooperative. Not like you.

MICHEL: Cooperative?

INTERROGATOR: I want a list of all your Jew friends who have been critical of our policies. We want to wipe out all counter-revolutionaries in our midst. Especially Jewish ones.

MICHEL: I have no disloyal friends.

INTERROGATOR: And don't even think of hiding or running away. We're everywhere. Watching. There is no place to hide.

MICHEL: Yes, Comrade.

INTERROGATOR: To make sure, let me have your identity card.

MICHEL: Left it home.

INTERROGATOR: I could lock you up right now for not having your ID card with you.

MICHEL: I have my student card.

INTERROGATOR: Good. I'll hold that until tomorrow morning.

SCENE TWO

The student lounge at the Music Conservatory in St. Petersburg. A large, well-worn sofa nearly fills the room.

SONYA: I'm getting nowhere.

BORIS: You can't give up now.

SONYA: It's no use. I've decided. I'm going home.

BORIS: We were going to give a recital together this winter, remember?

SONYA: Boris, my dearest friend. You have a great career in front of you. Some day people will pay to hear you play your violin. I…

BORIS: Yes, and you will accompany me on your piano.

SONYA: If I'm lucky I'll be able to give lessons to children back home.

BORIS: You had a terrible difficult few weeks, Sonya. You need to take a rest. We'll go visit Sasha at his dacha and have a good rest. You'll come back refreshed and have a good laugh about your talk of quitting.

SONYA: I'm through. Really.

BORIS: What will you do at home?

SONYA: I'm going home. I've been away three long years.

BORIS: I'm going with you.

SONYA:	Don't be foolish. You have to finish your studies here.
BORIS:	I can't let you go back alone. It's a long journey and not safe for a young beautiful woman to go all that way alone. Besides, I promised your father I would look after you.
SONYA:	I can't make you stop your studies. Impossible.
BORIS:	I'm not stopping, Sonya. I need a break, too. Neither of us has been home for three years.
SONYA:	I hope they remember who we are.
BORIS:	Maybe when we get home we could tell our families about our plans.
SONYA:	Which plans?
BORIS:	About our future.
SONYA:	I would wait until they get over the shock of having us both home again.
BORIS:	Will you continue to study? I've heard the conservatory in Harbin has been rebuilt and has an excellent faculty.
SONYA:	I'll never be a concert pianist, Boris. I don't have the discipline, the patience, or the single-mindedness that you have, Boris.
BORIS:	We'll see. When we get back home you'll change your mind.
SONYA:	Time will tell. Shall we go to our last piano recital at the school?
BORIS:	Who is playing and when is it?
SONYA:	Friday night. One of our postgraduate scholars is playing a new piece by Rimsky-Korsakov.
BORIS:	I wouldn't miss it.

SCENE THREE

Michel's parents' apartment in St. Petersburg.

MICHEL: I must go. I'm not going to spend ten years in one of their Siberian hell holes carrying rocks for ten hours a day.

MOTHER: There must be something else we can do.

MICHEL: I've thought of everything. If I go back empty-handed in the morning, I'll surely end up in Siberia. Then they'll go after Lyubov, Laser, and Eugenia. They'll never stop.

MOTHER: And if you bring back ....

MICHEL: It'll be worse. Then they will say I lied, keep the jewelry, and make us pay the tax plus an enormous penalty—and I'll still end up in a Gulag somewhere.

MOTHER: So...

MICHEL: Running away is the only answer.

MOTHER: You can't hide from the Bolsheviks. They're everywhere.

MICHEL: Not in Mongolia.

MOTHER: Where?

MICHEL: It's a long journey there and they'll get tired of looking for me by the time I get to the border.

MOTHER: What will you do there? We have no family there. No friends.

MICHEL: One of the engineers from our school went there last year and told us they badly need engineers and are paying higher salaries than in Russia.

MOTHER: And the civil war?

MICHEL: That's in China, Mother, not in Mongolia.

MOTHER: Is it safe there? What language do they speak? Have you
            a visa?

MICHEL: No. And they'll never give me one now. In fact, they took
            away my student identification card this afternoon.

MOTHER: So how will you ever get out of the country?

MICHEL: I won't have to cross any borders for at least eight or nine
            days.

MOTHER: And then you'll have no visa, passport, or even a student
            identity card.

MICHEL: Lots of people cross borders without papers.

MOTHER: Any persons we know?

MICHEL: They have thousands of miles of borders to watch. There
            are certainly places they're not watching.

MOTHER: It was my idea to hide the valuables, so…

MICHEL: They have already decided that I did it. So I'm the one
            who has to disappear from here.

MOTHER: What will you do there? How long will you stay?

MICHEL: Just long enough for them to forget about me. Then I'll
            come home.

MOTHER: The secret police have long memories. I don't like it.

MICHEL: Is it better to have you visit me in some God-forsaken
            prison labor camp in Siberia for the next twenty years?
            Send me bread and jam in packages that will never arrive
            anyway?

MOTHER: And what do I tell the police when they come?

MICHEL: Tell them you haven't seen me since I had the interview
            with the GPU. And you have no idea what happened to
            your jewelry.

MOTHER:	I have to tell them something.
MICHEL:	Tell them I've gone to visit our relatives in New York City in the United States and am planning to make my fortune there.
MOTHER:	Misha, you know what? Once you start running you'll have to keep running for the rest of your life.
MICHEL:	I'd rather run than sit in a jail cell rotting to death, Mother.

SCENE FOUR

"Hard" tourist-class train compartment in Vitebsk Station, St. Petersburg.

SONYA:	These compartments have gotten smaller since we took this train three years ago.
BORIS:	This time at least we have beds.
SONYA:	It was a good idea to come early to try to get a compartment for ourselves.
BORIS:	We can hope no one comes.
SONYA:	At least you can practice your violin. There are no pianos on this train, I guess.
BORIS:	Ten days will fly by. You'll see.
SONYA:	Why couldn't our parents have found a closer place to settle down in when they left Russia? Manchuria seems like the end of the world.
BORIS:	Well, it's not that far.

SONYA: What's farther, Japan? America?

BORIS: Still, it's our home.

(*PROVODNIK appears and shows MICHEL to his compartment*)

PROVODNIK: This is yours, Tavarisch. Have a good trip.

MICHEL: Thank you. [*Provodnik leaves.*] Good evening. It looks
               like we'll be sharing this cave for ten days. My name is
               Michel Michelovitch.

BORIS: Welcome. I am Boris Petrovitch. And this is Sonya
               Michalovnova.

MICHEL: I am pleased to meet you. I seem to have forced myself
               into what looked like your private compartment but…

SONYA: Don't worry. We can only hope that they don't put three
               more people into our little space here.

BORIS: Are you going far, Michel Michelovitch?

MICHEL: Well, [*hesitating*] I have no plans yet.

BORIS: Didn't you have to buy a ticket to somewhere?

MICHEL: Yes, I'm going to [*hesitating*] Novosibirsk.

SONYA: You don't sound sure. Is there a problem?

MICHEL: No, no. Novosibirsk is where I'm going.

SONYA: Well, we will be together for at least six days anyway.

MICHEL: So you've taken this journey before?

BORIS: Once. Three years ago but going the other way. We're
               going home. Home to Manchuria.

MICHEL: What about Chiang Kai-shek? Seems he is starting some
               sort of revolution.

BORIS: That's far from Manzhouli, thank goodness.

MICHEL: Anyway, a nice long train journey seems a pleasant enough way to spend some time.

BORIS: We'll see how you feel after a few days.

SONYA: Did the provodnik show you where to put your luggage?

MICHEL: No. I really have no luggage. I'm traveling light.

BORIS: Did you lose it? Did someone take it?

MICHEL: Yes, I … had to leave it behind. I have a few things in my little karsinka here. That should be enough for me.

SONYA: Would you like a window seat?

MICHEL: No, thank you. I'll be fine here.

(GUARD with a clipboard enters the cabin without knocking.)

BORIS: Is there a delay? We should have left an hour ago.

GUARD: We've been ordered to search the train for a student fugitive wanted by the state police.

BORIS: Nobody here like that.

GUARD: He is a Jewish engineering student. Neither of you seem to have a beard. I guess I'll keep looking.

(GUARD exits.)

BORIS: I didn't know that all Jewish engineering students must have beards.

SONYA: Didn't you say you were an engineering student, Michel?

MICHEL: How could I be? I don't have a beard.

SCENE FIVE

Six days later.

SONYA: Misha, you missed your stop.

MICHEL: What do you mean?

SONYA: I mean, you told us you were going to Novosibirsk

MICHEL: I changed my mind.

SONYA: Fine, so now where are you going?

MICHEL: Perhaps China. Or Ulaanbaatar.

SONYA: They aren't exactly in the same neighborhood.

MICHEL: Why is everyone so interested in where I'm going?

SONYA: That's what people do on trains—exchange life stories, gossip, tell lies, dream about other places, worry about the state of the train, and find out where other passengers are going.

MICHEL: Well, actually, I'm going to look for a job.

SONYA: While you were out this morning, Boris and I decided that you're either a very famous writer looking for a new plot for your next drama or you're running away from the police after an unsuccessful assassination.

MICHEL: You give me too much credit.

SONYA: Which is it, then?

MICHEL: I am just an unemployed, beardless Jewish engineering graduate looking for my first job.

SONYA: In Mongolia?

MICHEL: Why not? I'm told it's a land of great opportunity.

SONYA: And you think the police won't find you there?

MICHEL: I didn't say anything about police, Sonya Michalovnova.

SONYA: Did you steal something? Perhaps you strangled your girlfriend because you found her with another man?

MICHEL: You have a vivid imagination.

SONYA: Well, then, tell me.

MICHEL: All students have been ordered to do compulsory military training for at least two years. Army uniforms give me hives.

SONYA: That's not a good enough reason for running away. What's the real reason?

MICHEL: It's not really a very dramatic story. I was wrongly accused of something I didn't do. The police said I was lying and threatened to send me up for twenty years.

SONYA: So you decided to run.

MICHEL: Yes, that's more or less what happened.

SONYA: Couldn't you just go across the border to Poland? Seems closer.

MICHEL: I thought of that. But Poland is too close and crossing that border would be just like walking into a jail cell. And besides, the civil unrest there has made things difficult, especially for young Jewish engineers from Russia.

BORIS: And Pilsudski makes Stalin look like a pussycat.

SONYA: And you think Mongolia would be better?

MICHEL: It can't be much worse. But there is one big problem.

BORIS: Maybe we can help. What is it?

MICHEL: I have no identity card.

SONYA: That's all?

MICHEL: Or visa.

SONYA: Oh, I thought it was something serious.

BORIS: And you have no money to convince the border guards
            to let you out of Russia?

MICHEL: Well, actually that's right.

SONYA: There's a train going back to St. Petersburg in a few
            hours. Maybe you should go home and get your papers
            back?

MICHEL: Have you any other good ideas?

SONYA: I'll work on it. It seems we're having a longer than usual
            stop here.

MICHEL: Where are we?

SONYA: This should be Irkutsk.

MICHEL: Can we get off the train to stretch our legs here?

SONYA: Only if the provodnik says it is OK.

(The train public address systems blares out an almost unintelligible message.)

BORIS: You won't believe it!

SONYA: Stalin has resigned?

BORIS: Be serious, can't you?

MICHEL: They've run out of coal for the train.

BORIS: Close. The engine broke down and they have to send to
            Moscow for a replacement part.

SONYA: And what happens to us?

BORIS: We wait.

MICHEL: For how long?

BORIS: God knows.

MICHEL:	Isn't there another train?
SONYA:	That's the one that is bringing the replacement part.
MICHEL:	At least now it will be easier for you to practice your violin, Boris.
SONYA:	And since there is no piano on the train I can try to find a way of getting Misha out of the country.

SCENE SIX

SONYA:	Misha, we'll be in Zabaykalsk tomorrow. That's the border and we get off there. Have you decided how you're going to deal with the border guards?
MICHEL:	Can I hide in your luggage?
BORIS:	We could try to bribe the guard.
MICHEL:	That won't work.
SONYA:	Why?
MICHEL:	I don't have enough money.
SONYA:	Tell him you'll write a check.
BORIS:	Be serious, Sonya.
MICHEL:	Can I get off at the stop before the border and walk?
SONYA:	Good idea but it won't work.
MICHEL:	Why?
BORIS:	It's freezing cold outside and there's no city within a hundred kilometers.
SONYA:	You can just tell the truth. I'm told the jails in this part of Russia are rather comfortable and the work is not too hard.

BORIS: They'll take him to the local immigration office and make some replacement papers. It could take weeks. By then the police are sure to find him.

MICHEL: I'm sorry, dear friends, that I've gotten you so mixed up in my personal affairs.

SONYA: There has to be a way.

BORIS: How do they do it in books or in the cinema?

SONYA: Maybe we could talk our way into Manchuria.

BORIS: That should be easy for you, Sonya.

SONYA: I could say Misha and I have just become engaged to be married and I was coming home to introduce my future husband to his new in-laws, brothers, sisters, cousins, and so forth. And Boris, you'll say Misha is a close relative—a cousin you were bringing home to meet the family.

MICHEL: I really like that idea.

SONYA: And in Omsk, at the station, some hooligans stole Misha's pocketbook with all of his papers and money.

BORIS: Do you really think the guards are that stupid?

SONYA: Most of them.

MICHEL: And if they don't believe us?

SONYA: Then we'll join you in Siberia.

BORIS: You have to make the story more believable.

SONYA: I don't even have an engagement ring.

MICHEL: Maybe if they let us off the train I could buy one.

BORIS: Well…

SONYA: What is it, Boris?

BORIS:	I happen to have an engagement ring in my suitcase. I was rather saving it for…. But I guess I could loan it to you … just for this drama.
SONYA:	That's a most generous offer, Boris. What do you think, Misha? Shall we try it?
MICHEL:	I'll never be able to repay you for your kindness.

SCENE SEVEN

Inside the Manchuria railroad station in China

SONYA:	Well, we did it!
MICHEL:	*You* did it, Sonya. We were just the audience. Your performance was great. Perhaps you should give up the piano and go on the stage.
BORIS:	Bravo, Sonya. You had the border guard eating out of your hand.
SONYA:	I thought perhaps the story about how Misha lost the papers may have been a bit too dramatic.
MICHEL:	The more fantastic your description became, the more the guards became spellbound.
SONYA:	Well, dear friends, what should we do now?
BORIS:	Perhaps we can help Misha find which train he should take from here.
MICHEL:	Don't worry about me. I'll be fine here.
SONYA:	What will you do, Misha?
MICHEL:	My father used to say, "If you don't know where you're

going, it doesn't matter how quickly you get there!" I'm in no hurry, now that we're out of Russia.

BORIS: There's nothing much in Manchuria these days. It's practically deserted. It's mostly a border crossing. I think you should head for Ulaanbaatar. It's a big trading center and there's lots of commercial activity there.

SONYA: Manchuria is actually a lovely little city. Not very big. But it was where my father first settled when he came from Russia.

MICHEL: Why here, Sonya? It's in the middle of nowhere.

SONYA: It was easy to get to. You could walk across the border if you had to. And in 1885 the Russians received a concession from the Chinese to build the Chinese Railroad that would go as far as Port Arthur.

BORIS: I didn't know your family went to Manchuria.

SONYA: Not everyone came. Uncle Machi decided to go to America instead.

BORIS: What was the attraction of China?

SONYA: Many Jews landed up here. In Moscow, Jewish workers were expelled. Pogroms were still common. So, many left in search of a better life.

MICHEL: Why were the Russians so generous?

SONYA: They wanted rapid economic development and so encouraged investors and entrepreneurs to immigrate to Manchuria.

BORIS: So the whole family packed up and fled Russia?

SONYA: Uncle Abraham came first, and after getting started he sent for the rest of the family.

MICHEL: And what did they all do?

SONYA: My father started the first printing shop here, after he came from Russia. After that, the community started a newspaper and he printed that, too. Later, he became the head of the Jewish community.

MICHEL: Is there a big Jewish community in Manchuria?

SONYA: No. Once the Russians and Chinese agreed to extend the railroad, Harbin became the center point for all railroad enterprises—a hub for all train connections—and a center for trade. Many Jewish families moved there.

MICHEL: And they stayed there?

SONYA: Harbin had already become the Jewish cultural capital of the Far East by the time the railroad was finished. It has maybe twenty-five thousand Jews.

BORIS: Well, getting back to where Misha should go, I still think Ulaanbaatar makes the most sense for you.

SONYA: Misha knows no one there, Boris. What will he do?

BORIS: Begin to knock on doors looking for a job. He's an engineer. He speaks Russian, German, and French. That should be enough to get him started somewhere.

SONYA: I have an idea. Why not come with us to Manchuria, or Manzhouli, as they now prefer to call it?

BORIS: That's just putting things off. He needs to get a job.

MICHEL: Boris is right, Sonya. The invitation is most generous and tempting, but I've imposed on you both long enough. I must let you get on with your lives.

SONYA: Maybe you'll have some better opportunities in Manzhouli. It's exploding with new opportunities since the railroad became a reality.

BORIS: Mostly people are still struggling to make a living there.

SONYA: You haven't been there for three years.

MICHEL: Before I left, my mother gave me some names of people I
             might look up if I ever needed help.

BORIS: In Ulaanbaatar?

MICHEL: No, actually, in Manzhouli. She said it had a lively,
             sophisticated, and friendly Jewish community.

SONYA: Well, then it's decided. We'll go to Manzhouli. OK?

BORIS: What are the names of people you want to contact,
             Misha?

MICHEL: I'll have a look. [*MICHEL reaches into his inside jacket
             pocket and carefully unfolds a piece of notepaper.*] There is
             a family that came from St. Petersburg called Klebanoff.
             Do you know them?

SONYA: Of course! They own a musical instrument store on the
             main street. I was in school with one of their daughters.

MICHEL: Let me see. Then there is a large Jewish family called
             [*reading from his notes*] Dinaburg.

SONYA: Are you joking?

MICHEL: No. That's the name my mother wrote down just here,
             look. Why are you surprised?

BORIS: Tell him, Sonya.

MICHEL: Tell me what?

SONYA: That's my family's name.

MICHEL: Are you serious?

SONYA: Do you want to see my visa?

BORIS: She's telling the truth, Misha.

MICHEL: Why would my mother know your family's name?

SONYA: I can only imagine that Uncle David met your father on one of his buying trips to St. Petersburg.

MICHEL: Would your uncle be buying cloth for making suits and costs?

SONYA: Yes, and other things, too.

MICHEL: Well, maybe that's how they knew his name. My father had a shop selling cloth and woolen goods.

SONYA: Now it's settled. You have to come home with us.

BORIS: Are you sure you want to do this, Misha? I'm sure you'd be welcome in Manzhouli any time. You don't have to rush there now. I'd find a job first, and then come and visit.

SONYA: When you taste my mother's borscht, you'll never want to leave.

MICHEL: You're a very convincing young woman, Sonya.

SONYA: My heart is my compass. Should I return the ring to Boris?

MICHEL: I like the way it looks on you. Boris doesn't need it—just yet.

SCENE EIGHT

Dining room in Sonya's house in Manzhouli

FATHER: So, Sonichka, you've been home for a few weeks. Are you sorry you left your school in St. Petersburg?

SONYA: No, Father, it's lovely to be back home.

FATHER: And have you seen lots of changes since you left?

SONYA: It's amazing. Manzhouli has grown in practically every dimension. New people, more streets, new houses, grand public buildings, bigger shops. It's like a miracle.

FATHER: It is a miracle. But still, as our life here gets better and more secure, people are leaving. Even some of our own family has moved away since you left.

SONYA: Are they leaving because they're looking for better opportunities?

FATHER: No. There are plenty of opportunities here. I think they're scared.

SONYA: Of what?

FATHER: The unknown. Rumors scare people. Regardless of how obscure and unfounded or far-fetched the stories may be, people hear what they want to hear and often block out the truth.

SONYA: May I change the subject for a minute?

FATHER: Of course.

SONYA: Did [hesitatingly] Misha come to see you yesterday?

FATHER: You mean Michel.

SONYA: Did you talk with him?

FATHER: Yes.

SONYA: And?

FATHER: We had a nice walk and long chat.

SONYA: And? Did he say anything else?

FATHER: Let me think…

SONYA: Father, please, you know…

FATHER: Oh, yes, he did ask me if I would consent to have him marry you.

SONYA: And what did you say?

FATHER: I asked him if he didn't think that things were moving a bit too quickly, since you've only known each other for such a short time.

SONYA: And what did he say?

FATHER: He said he'd made up his mind the first time he met you in the train station in St. Petersburg.

SONYA: Did he say anything else?

FATHER: He felt very sad about disappointing Boris.

SONYA: Boris will always be our best friend.

FATHER: I asked him how he was going to support you after you got married.

SONYA: And what did he say?

FATHER: He was a bit vague, but assured me that you would always be well taken care of.

SONYA: I love him very much, Father.

FATHER: Are you sure?

SONYA: I can't imagine spending the rest of my life with anyone but Misha.

FATHER: I told him he would be most welcome in our family.

*   *   *

Boris enrolled at the conservatory of music in Harbin, where he continued his studies with some of the great violin teachers from Odessa, and then, for several years, he traveled around the world giving concerts. Unfortunately, he was killed soon after in a car accident in Berlin.

Sonya and Michel arrived in Manzhouli and were married four weeks later. Their first child, Mark, was born two years later. Some six years later, they had another son, Henri, born in Brussels, Belgium.

ACT 2 of the play *A Manchurian Odyssey* is a work in progress.

Geoffrey and I standing outside the front door of the apartment house in St. Petersburg (2009) where my father grew up. I tried to imagine my father's emotions that evening in 1925 when he bid his family farewell, not knowing if he would ever see any of them again.

10

Going Posh

On the night my father, Michel, hurriedly left Leningrad in 1925, only his mother came to see him off. As he boarded the train, he promised her that he would be back to see her as soon as it was safe to come home.

Four years later, now living in Manchuria, married with one small child, he decided to fulfill his promise. After almost three years without a holiday, he made a plan to use some savings he had accumulated and take his wife and son to Europe. Instead of making the two-week journey by train, he thought it would be more relaxing to go by sea.

He diligently collected some photographs to show his family

a glimpse of the life he had made for himself in Manchuria, and carefully filled a small photo album with them. Many of the photos in this book came from that album, which is preserved in our family archive.

En route to its final destination, the passenger ship stopped in Port Said, Egypt, for a few days.

The world's political and economic situation that greeted the young family when they landed in Port Said in January 1930 was depressive and worrisome. The aftermath of the 1929 stock market crash in the United States had impacted the economic climate throughout the world. Double-digit inflation was considered the norm in most countries. High unemployment throughout the continent cast an aura of gloom wherever they went. In Germany, the seeds of Fascism were well sown and in some places thriving.

Whatever plans that had been made before the family left had to be cancelled. The visa required for travel to Russia carried a serious possibility of becoming a one-way ticket, a risk Michel was not prepared to take.

The situation was further complicated when he received a long cable from his family in Manchuria....

My big brother, Mark, with his proud parents, for the obligatory first family portrait, February 1928

*A welcome
stopover in the
Middle East on
the voyage from
China to Europe
in 1929*

*Father never missed an opportunity to explore places. In Port Said,
Egypt, the stay was brief but he made time for a private guided tour of
the city.*

*It did not take long for everyone to adjust to the
formality of a European capital.*

PART II

BRUSSELS SPROUTS

*Precious hours with Father, during one of his weekend
visits to our summer house in Knokke*

Introduction
A Cable from Home

December 1929
Manzhouli, Manchuria

Dearest Children,

As much as we are all anxious to see you come back home I think on balance it is best that you delay your return to Manchuria for a little time. The political and economic situation here is becoming more complicated and seemingly unsolvable. We all feel that things will get worse before they get better. Many businesses have had to close their doors and even the most basic commodities are becoming difficult to find, and very expensive. It makes no sense for you to travel all the way back and find yourselves in the middle of terrible political storms with all of their related consequences. I think it is simply not safe here anymore.

Ever since Chiang Kai-shek broke off diplomatic relations with Russia two years ago, his Kuomintang government has been trying to expand its authority and control to Manchuria. Chiang's government has posed a real threat to the Soviets and their ownership of the Chinese Eastern Railroad (CER). You will remember that while you were away in 1924 the Russians secured the title to the railroad via a treaty signed in Mukden.

A few months ago in May, the Chinese organized vicious attacks on Soviet consulates as well as several important locations along the CER line, and eventually took complete control of the railroad and many of its ancillary service centers. Misha, you would almost certainly have been directly involved if you were here.

In September, the Russian army under General Bliukher arrived in Manchuria and drove all the Chinese forces out, and re-established Russian presence here. These have been difficult times for all of us as you can imagine. Several of our family have already planned to leave. Many of our friends have also decided it was time to move on. Amazingly some are going to Australia and even Mexico or Cuba.

At the same time, the Japanese invasion of Northern Manchuria has served to complicate the situation and frankly, nobody knows for sure what will happen next. I fear for the worst.

I know that you will be anxious to get back home after all these weeks away and no one is more anxious than I to see you back. But for now, please find some temporary home in Europe and wait for the storm clouds to take their course. We of course have close family in America but I am told that visas are almost impossible to get at the moment.

Please let me know if there is anything I can do to help.

All my love,
Father

11

Homeless and Stateless

The year 1929 was not a particularly good year to be Jewish and stateless in Europe. Most countries there and in North America were struggling with high inflation, unemployment, high interest rates, and growing national debt. And finally, on October 29, Black Friday, the New York stock market crashed, which had immediate repercussions throughout Europe and the rest of the world.

This is the Europe that greeted my parents and my brother, Mark, as they stepped ashore in Marseilles after a long sea voyage from Shanghai. They were on my parents' first holiday since they had married in 1925 in Manchuria. What they saw and heard made them glad they could go back to their life in China, enjoying a stable, although slow-growing economy, a peaceful environment, and a comfortable lifestyle.

But shortly after they arrived, the news from their family back in Manchuria was that things had deteriorated rapidly at home, politically as well as economically, and the future was fraught with potentially devastating consequences. They were urged by their family and friends to stay in Europe for a little while, until things calmed down and political stability re-established itself. It did not. Things got worse. Much worse. The options of where to settle down, even for a few years, were narrowed when it became clear that most countries in Europe no longer allowed even limited immigration. Great Britain and France had repressive quota systems, as did the United States, that essentially closed their borders. Belgium was one of the only countries into which they were allowed.

On May 13, 1930, Father finally was able to "arrange" an official identity card and passport at the Lithuanian Embassy in Brussels. Despite using three different spellings of the family name and some questionable entries in the "nationality" line, these papers permitted the entire family to settle in Belgium. One can only guess how much they had cost to acquire.

My parents' new home, in May 1930, was in Antwerp. Like so many refugees, their initial thoughts concerned how to earn a living and how to establish contacts with friends and family who might provide some ideas and connections for starting an enterprise or trade. Shanghai would have been a natural first step to search for commercial contacts. But the emergence of the Communist party

Until Father was finally issued an official permit to live in Antwerp, the family were considered stateless aliens.

"Official" identity card and passport from Lithuanian Embassy, Brussels

and the fallout from the Russo–Japanese War made normal international commercial relationships highly unreliable.

So Father turned to his friends, siblings, and cousins in Finland for advice and help. With no capital, only a modest command of the local language, and hardly any network of business or commercial contacts, his options were limited.

Antwerp was a thriving metropolis with a large Jewish population, mostly East Europeans who had arrived in the late nineteenth century, fleeing from pogroms. It was these Jews who created what was to become one of the world's largest centers for uncut diamonds, being at its height responsible for four-fifths of the world's uncut diamond trade. In addition to four individual bespoke trading markets, there was even a separate metro stop called "Diamont." As the diamond industry grew, so did the need for supporting commercial and financial services. Large national and international banks found that it was not profitable for them to provide small businesses, often sole proprietorships, with services, such as executing foreign exchange transactions, providing letters of credit, certificates of origin, bills of lading, insurance, and other trade documents.

Although he had had no direct experience in any of these commercial transactions in China, Father was certainly familiar with most of the basic forms of documentation. So the newly arrived immigrant from China decided to earn his livelihood in the illustrious world of banking—or at least in a very specialized corner of the business.

Starting all over again must have been a wrenching choice for my father and mother. They spoke very little French and even less

Flemish. The year 1929 was not a good time to start a new career, especially in banking. And while they may have had some modest financial resources to get started, there was no family to support them in difficult times. For the next few years, Father worked in a commercial bank preparing himself for a new career.

Then, in 1932, he had an opportunity to change employers and help create a new foreign exchange bank in Brussels, the capital of Belgium. It was the center of the country's financial institutions, and a larger, more cosmopolitan city than Antwerp. He and his new partner, Mr. Bernstein, co-founded the Nord Exchange at 85 Boulevard Adolphe Max, in the heart of Brussels.

I joined the family late one night, on 24 October 1933.

12

In the Beginning

My first home in Brussels, at 41 Avenue Jamblinne de Meux, was a five-bedroom apartment on the second floor in a prosperous neighborhood surrounded by tree-lined boulevards and nearby public parks. In addition to my mother, father, brother, and myself, the household included Fima, Isa ("Jack"), and Shura. Fima was my mother's brother and Isa, his closest friend and cousin. Shura was our residential nanny, cook, and housekeeper. Shura, similar to many other middle-aged, unmarried Russian immigrants, was sure she was Anastasia, daughter of the recently murdered tsar, waiting eagerly to be recalled to the soon to be re-established Romanoff court in St. Petersburg.

My first and only home in Brussels was a rather grand second-floor apartment in a suburb. My stylish mod carriage appears to be capable of being converted to a bathtub.

My earliest memories were of a happy, stress-free, busy, active household with people coming and going and what seemed to be an endless stream of visitors popping in and out, usually without much ceremony or special occasion.

While we had no immediate family living in Belgium, the community of Russian-speaking recent immigrants made up a closely knit social group. I well remember the Mosieffs, Vilkomers, Bagins, Stolloffs, Rosovskys, and the family of my father's partner in business, the Bernsteins. Amazingly, with the exception of the Bernsteins, I was able in later years to meet all of these family friends. One of them,

Henry Rosovsky, is still today a close friend, living in Cambridge, Massachusetts.

My first language was Russian, which is what we spoke at home. I remember Father explaining that we would all learn to speak French, which he called the "language of the streets," but if we did not speak Russian at home we would soon forget it. He was right. While my Russian vocabulary today is limited, essentially, to that of a six-year-old, my Russian pronunciation and accent are, apparently, practically "native."

In the absence of nursery schools, pre-kindergartens, kindergartens, special infant tutors, and a bevy of other professionals anxious to assist young children, I had to wait until I was five and a half before I was able to attend a proper school. Somehow I survived this deprivation.

Our family lifestyle might well be described as upper middle class. Our apartment was well furnished, with a fair share of contemporary paintings, oriental rugs, all types of books, and a fashionable "wireless," or radio. Mother's piano was in a prominent position in the living room, and was home for our friendly ceramic white horses. Father drove a large Mercedes convertible and Mother was usually decked out in the latest fashions, often from Paris.

We took our summer holidays at the beach in Knokke or Ostende, and throughout the year made weekend visits to various Belgian sites of special interest. Sometimes we even traveled beyond the Belgian borders—I remember a nip down to Nice, France, for the famous Bataille des Fleurs. There was at least one trip by train to Paris to see

Flower parades, rocky beaches, exotic gardens, and plenty of sunshine were happy memories on our spring holidays in Nice.

the Eiffel tower, the Jardin d'Acclimatation, and the Bateaux Mouches. In winter, our skiing and other winter sports destination was usually the resort town of Engelberg, Switzerland.

Our apartment was close to the military school, and a great treat I remember was going to the school and watching the students drilling in the yard. The precision of the soldiers' movements fascinated me, and I am sure at some stage I was hoping I could be one of them!

Weekends in Belgium were always family affairs. Where we were going was not as important as the fact that we always went as a family, and usually with a number of close family friends as well. Whether it was an overnight farm visit, special trips to the zoo in Antwerp, picnics, miniature golf, watching windmills in northern Belgium, or just excursions to parks, there was always something happening to keep one busy and occupied.

Close to home were weekends at the farm. As dedicated city dwellers, being able to stay on a real farm with live animals and a real farm family was a special treat. I don't remember how often we stayed there, but it must have been one of my favorite outings.

I was also particularly fond of the massive zoo that was right in the middle of Antwerp. It was very special because most of the animals there lived in vast areas and, instead of fences separating them from the visitors, there were natural barriers, usually moats, so you could imagine the animals in their real habitats.

Engelberg, Switzerland, winter 1937. You were never too young to start learning how to ski.

Mark and I on our way to help Father in his office on a Saturday morning, wearing our smart matching camelhair coats. Father is lovingly looking on from the side.

A visit to my father's office on Saturday mornings was always a memorable occasion. It was a chance to dress up and feel very special. The office, which was actually small, to me, was like visiting my father's own special multi-roomed palace. There were several neatly arranged desks, each with its own clear surface except for a variety of calculating machines with shiny keyboards and a unique assortment of handles to crank, wheels to turn, and knobs to spin. As you sat at each desk, it wasn't hard to imagine you were sitting at the controls of a fast-moving train or a high-flying airplane.

Without TV, computers, iPads, Game Boy, and the array of

Mother's piano, although in the living room, was often an alternative form of entertainment for Mark and me. Our two white ceramic horses look on knowingly from above.

electronic toys available today, how did I spend my time at home? My earliest memory, supported by photos and legends, was of my collection of wooden farm animals, fences, and farm buildings. The collection must have started with a single animal and over time was augmented by gifts from family and friends on appropriate occasions. All of the wooden pieces lived on a small wooden table and I continuously rearranged them.

When we escaped from Brussels in 1939, I was told there was very little room for my toys and books. I did take several of the animals, which have long since disappeared, and five or six books, which surprisingly have survived to this day, including the French versions of *Snow White and the Seven Dwarfs* and *Little Red Riding Hood*, several *Le Prince Riri* comic books, and two splendid *Felix the Cat* cartoon storybooks. Mother also brought some of my much-loved Russian children's books, which were always about animals.

*   *   *

While we were enjoying ourselves on the farm in the spring of 1938, Europe was in turmoil and the winds of war were blowing hard. Hitler marched unopposed into Austria, Chamberlain returned from Germany, triumphantly announcing that he had met with Hitler and "it is peace for our time." The Japanese destroyed Canton in a merciless bombing raid. And laws were passed in Germany making it illegal for Germans to play with or even speak to Jewish children.

Father was looking at what he could do to get the family out of Europe before war started in earnest. Having escaped from Russia in 1925 and having left Harbin in 1929, he was certainly under no illusions, as so many other Europeans were, that things would get better soon. He was determined to protect his family and survive.

I now know that one of the things he initiated as far back as 1934 was the transfer of funds from Belgium to the United States. My archives contain detailed bank statements, from Guaranty Trust Company of New York, showing that he sent a modest but constant trickle of funds to America so that when and if we managed to get there, we would be financially independent and not have to rely on relatives, charities, or other handouts. The statement from September 30, 1939, one month before we left Brussels, shows that he had indeed been able to transfer a substantial sum.

13

My Big Brother, Mark

Mark was born in 1927, six years before me almost to the day. It is a curious fact that as we grew older, the relative differences between our ages became smaller. When we arrived in America in 1939, Mark was twice as old as I was. It would be some years until I was no longer considered the baby brother. By the time I graduated from university, I was almost three-quarters his age.

Despite our age difference, I cannot recall any sibling rivalry between us. We had a comfortable, warm, harmonious household, and the presence of Fima and Isa provided several centers of serenity in the exceptional cases when conflicts arose and one needed a safe haven or a trusted arbitrator.

It was clear from an early age that I was destined to be slightly overweight—well, at least pudgy.

In my first official photograph, Mark did not seem thrilled to be sitting for a portrait with his four-months-old brother. Obviously, my proclivity for weight gain was a problem right from the beginning. Mark's made-to-order sailor suit was eventually handed down to me and today remains intact, except for a few moth holes, in our long-term hanging storage closet (and available for loan for costume parties).

Although my rightful legal name was Henri for as long as I can remember, I was called "Riri" in Belgium. Perhaps I had difficulty pronouncing my given name when I began talking, or perhaps it was the French comic book character Prince Riri—we will never know the origin of my nickname. In any case, it was a lot easier to say "Riri" than the Russian equivalent, which was "Ondrushinka." Nevertheless, I answered to that mouthful as well.

As I grew bigger, I idolized my older brother. I wanted to do all the things he did—play with his friends, go on camping trips with his Boy Scout group, and I always wanted to be wherever he was. On one occasion, despite using all of my powers of persuasion, I was unable to convince anyone that I should be allowed to go with the big boys on an overnight excursion, although I was allowed to see them off at the central railroad station. I am sure Mark was not thrilled with this hero worship.

I could never understand why I could not go on an overnight hike with the big Boy Scouts.

During our last few months in Brussels, Father decided to send Mark to an English-speaking boarding school. Almost certainly this was in anticipation of fulfilling his hope someday to move to the United States and settle him into an English-speaking school. For a few months, I was able to play the only child in the family, and I didn't like it very much.

When I was finally old enough to go to school, I was thrilled to be in the same building as Mark, albeit in different classes. In fact, the best part of going to school was being able to walk to school together. Even though I probably attended for only a few months, my first school left a tremendous impression on me. (Twenty-five years later, when Alberta and I were in Brussels, I decided to visit it. The evening before our planned visit, I tried to draw, as best I could remember, a floor plan of the school and my classroom. My sketch proved to be surprisingly accurate.)

Later, when we were finally settled in America, it became difficult to follow Mark around. We quickly established our own circles of friends and our own unique activities. But we did have one common venture, about which I have fond memories. Mark somehow arranged to have a daily newspaper delivery route in the neighborhood. A carefully wrapped package of morning papers arrived on our doorstep every morning, with labels indicating the address to which each of the papers should be delivered. Mark began by fixing the newspapers to his bicycle in specially provided saddlebags, and as he cycled down the street he would stop, fold the newspaper, and from the curb try to throw the paper as close as possible to the front door. Most houses had rather large front lawns, and newspapers propelled towards the front door typically fell well short of their target.

As complaints from customers began to accumulate, it was clear that the strategy of "airlifting" the papers from the curb to the front door was not an option. Mark would be obliged to get off his bike, put its kickstand down, and hand-carry the newspaper to the designated front door. Eventually, he determined that he could outsource or subcontract the last stage in the newspaper delivery process. I was the subcontractor. My compensation was the privilege of each morning having a ride on the back of Mark's bicycle. I don't remember how long that lasted. I suspect Father intervened on my behalf and insisted that I be properly compensated.

14

Fima and Isa,
aka Ephraim and Israel

When I was growing up, I considered Fima and Isa my older brothers, and it was many years later that I realized that Fima was my uncle (Mother's younger brother), and Isa was my cousin, also on my mother's side. But it did not really matter; both Fima and Isa lived as an indivisible part of our household all the years we lived in Brussels. They shared our lives as an integral part of our family. We had dinner together and went on holidays together. It was Fima who introduced me to Jules Verne. I am sure he became bored of reading *Around the World in Eighty Days*, *Journey to the Center of the Earth*, and *Twenty*

Being an integral part of the household meant that we were able to spend a lot of time together, both at home and on trips. Isa, Mother, Henry (in front), Fima, and Mark.

Thousand Leagues Under the Sea out loud to me, but they remain some of my favorite books.

How Fima and Isa came to live with us is a complex saga. Both of "the boys," as Mother always referred to them, were born in Manzhouli and grew up together as close friends there. They went to school together and both wanted to study engineering.

Unfortunately there was no way they could study engineering at a higher educational level in either Manzhouli or Harbin. The possibilities open to them were limited, and eventually they decided to study in Europe. Why they chose the university in Grenoble is not clear. It was a strange choice. Neither of them spoke French particularly well.

Grenoble is in the mountains of central France and not particularly accessible. Nor was it particularly cosmopolitan. But strangest of all was the fact that it was not likely that either of them could ever find a job in France at that time, the early 1930s. Obviously they must have planned to return home after their studies and find work in China.

They chose to leave China as political unrest escalated into armed conflict. Although there was no military activity near Manzhouli, no one could be certain of the future. They hoped to stay away long enough to get an education and avoid the bloodshed and instability.

The five-year program in France was a big success, and both Fima and Isa graduated close to the top of their class. Not being able to find work in France, but deciding that going back to China in the middle of a revolution was impractical, the "boys" came to visit us in Brussels and try to work out their future plans. They must have come just after I was born, in 1933, because I have photographs with them when I was just a few months old.

Back in Manzhouli, the inevitable exodus of family had become a veritable flood. Most went first to Shanghai and then to either Japan or Australia. By then, it must have become obvious to Fima and Isa that returning to China was not a feasible option, and when it became clear that there were few employment alternatives for Fima and Isa in Belgium, Father gave them a job in the Nord Exchange Bank. They must have done well because after a few years, they opened a branch at 156, Rue Neuve, in a busy arcade in the financial district. I suppose to call it an office is a slight exaggeration, but at least it was a viable commercial location in a busy, covered shopping arcade in the center of Brussels, and it gave the "boys" a chance to be on their own.

When, in 1939, we left Brussels without them to come to America, it was an enormous trauma for all of us. I was exceptionally affected because I was too young to understand why they couldn't come along with us, just as they had come on family outings, picnics, and holidays. Father was able to promise me that they would soon follow and would join us in America. He could not know that, in fact, it would take almost six years before they were able to join us. And by that time, in late 1945, Father had died.

On Friday May 10, 1940, the Germans invaded Belgium, marched into Holland and Luxemburg. Finally, on the morning of Sunday May 12, after months of Father pleading with them to leave Brussels, Fima and Isa packed a few personal items into Father's car and, along with thousands of others fleeing the Germans, began the hazardous

Father's Mercedes never seemed to have any limit on how many people could fit in the back seat.

journey by road southward. The entire Bernstein family of mother, father, and three children joined them in the car.

On their way out of Brussels, the last stop they made was at the bank on 85 Boulevard Adolphe Max. As Mr. Bernstein was co-owner with my father of the Nord Exchange Bank, he made the decision to open the large safe at the back of the office and collect all of the currency, both local and foreign, that they could find. The cash was removed in bags and suitcases, and then he carefully secured the premises. It was impossible to remove money from the corporation's bank account, however, as May 12 was a Sunday.

Their plan was to drive until they reached an Atlantic port, where they hoped to find passage out of Europe. Fima and Isa were anxious to see their parents, after twelve years away from them, and hoped to return home to China. The Bernsteins decided to try to reach the Belgian Congo. The closest ports of Calais, Cherbourg, Brest, and Saint Nazaire were already in a war zone, so the safest bet was to make for Bordeaux and, in fact, that is where their retreat halted, as travel further south was impossible. When it became clear that their journey could not continue, Mr. Bernstein made arrangements to charter an entire merchant vessel in order to leave France safely and to take everyone to a neutral port in Portugal.

In these far-from-normal times, it was impossible to buy passage through normal channels. It was necessary to make off-the-record arrangements. The small group of seven escapees from Brussels was joined by another group of refugees, and they were finally able to make arrangements to sail to Africa. Being desperate times, the captain demanded $40,000 for the group, which, fortunately, Fima and Isa were able to pay out of the funds from the Nord Exchange Bank safe.

The S.S. *Dora* was a modest tramp steamer but the forty-five passengers who boarded her, including Fima and Isa, were happy to be on their way to a safer environment. Unfortunately, the Turkish captain had other plans. When the ship arrived in the Port of Lisbon, he demanded more money from the passengers. The passengers were unable to meet the captain's demand and decided to leave the ship.

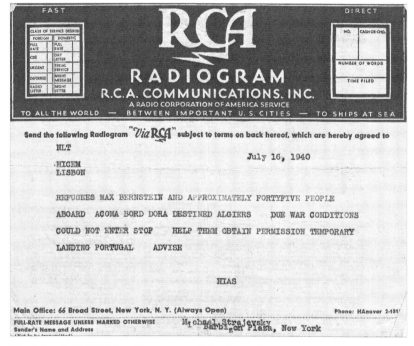

The July 1940 HIAS cable arranged for forty-five passengers to stay under police control in a small Portuguese village until they could arrange onward passage

Unfortunately, however, the Portuguese authorities would not allow any of them to enter the country. It was Father's intervention, with the help of HIAS (Hebrew Immigrant Aid Society), that finally broke the impasse. In late July 1940, under heavy police control, the passengers of the S.S. *Dora* stepped foot on land in Lisbon.

One of those passengers found his way to New York later that year and gave us a first-hand report of the tribulations the group had faced in Lisbon. Mr. Maisel became a close family friend, and for years came to our home for Sabbath dinner. The Bernsteins eventually reached the Belgian Congo, where they spent the remainder of the war years. Fima and Isa were determined to see their parents in China and, after waiting a few months in Lisbon, they boarded the *Hakana Maru* for Tokyo. On the way, the ship moored in the New York harbor for a few days. Without a proper visa, neither one of "the boys" was allowed to leave the ship. But they could have visitors, and our whole family went to New York and visited them on board.

Not long after that, Father succeeded in arranging visas for them, and plans were made for them to return to the United States after the visit in China. But when they finally made their way to China, it proved to be impossible to travel north to Harbin to see their parents and, sadly, their parents were unable to travel south to see them.

The final act of their saga involved their return trip to the United States. Given the uncertainty of the times, Father had arranged passage for them on a passenger ship from Shanghai to San Francisco. Their ship, unfortunately, landed in Manila, the Philippines, on December 8, 1941, the day the Japanese invaded the Philippines and ten hours after their surprise attack on Pearl Harbor. As a consequence, both Fima and Isa were obliged to stay in Manila for the next four years. While not in a formal prisoner camp, they and several thousand others were confined to a carefully guarded refugee camp under severe conditions. Travel outside the compound was not possible and food supplies were barely adequate.

Happily, Isa met Sophie Greenberg in the camp. They fell in love, decided to marry after the war, and when the war ended they continued their journey to America. I guess it was perfectly natural that they should live with us in New York, just as they had done in Brussels. Ironically, their situation was not too dissimilar to the time when they had graduated from university in France—they could not go home, they had no jobs, they had very little money and even fewer assets.

The big difference was that when they rejoined us in 1946, they brought along a third person—Sophie. In fact, Sophie arrived on our doorstep about six months before the others. We all immediately fell in love with her and were delighted that Isa had decided to settle down and start a family. I still have fond memories of how she would frequently arrive home from her day job at a nearby Broadway bakery called Cake Masters, bringing a large and overflowing cake box of Napoleons and chocolate éclairs.

When Fima and Isa finally arrived, we all somehow managed to fit into our apartment, which was on Riverside Drive. It soon doubled as the office of a new trading venture known as Dunster Trading Company, and very quickly a new enterprise was born.

In 1946 I was thirteen, twice as old as when I had last seen Fima and Isa. I still looked upon them as older brothers, and since Father was no longer with us, in some small way they filled a gap in my life, for which I will always be grateful.

No one could explain to a six-year-old why Fima and Isa could not get off the boat, when it was moored in the harbor of New York City, and come home with us.

No one would even think of coming to the dinner table without a jacket and tie.

15

Come In, It's Time to Eat

Without doubt, in our home the evening meal was always the highlight of every day as we were growing up. It was a time when the whole family came together in what was essentially a family board meeting. Dinner was always in the dining room. There were always linen napkins, a fine tablecloth, elegant china, and exquisite silverware. Somehow, the actual menu seemed of secondary importance.

I do not recall prayers being said, but no one would dare pick up a spoon or fork before Father did, and that usually did not happen until he had shared with us some current news, topical gossip, or an amusing anecdote. Those few minutes before the meal made us all feel very important and somehow brought us all closer together. This ritual continued for as long as I remember.

When the war started and we were living in Cleveland, Ohio, these evening briefings were a substitute for the seven o'clock news. Once the meal began, everyone chipped in with questions, remarks, and most importantly their personal views. Disagreement was not only allowed but encouraged. Heated arguments were usually resolved by my father's Solomon-type judgments.

Until my fourth birthday, except on special occasions I ate all of my meals in the kitchen with Shura. On my fourth birthday, I graduated to the dining room with the big people. As you can imagine, graduation for me was a momentous occasion.

At that meal, which I remember with clarity, the first course was not our usual borscht or chicken soup but rather a thick cream of cauliflower soup with several grotesque bits of white cauliflower floating peacefully in the soup bowl. I did not like the smell of it, the look of it, the texture, or, of course, the taste. As politely as I could, I asked to be excused from the soup course. Unfortunately, my polite plea was denied by the "higher authorities" for reasons that are still to this day not clear to me.

I realized that rejecting one's soup would also almost certainly mean I would have to forego the rest of the meal, but this was a price I was prepared to pay. I was reminded that children in Armenia were starving, but it made little impression on me. And worse was yet to come.

The others finished their soup and went on to the main course, and eventually the dessert arrived. I was invited to stay at the table with the cauliflower soup in the bowl in front of me while the others finished their dinner. By this time the soup was not only ice cold but had morphed into something resembling an atomic bomb mushroom cloud. I made a calculated decision that it would be better to starve and miss a meal than get sick. What I did not know then was that another part of the "sentence" for not eating one's soup was instant relegation back to the kitchen.

The next day, dear Shura welcomed me back to the kitchen at dinnertime. I am sure she was secretly happy—she never liked to eat alone, as I recall. I cannot remember how long my "sentence" was.

Today, all of our evening meals at home, whether elaborate or simple, are always taken in our dining room. Is this a reaction to my experience as a four-year-old? I will let all you armchair psychiatrists decide.

This image is permanently etched into my personal memory bank.

The hair, well... but the dress must go.

16

No More Fringe Benefits

In Belgium, it was considered politically correct and patriotically fashionable to follow the Royal Family's lead in respect to dress, hairstyle, and holidays. For example, no matter how cold it was in November, if the Crown Prince was wearing short trousers, it was considered unpatriotic and politically incorrect to wear anything else. If the Queen went to a concert in a short skirt, you can be sure that there would not be a long dress in the hall.

Where this practice of playing "follow my monarch" had the most pronounced impact for me was in terms of hairstyle. Throughout the country, in castles and palaces in Belgium, all royal children had bangs, or fringes, covering most of their forehead. This was not to cover up their wrinkles. It simply was Le Mode du Jour.

When the young prince finally had his fringe cut, there was a dash to the barbershops, which probably had to stay open late that fateful day to meet the demand. I was no exception and asked to have all my hair cut off. In fact, I was practically shaven. It was a great day. I was getting annoyed at being mistaken for a girl. I suppose Mother's choice of clothing for me did not help to dispel this impression.

A curious consequence of my new hairless look was that I was apparently able to imitate Laurel, the skinny guy of Laurel and Hardy film fame. I am not sure who made the connection or if it were accurate, but I do remember that from time to time, I was encouraged to give visitors my special "Laurel look." Too bad I couldn't keep his physique as I grew older.

Resemblance to Laurel and Hardy was totally intentional.

17

Knokke, Belgium's Miami Beach?

Every August, the family moved to the seashore. That is because August was probably the only month that the water along the Belgian coast was even remotely warm enough to go into the North Sea, and even then one had to choose the days carefully for bathing to avoid frostbite. Wet suits had not yet been invented. Usually we spent four or five weeks each year *sur la mer*.

Belgium has three principal beach resorts—Knokke, Ostend, and Blankenberg—and all of them were within commuting distance from Brussels, about an hour and a half by car and a little less on a fast train. This meant that while Mother, Mark, Shura, and I spent all of our time at the beach in August, Father, Fima, and Isa typically would come down just for the weekends.

While today the Knokke beachfront is practically encircled by high-rise apartment buildings and hotels, in the 1930s one found a small number of summer homes, wild grassy dunes, and open spaces there. My unforgettable memory of Knokke, apart from the frigid water, is the extraordinarily wide beach and seemingly endless shallow water. This combination made it especially suitable for young children, who could walk out into the sea for miles and still be in water just up to their waists—while it was good for kids, it was not so good for serious swimmers, except at high tide.

Every summer Father would rent a simple house, within walking distance of the beach, with lots of rooms for visitors. At the beach, every family had their own private beach cabana, in which they were able to stuff every possible piece of essential beach furniture, including chairs, umbrellas, tables, and footrests, plus, of course, towels, cushions, and beach robes. In addition, there was an assortment of shovels, beach balls, pails, and other indispensable equipment. Everyone had extra bathing suits, which were mandatory to change into after even the briefest immersion into the frigid North Sea. I am sure we had no refrigerator in our beach cabana, but there always seemed to be a generous supply of food to suit every appetite at any time of the day.

Every day on the beach there was a frenetic schedule of activities for beachgoers of all ages, genders, skills, and interests. The activities were very well organized by counselors and guides, who seemed to be an integral part of the beach scene. Most of the activities were

Each family had its own private beach cabana which, among other beach necessities, is where they stored warm clothing, just in case.

designed as group events, typically in the form of a competition of one sort or another. While yoga had not yet arrived at the Belgian shore, yoga-type exercise classes certainly had, and they were always popular.

A long, flat, hard beach made running games particularly popular. Relay races, obstacle courses, potato sack races, and spoon and egg contests were standard weekday events. Finals were scheduled for weekends, when there were certain to be more spectators to cheer all of the contestants to victory.

Of the entire panoply of beach competitions and entertainment, building sand castles, topped with bespoke identifying flags was always my favorite. The basic concept was to see whose flag could withstand the ravages of the incoming tide for the longest period of time. You protected your flag with a highly sophisticated array of moats, walls, reservoirs, and cleverly designed abutments. Construction would

All ages joined in frequent rope pull challenges.

As the tide starts to rise, the last flag remaining upright is declared the winner.

begin when the starter blew his whistle and stopped after a predeter-mined time, typically when the tide first began its relentless approach to the line of carefully constructed citadels. Once the tide started to come in, no repair of your magnificent structure was allowed. The winning team was the one whose flag was left standing after all others had fallen.

Mark and I usually did very well in these contests, as I remember.

Our secret, which I can now share with the world for the first time, was not to worry too much about building a high mountain stronghold for the flag to fly from, but rather to put all one's energy into the construction of intricate and extensive networks of moats, barriers, and reservoirs designed to slow the flow of water, make it bypass your flag, and, hopefully, divert it away from your citadel. It was also possible, if one were clever, to arrange your walls and moats so that excess overflow would pass directly to the competitor's structure on either side of you. Yes, all is fair in love and sand castle building.

The alternative to the sand castle challenge was to build sand cars, sand airplanes, or sand sofas. Once completed, one's masterpiece would be embellished with appropriate accoutrements to represent steering wheels, instrument panels, cushions, armrests, and back seats.

Most of the Knokke beach's length, while sandy, was extremely hard-packed. As a result, horseback riding was often allowed. My equestrian experience was limited to sitting briefly on a horse for a photo op. Another much more popular form of locomotion was via sailboat and other basic waterborne craft. I remained, in the main, an expert dry-land sailor.

Despite the fact that hot sunny days were relatively rare in Knokke, a constant problem at the beach was getting sunburned. Suntan lotions existed but were not yet generally available commercially, and no one knew about the connection between sunburns and cancer (or that even on cloudy days, the bad infrared rays can get you into potentially serious trouble).

156

Horses, sailboats, and canoes were popular distractions on most days since the water was usually unbearably cold. Mark, my mother, and I.

157

The treatment for severe sunburn was something we all dreaded. It was so memorable that it was enough to make you wear a hat, use sunglasses, and wear a long-sleeved shirt, or stay under the beach umbrella, or hide in your cabana, for most of the day. The cure for serious sunburn consisted of being entombed in a specially prepared paste, made by mixing common baking powder and water. The theory was that once it was applied, the harmful elements in your skin that were causing you to turn bright red would abate and become absorbed in the slush being liberally applied to all parts of your body. At the beginning, this process was deemed amusing since we could all pretend to be King Tutankhamen. As the moisture in the paste evaporated, however, one felt more like a half-baked chocolate cake than an Egyptian pharaoh. When the baking powder began to crack all over your body the advice about staying out of the sun became an eleventh commandment.

Despite the fact that there was a fine train service from Brussels, most people arrived in Knokke by automobile. It became a favorite Friday late afternoon ritual to greet Father and whomever he had brought with him as weekend guests. In fact, our house and beach cabin was a magnet for what seemed like a continuous stream of friends. Some I knew from seeing them at our home in Brussels, but others seemed to be strictly beach friends. I knew everyone only by the family name. Some of the guests I remember were Mr. and Mrs. Sinai, Mr. and Mrs. Stoloff, the Mosieffs, the Bernsteins, and the Meltzers—that was the way I had to refer to them, as first names were strictly reserved for adults.

One year, our beach holiday home was in Ostend. While the beach there was similar to Knokke's, the amenities were much more sophisticated. There were mini-golf courses, amusement parks, and miles of esplanades or boardwalks with all types of rentable transport devices—bicycles, tricycles, six-person go-carts, and tandem bicycles.

The dress code left little to chance. Fima, Mother, Sinai, Mrs. Stoloff, Jack (with Mark on his shoulders), Mr. Stoloff (with me on his shoulders)

18

How I Lost My Favorite Toy

The summer of 1939 turned out to be an infamous time in modern history. In September, the German army marched into Poland, which was the start of World War II. For this little boy, however, the big event of that summer was a holiday in Switzerland with his mother. I had a bad cough that was diagnosed as asthma, and the doctors convinced my mother that I needed to spend some time in the fresh mountain air to clear my lungs. Mother took me to Engelberg, where we had so much enjoyed skiing in the winter.

One of my most favorite activities in Engelberg was riding up, by cable car, to one of the peaks surrounding the village. When I saw a toy model of the cable car in a local store window that summer, I was very excited. It was a rather simple toy—no batteries, no electronics, no ninety-page instruction book. A wire holding the cable car was attached at one end to a nail (or hook) in the wall, while the other end was fixed on the floor. A tiny wheel, turned by hand, moved the cable car along the wire from the "mountaintop" to the floor (or base station) and back up again. Some small figurines were provided to fill the car. It did not take long for me to decide that my life would fall apart if I could not take this toy cable car home with me to Brussels.

I convinced my mother that my asthma would get better much quicker if she bought me this little toy cable car. Eventually she did, and I played with it for hours at a time. I put the little people inside and moved them up and down the make-believe mountain I had constructed in my mind. Soon the cable car and I became insepa-rable, and I was then anxious to go back to Brussels so that I could share my new acquisition with the rest of the family.

When we got home, the ominous war clouds of the daily news overshadowed the excitement of a small boy and his new toy. The invasion of Poland was only the latest in a long catalog of German atrocities. Kristallnacht, anti-Jewish laws, concentration camps, the Anschluss of Austria, and the annexation of Sudetenland—the collective name for areas of Czechoslovakia with significant German populations—all were harbingers of tragedies to follow. I, of course, was well insulated from any of the horrible details of these events.

The first day Father saw me playing with my new toy, he was curiously silent. He did not share in my obviously passionate zeal, unlike the others in the family, and even left the room without a word.

162

Asthma may not have been the reason I was sent to Switzerland, but it was a lot more fun being there than in dreary Brussels.

Later, he returned to my room, disconnected the two ends of the cable car, and carefully returned them to the box in which they came. He left the room with the box under his arm, without saying a word.

To say that I was devastated would have been an understatement. I thought I must have done something terribly wrong to deserve such a dire punishment.

At some point, I can't honestly recall when, my father explained to me that the cable car was made in Germany, and given the current situation, it was his decision that we should not buy anything German. My precious cable car was a casualty of the war. Was my father's reaction rational? The people who built the toy were not concurrently waging war….

The episode of the cable car was etched into my memory. Not so much as a severe decision by my father but as an everlasting reminder of how strong personal and moral feelings can and should motivate one's actions, despite the consequences, which in this case was the disappointment of a five-and-a-half-year-old boy.

That was my first contribution to the war effort.

The design of my toy hasn't changed much in the last seventy years, as this photo taken in 2011 clearly shows.

19

The Calm Before the Storm, 1936–1937

In 1937 the Spanish Civil War captured the world's attention and the front pages of newspapers. Hardly anyone noticed that Mussolini had invaded and occupied Ethiopia. The Sino-Japanese War had erupted into a full-scale conflict, and Japanese bombs fell on Shanghai. Meanwhile Hitler had denounced the Locarno pact, which in 1926 had re-drawn borders in Europe, and had quietly occupied the Rhineland. The *Hindenburg* had exploded in mid-air, Roosevelt had been re-elected, and Edward VIII had renounced the British crown and wed Mrs. Wallis.

Brussels in 1937 enjoyed an uneventful, peaceful period. At home, a Sunday walk in the park was always a special attraction and an occasion to dress up. Father's bowtie was considered very avant-garde in those days, as were my shiny white "Sunday" sandals, reserved for special events. Father would put away his formal weekday banker's attire. His pitch-black bowler hat, no doubt imported from London, would peacefully rest on a tall clothing rack in the front hall. Mark was allowed to bring his new scooter, but had to wear a jacket. The park was actually a tree-lined central walkway between two sides of a road next to our apartment house.

Being six years younger than Mark meant that I always looked up to him and could not wait until I would reach his age and follow his example. Always, that is with one exception, which is still fresh in my mind.

One weekend, Father had forgotten to buy the weekend newspaper and decided it would be safe for Mark to walk to a nearby shop to buy the paper for him. While the shop was not very far, it did require crossing several streets that typically had light traffic. Without traffic lights, crossing a thoroughfare like that had to be done with some care and attention. This was going to be a big treat for Mark—doing an errand for Father without any supervision. In my eyes he was now practically an adult.

I remember Father carefully giving Mark detailed instructions on how to reach the shop, even though we had walked there with him or Mother many times. He gave him some money, and Mark was to go and return, without making any stops along the way, and bring back

Sunday was always Father's day.

the change that the shopkeeper would give him.

When Mark returned with the newspaper, Father asked him for the change. Mark calmly announced that as he was walking home as instructed, the few coins he had received in change slipped from his hand, fell on the street, and, unfortunately, rolled into an open sewer drain in the street, lost forever. Mark said he was sorry but it was just an accident. Father at first accepted his account, but a little later called him back and asked him to repeat his tale of woe, pointing out that he should tell him exactly where this terrible event had taken place. Mark repeated his sorry saga in an even more convincing tone than the first time.

Father apparently called the shop a while later. "Thank you for helping Mark with his errand," he said. "Did you by any chance give him any change from the money he brought you?"

"Well, I was going to, but since it was just a few centimes, Mark asked if he might have the change in sweets," came the reply. "I had no problem with that."

I was never told exactly what punishment Father arranged for Mark for his misdemeanor. For me, I could not believe that Mark had actually lied to Father. I am certain, however, that the punishment was not in any way physical. I cannot remember any time that either Father or Mother ever so much as laid a hand on me. Besides, a stern look of disapproval from Father was ten times more effective than any spanking could ever be.

*   *   *

While the drama of the missing centimes was unfolding in the peaceful suburbs of Brussels, Hitler was burning books, operating concentration camps filled with "undesirables," and the notorious Nuremburg laws for the Protection of German Blood and Honor were being mercilessly enforced. Jews were no longer considered German citizens. They were deprived of all basic rights, banned from all professional organizations, and barred from attending German schools. The handwriting was clearly on the wall.

If anyone needed confirmation of Hitler's master plan, the night of 9 November 1938 left no one in doubt. The atrocities of Kristall-nacht turned out to be only a dress rehearsal of what was to come.

20

Goodbye Brussels, Hello America

October 8, 1939. That was our last day in Brussels. I don't remember much about the preparations for our trip. My only role in packing and getting our things ready was to decide what books and toys I wanted to take with me. Of course, I had no idea that we would never come back to our home in Brussels. We often went on an "adventure trip" as a family, and I assumed this was such a trip and that we would be home soon.

Almost everyone we knew in Brussels came to the station to see us off that morning. The scene at the station was probably being repeated in railroad stations all over Europe, for those lucky enough to read the handwriting on the wall and with enough resources and

Only a few people who came to the Brussels railroad station in October 1939 to see us off survived the war.

contacts to arrange their "escape." I was too young to understand what was happening. It was just another holiday and a chance to see many family friends. We never saw many of these acquaintances again.

I must have asked Fima and Isa many times why they were not coming with us on our trip. Father asked them the same question. They answered that they would leave soon and join us, but for now they wanted to stay and close my father's business and premises in an orderly fashion. In any case, they argued, there was plenty of time because the Germans were busy fighting the Russians and there was no reason they should bother to attack little Belgium. "The boys" would first to go to Harbin to see their parents and then they would join us in America or wherever we ended up.

The train took us all to Rotterdam, where we would shortly board the S.S. *Statendam III* for our trip to America. Launched in 1929, the *Statendam III* was considered the best of its class. But unfortunately, it was not immune to attacks by U-boats.

We did not have to wait long in Rotterdam. I do not remember whether the ship stopped in Southampton, but I do remember walking around the deck wrapped up against the cold wind, with Father tightly holding my hand in case the wind might blow me into the sea. This was a great adventure for me because it was my first trip on an ocean-going liner. I remember that Mark and I had our very

On our way to the "New World" and a new home

173

own stateroom with a real porthole. Well, it seemed like a stateroom to me.

One day there was big excitement on board because a famous passenger was making himself known to everyone and was happily posing for photographs and giving autographs. It was only years later, when looking at the photos, that I discovered who the celebrity was— President Franklin D. Roosevelt's son, Franklin Junior, and his wife.

I imagine I was the only one on board who was not concerned about the rumors that German U-boats were beginning to operate aggressively in the North Atlantic. And in addition to the danger of submarines, the Germans had peppered the North Atlantic with deadly floating mines. (On its return voyage from America, the *Statendam III* arrived in the Netherlands in December 1939, at which time the owners decided it was too dangerous to make any more Atlantic crossings. The ship remained docked in the Rotterdam Harbor waiting for the war to end. In the months that followed, however, German bombers left the port in shambles. The *Statendam* suffered irreparable damage and never sailed again.)

Despite the fact that a war was being waged, the opulent style of the *Statendam* was not compromised. Everyone dressed up for dinner every night. It was a special treat for me—a posh restaurant every night. Unfortunately, I discovered that I was not that good a sailor, especially in October in the North Atlantic. All dressed up, I ate many of my meals in my cabin.

My parents planned a special dinner for my sixth birthday, on October 24, 1939. I was determined not be sick on my birthday. I do not remember the menu but I do recall at least one, perhaps two strolling violinists playing songs I requested at our table. Everything was fine until the birthday cake arrived. Exactly what happened then is unclear. But I ate my little bit of birthday cake back in my cabin that night, not at the table.

As the ship came closer to its final destination, New York City, there was much discussion about America and especially about Uncle Max, who would meet us at the dock when we landed. Uncle Max was my mother's older brother, who had left Manchuria to go to America in 1918 and eventually settled in Cleveland, Ohio, joining several uncles and other relatives who had arrived there fifteen years earlier.

When we arrived, Max was waiting for us. To a six-year-old, Max seemed like a real live giant, especially since I was frequently told that soon after he came to America he had become a professional boxer. Up until then, the only image I had of what a boxer might look like came from reading *Popeye* comic stories, so I had expected to see a muscle-bulging, tattooed, pipe-smoking sailor—a spinach-eating Goliath.

Max had come to New York from Cleveland to meet his "kid" sister, my mother, whom he had not seen for more than twenty years, and her family. He was my first contact with a real American. Over the ensuing years, Max became a favorite not only to me but to the whole family. He was always smiling, always cheerful, generous, and thoughtful. I was to visit him often in Cleveland.

One of the first things that struck me when we arrived in New

York was that everyone was speaking a language I did not understand. Apparently, despite all of the briefings and preparations, no one had pointed out to me that Americans spoke neither French nor Russian.

What was the reaction of the rest of our family?

Mark was probably anxious to get off the ship and practice his English. Mother would have been worried about how long it would take for the family to find a permanent home. Father was almost certainly wrestling with the various commercial or professional options that might be open to him in the New World.

21

A Dialogue with My Father

It was only after I became a father myself that I began to appreciate the enormous tragedy of growing up without a father. I realize that, being only eleven years old when my father died, I know very little about him. If he were alive now, I would like to ask him some questions.

HENRY: What would you say was the happiest moment in your life?

FATHER: When I boarded the Trans-Siberian Express in St. Petersburg one dreary March evening in 1925, I wondered if I would ever see my mother, brothers, and sisters ever again. I felt alone, depressed, and frightened. Hopefully, my decision to travel eastward rather than west to try to reach Poland would keep the police from finding me and putting me in prison for twenty years or more.

It was on that train that I first met your beautiful mother and knew at once that I wanted to spend the rest of my life with her. That was the happiest moment in my life.

HENRY: Mother was living in St. Petersburg for almost three years while she was studying at the music conservatory. How come you never met her during all those years? The Jewish community was not that large.

"When I first met your mother on the train, I knew at once that I wanted to spend the rest of my life with her."

FATHER: It was my bad luck.

HENRY: You finally disembarked the train in Manzhouli. How did you choose that city? Did you feel you were safe from the police then?

FATHER: I couldn't be certain. But I think it had been almost three weeks since I'd boarded the train in St. Petersburg and I was now in China, so I felt I would be safe at least for a while. And more importantly, that was your Mother's last stop and having found her, I was not going to let her get away.

HENRY: How did you manage in a strange country, without a passport, with very little money and no obvious employment prospects or means of support?

FATHER: Your grandfather, Misha, in the beginning arranged for me to work in his printing shop. But I was anxious to make my own way and so after a few months, I found a job working for a small company that was doing various construction projects connected with the building of the new Chinese railroad. A steady job meant that I could get married and support a family.

HENRY: But you didn't speak Chinese?

FATHER: Most everyone in Manzhouli spoke Russian. I had a special advantage because I also spoke perfect German. When we were growing up, my father made all of the children learn German. We even had a German tutor who came to our apartment to give us special lessons. That turned out to be very useful. Many of the subjects in the engineering university I graduated from in St. Petersburg were taught in German.

HENRY: How did knowing German help in China?

FATHER: Most of the materials going into the construction of the railroad and various supporting facilities came from Germany, and all of the assembly instructions were in German. A fluent German-speaking engineer was not easy to find, and a valuable asset in those days.

HENRY: Soon you were married, well settled, and had a young son, my brother, Mark. How did you end up in Brussels?

FATHER: In 1929 your mother and I decided that we should take a holiday in Europe. I'd been working without a break for some time and we'd saved enough money to afford a vacation in Europe and perhaps a chance to see my family again. We were only going to be away for five weeks, but once we arrived in Europe the political situation in China began to deteriorate rapidly and our family wrote to us saying that we'd be wise to delay our return until things settled down.

HENRY: So you decided to continue to tour around Europe for a few weeks?

FATHER: No. We wanted to find a safe temporary home and I needed a job.

HENRY: Of all the places in Europe, why did you choose Belgium?

FATHER: We didn't have much of a choice, frankly. In 1929 most countries in Europe required people to have proper visas. I wasn't too keen to return to Russia. Belgium was the only country that had opened its doors to Jewish immigrants.

HENRY: So you decided to move temporarily to Brussels?

FATHER: Antwerp.

HENRY: Why Antwerp?

FATHER: Before making a final move, I decided to speak with
            some relatives who were living in Helsinki. My uncle,
            Lasar Stracheffsky, was a successful merchant in Helsinki
            and had some good commercial contacts in Antwerp,
            and he encouraged me to settle in Antwerp. He knew
            people there and felt he could help me find some good
            opportunities.

HENRY: You found another engineering job?

FATHER: Not exactly. Antwerp was a busy commercial trading
            center in 1929. There was a depression in Europe and
            so there were few construction projects that needed
            engineers. After a few weeks of meetings and talking
            to people, I decided to accept a position in the foreign
            exchange office of one of the small commercial banks.

HENRY: What did the family do?

FATHER: We rented an apartment not too far from my office.

HENRY: It must have been difficult to settle in a strange country
            without friends or relatives, having to learn a new
            language. How did you manage?

FATHER: It was easier than I thought it would be. Belgium was full
            of Jewish immigrants from all over Europe. We quickly
            found many new friends, most of whom spoke Russian,
            so we felt very much at home. There were Russian restau-
            rants, newspapers, even a Russian radio station. I also
            spoke some basic French and, of course, German. And
            Mother was able to arrange to teach some students who
            wanted to take piano lessons.

HENRY: Did you find it difficult learning how to become a
            banker?

FATHER: Work was very interesting. I had never worked in a

"We had a busy social life."

proper office before, so at first it was a little awkward for
me. Wearing a white shirt and tie every day was, well,
different from what I was used to wearing in China. It
was hard—but interesting.

HENRY: So people came to your office to exchange currency?

FATHER: Not exactly. The bank was strictly a commercial bank,
            so we only dealt with businesses and companies, and
            usually by telephone, mail, or cables. Every country had
            its own currency, so if someone, say, Mr. Karl in Sweden,
            wanted to buy Spanish leather luggage, he would have

to find someone who would exchange his krones for the equivalent value in pesetas. We acted as the agent or middleman who made the transaction possible.

HENRY: Without the Internet, how did you know what the correct exchange was on any specific day or hour?

FATHER: That was the banker's job. You see, even without the Internet there were a lot of sources, but the most reliable was the country's central bank. Banks released daily reports on currency rates and they were published in the financial newspapers, just as they are today. Our little bank, in addition to exchanging currency, had to provide all sorts of other documentation to support a growing export-import trade.

HENRY: Like what, for example?

FATHER: The most common papers were called "guaranteed letters of credit."

HENRY: Were you still planning to return to China?

FATHER: No. The world's economic condition was deteriorating rapidly. The stock market in the United States crashed in 1929, and all over the world depression, unemployment, and bank failures were the order of the day. In Belgium, we were fortunate to be in a relatively good, stable economic environment. Our little bank was quite permanently active, and the family was well settled. Frankly, China, while still in our minds, seemed more and more unlikely as a place for us to live.

HENRY: If things were so fine in Antwerp, why did you move to Brussels?

FATHER: A colleague in our bank, Mr. Bernstein, convinced me that we should open our own foreign exchange office, but it would have to be in a different city. He suggested Brussels, which was the capital of Belgium.

HENRY: So you collected your things and moved the family to Brussels?

FATHER: We didn't have much to move. Yes, and we started Nord Exchange in 1933 there. Although the financial world was in turmoil, we seemed to have chosen a good time to make the move and start a new boutique bank. We found a bigger apartment in a nice neighborhood and, later that year, as you well know, you joined the family.

HENRY: How did you decide on the name Henri? That was very French.

FATHER: We looked for a name that could be easily adopted in any country we might be living, in case we had to move again. But there were also some close relatives in our family called Henrietta. And your Hebrew name, Aron, was the name of your great-grandfather.

HENRY: Why were Fima and Isa living with us in Brussels when I was born?

FATHER: Well, Fima was Mother's brother and Isa was her close first cousin. They had left Harbin together to study engineering at the University of Grenoble in France. When they graduated in 1933, going back to Harbin was not a real option, given the political situation there, but there were no jobs available in France. So we invited them to come and live with us for a while until things got sorted out.

HENRY: Why didn't they come with us when we left Brussels in 1939?

FATHER: Things seldom work out the way you plan. I needed

some help in our office and gave both Isa and Fima jobs in our bank. In fact, after a few years I encouraged them to open a branch of our bank, which they did and were very successful. I begged them both to leave Brussels at the same time we did, but they felt an obligation to me to keep the bank open, and they couldn't believe that things were going to get a lot worse in Europe. By now, Germany had invaded Poland, annexed a good part of Czechoslovakia, and was soon to begin sinking ships in the North Atlantic—the handwriting was certainly on the wall for everyone to see.

HENRY: What was the happiest period in your life?

FATHER: I always enjoyed whatever I was doing and, with the love and support of the family, our life was always happy and cheerful.

HENRY: Were you seriously thinking of settling in Brussels permanently?

FATHER: Brussels in the 1930s was a wonderful place to live. The economic situation had settled down; we were living comfortably; we had lots of wonderful friends; we were able to take both winter and summer holidays; Mother had some help in the apartment; and you and Mark were a great joy for us.

HENRY: If things were so tranquil and life so pleasant, why did you start quietly transferring some of your personal funds to the Chase Bank in New York in 1933?

FATHER: In 1933 I felt the European economic and political situation was becoming unstable. The German National-ists had taken power in Germany. Most Jewish civil rights had begun to disappear. Jews were no longer allowed to own shops or go to most universities. Concentration

"You and Mark were a great joy for us."

"We were able to take both summer and winter holidays with the entire family."

camps had sprung up. Books were being burned. You didn't have to be Nostradamus to predict the future.

HENRY: How would money in a bank in the United States help?

FATHER: I was almost forty, had a good position, a wonderful family, and was living very comfortably. I already had had experiences of being forced to flee two different countries, almost penniless, to escape unpleasant political situations. I was a reasonably qualified professional. I was determined that if this should happen again, I would be prepared.

HENRY: Why America and not some other country?

FATHER: First, we had lots of relatives in Cleveland—uncles, cousins, and Mother's older brother, Max. America seemed far away, and somehow it seemed to have remained immune from the political disease spreading in Europe. I was told that if you could show that you had enough money to support yourself and your family, or were sponsored by someone, your chances of getting a visa were greatly improved.

HENRY: You had created and built up, over many years, a thriving business in Brussels and your life style was comfortable, you had many friends. It must have been a difficult decision for the family.

FATHER: My real wealth was tied inexorably to my love for my family. That was always what really mattered most to me. Financial and material wealth were always a secondary consideration.

HENRY: When did you finally decide you would leave Brussels and move the family?

FATHER: While we did not have television, of course, news from

	around Europe was broadcast frequently on the wireless and newspapers were always well informed. Things were getting worse and worse every year. In March 1938 Hitler marched into Austria and declared it a part of Germany.
HENRY:	Was that when you decided it was time to flee Europe?
FATHER:	No. Actually, what finally decided me was Kristallnacht. That was later that year. In November, the Germans killed about one hundred Jews and destroyed two hundred synagogues. They later called that atrocity "Kristallnacht." How many more signs did people need to see what was happening?
HENRY:	But we didn't leave Belgium until almost a year later. Why did it take so long?
FATHER:	Leaving wasn't so straightforward. Belgian citizens were the only ones who officially and legally could enter the United States. All other nationalities had to apply and be put on a waiting list because America had established a quota system for immigrants from every country. The Belgium quota was, happily, never filled.
HENRY:	I can imagine it was a terrible dilemma. You had no official passport. Mark and Mother were born in China…. What was the solution?
FATHER:	Officially, there was no possible solution to our situation. Fortunately, the Belgian administrative bureaucracy was full of people who could be "flexible." We were able to "officially" become Lithuanian citizens. It was an arrangement which could be organized if you knew the right people and had some funds available.
HENRY:	How did that work out?

FATHER: The Americans would under no circumstances allow us
            to immigrate, except, of course, for you, Henry, since you
            were born in Belgium and were a Belgian. But Lithua-
            nians could visit America if they had good reasons and
            were willing to travel and enter as tourists. A good reason
            did, astoundingly, present itself. In Cleveland, our cousin
            Helen Teplitz was going to get married and we were
            cordially invited or got ourselves invited, I forget which,
            to the wedding, in the winter of 1939.

HENRY: So you used Lithuanian papers?

FATHER: It turned out that the "only" unfilled United States quota,
            besides Belgium, was for Lithuanians.

HENRY: So you became Lithuanian?

FATHER: It was the only possible way to get to America. We didn't
            have much time, either—our Cartes d'Identité arrived
            only a few days before our ship was scheduled to leave
            Rotterdam for the U.S.

HENRY: What other plans did you have to make?

FATHER: First, I decided to improve my English. I knew enough to
            operate my bank and even write letters, but I needed lots
            of improvement. We sent Mark to an English boarding
            school near Brussels. Most importantly, we had to
            find suitable transportation, which, of course, meant a
            passenger ship. This was a major obstacle. At the same
            time, I made arrangements to create a Nord Exchange
            branch in America. That helped us get permission to
            enter America.

HENRY: Without planes crossing the Atlantic Ocean, I would
            have thought there were many passenger ships available.

FATHER: The problem was that German submarines were already making the Atlantic an unsafe place. In addition, of course, we weren't the only ones wanting to go to America. British passenger ships had stopped sailing after England declared war on Germany. The only possibility was to find a Dutch ship. With the help of some of my banking contacts, we managed to book passage on Holland America's *Statendam*. You might remember that after its return voyage from America, the *Statendam* was destroyed in the port of Rotterdam by German Luftwaffe bombers.

HENRY: When you left for a "visit," did you expect to stay permanently?

FATHER: No. We expected to come back, but after we arrived in the U.S., we realized that the war would not be resolved easily, so we asked Fima and Isa to pack and ship us a crate of our possessions.

HENRY: I remember that when we were getting ready to pack for the trip I was allowed to take only two toys and some of my most precious books. How did you decide what to take with you and what to leave behind?

FATHER: It wasn't difficult. Most of our furniture and Mother's piano had to stay. In fact, since Isa and Fima weren't coming with us, we could leave most things in the apartment, and I left our Mercedes convertible for them to use. We had to take some formal clothing, since the wedding in Cleveland was formal and dinners on the ship were also formal, so I brought my smoking jacket. Mother took some long dresses and her jewelry.

There were, however, a number of possessions that we wanted to bring to America but that certainly would not be allowed on a passenger ship as the belongings of a family going to America for a visit. We made very difficult choices, deciding which things we would ask Fima to ship to us in America in a small wooden crate.

HENRY: What did you decide to pack in the crate?

FATHER: First, six paintings that hung in our living room. They were not that special or valuable, but we felt they would always remind us of home. Mother chose to pack our silverware, some photo albums, a few crystal bowls, and some candlesticks. Our two white ceramic horses also had to come.

I put some precious paper, letters, and business papers in my personal suitcase, as I had decided that I could continue to manage Nord Exchange, or at least some parts of it, from America, by cable and letters. Banking was one of those businesses that was truly international in those days.

HENRY: If that didn't work out because of the war, did you have some other plans?

FATHER: Well, I had many ideas but, frankly, there was little time to explore options. Getting out of Europe was my prime objective. The rest would have to wait.

HENRY: Once you decided to leave, it must have been difficult to wait and watch the situation in Europe getting increasingly more dangerous.

FATHER: It was worse than that. All established ships' schedules were useless and we had to wait, at home, until the shipping line called to tell us to come to Rotterdam immediately.

HENRY: I remember having my sixth birthday on board the ship. How did that work out?

191

FATHER: I'm afraid you weren't a very good sailor. For much of
            the trip, you were in your cabin in bed, which was too
            bad since it was a grand ship and the meals were really
            wonderful. You did manage to get to dinner, or maybe it
            was lunch, for your birthday, and three violinists came to
            our table and played "Happy Birthday" to you.

HENRY: Were you worried about the German submarines that
            had already done so much damage in the North Atlantic?

FATHER: I think everyone knew what the situation was, but no
            one spoke about it. In fact, this was to be the ship's last
            crossing.

            It's getting late. Let's continue the saga on another day.

PART III
A NEW CLEVELAND INDIAN

Practice makes perfect

Introduction
Why Cleveland?

While leaving Brussels was in Father's long-term plan for some time, it was only when we received an invitation to a family wedding in Cleveland that the dream began to take tangible shape and a destination was identified. Uncle Meyer Teplitz's oldest daughter, Helen, was getting married to Dr. Ralph Maier. A cousin's wedding four thousand miles away hardly seems noteworthy enough to justify packing up the whole family, traveling across the submarine-infested North Atlantic, and then taking an overnight train to Cleveland. However, it was enough to convince the American consul in Antwerp to grant the Strajevsky family a U.S. visa.

Cleveland must not have been an obvious place for us to settle, however.

"Cleveland should be a nice city," Mother suggested. "We have lots of uncles and cousins who have been living there for years."

"I know that," Father replied, "but New York is a worldwide financial center. Cleveland is in a different league."

"Let's go and see, and then decide," Mother replied. "We have time."

For Mark and me, it was just the start of another great adventure. It would be a chance to make new friends, meet some relatives, explore new places, and face new challenges. Mark had an advantage, as he already spoke some English. I spoke not a word.

While Father was beginning his search for employment in the

U.S., the situation in Europe deteriorated. Denmark surrendered to the Germans, who then went on to invade Norway. On May 10, 1940, the Germans invaded Belgium. A month later, Hitler marched his troops into Paris.

22

Discovering the New World

Given the uncertain conditions in the North Atlantic, not surprisingly the S.S. *Statendam III* docked in New York two days behind schedule. Despite that, Max was on the dock to greet us. It was an emotional moment, since Mother and Max had not seen each other for more than twenty years.

While the American Consulate in Antwerp had granted Father the visa for the family, ostensibly to attend our cousin's wedding in Cleveland in December, no one was expecting us to return to Belgium after the wedding, given the political situation in Europe. It was unlikely that the American authorities would take too much notice because Father was able to provide evidence of his ability to be financially self-sufficient.

While there was a certain element of uncertainty about our longer-term plans, Father was probably looking at a five- to ten-year window of opportunity for our extended stay in America. In casting his net out in search of business opportunities, Cleveland was by no means the only location he was considering. His file of inquiries covers almost every corner of the United States. Someone had suggested that the retail wine and spirits business would be an attractive investment, and that was one of several areas he was looking into very carefully. Not being an American citizen, however, proved to be a major handicap, especially being here on what was essentially a visitor's visa.

Uncle Max had decided that before he drove us to Cleveland, we should see some of the attractions of New York. What could be a better location to explore the city than the Barbizon Plaza Hotel on Central Park South, in a huge suite facing Central Park? He must have picked the Barbizon because it sounded European and would make an easier transition for us than other hotels.

One of the memorable features of our stay was the restaurant a few doors from our hotel. Rumplemeyer's was an upscale coffee, tea, and ice-cream parlor that was copied from the original in Paris on the Rue de Rivoli. It was supposedly designed exclusively for children, and after the first time I was taken there, I begged to have all of my meals there. All of the ice-cream dishes had mesmerizing names to capture the attention of every six-year-old lucky enough to be taken there. The fact that I neither read nor understood English was not a handicap since each dish was beautifully illustrated on the menu in mouthwatering details.

There was even more excitement when Max took us all to the automat at Horn & Hardart. He gave us each a handful of nickels and told us to go get our own lunch. All of the food was behind small glass windows, so you could see what was on offer. Inserting one or more nickels, depending on the dish, activated the door to swing open so that you could remove the dish you had chosen. When the plate was lifted up, the door closed and a fresh portion mysteriously appeared, filling the empty space. All of this took place on a tiny rotating platform.

Food, glorious food.

I did not need to understand English at Horn & Hardart. However, many of the dishes in their little glass houses were completely out of the sphere of our family's experience. Corn on the cob in Belgium was only served to pigs. Fish cakes and chicken pot pies turned out to be main courses, not desserts. And hot dogs were not a breed of family pet. I was upset with a popular dish called "chicken a la king." I was certain that my king had nothing to do with this dish.

Mark and I had a spirited competition for who could find the biggest slice of cherry pie. I was disappointed later, when I discovered that not every restaurant in New York had food in little glass-enclosed cubicles.

While Father knew we had relatives in New York, he was unable to locate them from Belgium. Once we arrived in America, he wrote many letters to people whose family names were similar to what he remembered as his relatives' names. There were just too many lawyers with the last name of "Joseph" in New York City to contact, and even more businessmen named "Halperin" from Poland. But he continued his search, and the next time we went to New York, he collected several strong leads. Eventually, he did find them.

New York in the fall of 1939 was the site of the World's Fair. A few days after we arrived in the United States in late October 1939, we were taken to Flushing Meadows to see what wonders the Fair had in store for us. Despite the fact that I did not know a word of English and certainly could not read a word, the Fair made a big impression on me.

All six-year-old boys, and I was no exception, love to turn handles, push buttons, and watch machines turning, and to see airplanes close up, and to look inside lovely new cars. If this was what America was like, I was sure I would love every minute of our stay.

When I was told that there was a special building for Belgians, I asked to go there first. I cannot remember what was inside but I was proud that "my country" was represented, and asked for a picture to remind me of the event. The building was designed by a world-famous Belgian architect, Henri van de Velde, and when the Fair closed, it was dismantled and moved to the campus of Virginia Union University. Its very special thirty-five-bell carillon was later sold to Stanford University, where it is now installed in Hoover Tower.

The Belgium Pavilion at the 1940 World's Fair had to be our first stop.

Several exhibits remain in my mind as highlights. I particularly remember my fascination with moving walkways and stairs. To actually stand still in one place and somehow be moved forward was truly magical. And to stand still and be moved upwards was altogether unbelievable.

Then there were the "moving pictures." I may have seen some movie pictures in Belgium but they certainly were limited to cartoons—Mickey Mouse, Snow White, or Popeye. You can imagine my surprise when I saw real people, not cartoon characters, talking to me. Mother had to drag me, literally, out of the theatre. Later, as we walked around New York, there seemed to be moving pictures everywhere.

Then there were rooms full of enormous shining machines turning, sliding, and making wonderful mechanical music. But it was the room-sized erector set that I remember the most. Constructed of thin little pieces of colored silver metal held together with tiny screws, it seemed as if every piece was moving—up and down, backwards and forwards, round and round, but producing nothing, just moving in an orderly, prescribed direction. I secretly decided I would someday ask for an erector set of my own so that I, too, could build such a wonderful machine. Several years later, my dream came true.

Perhaps my visit to the 1939 World's Fair was the genesis of my lifelong interest in science and engineering. Alberta seems to remember being taken to the World's Fair in 1939 as well—perhaps we passed each other on the moving walkway! We had to wait almost twenty years to meet properly.

My wardrobe was just barely practical for New York. Short trousers for a six-year-old were allowed but long white socks, gloves, and white buckle shoes were not often seen there. Before going to the Fair, I was taken by Mother and Uncle Max to buy some proper little boy's shoes—perhaps something like Buster Browns. Shoelaces were going to be a problem, at least at first, and to this day I still have trouble tying shoelaces. But what for me was more fascinating than seeing a huge store full of shoes was that wonderful machine that showed you exactly how your toes fit into the shoes you were trying on. Incredibly, as you looked down at your feet, instead of your new shoes you saw a glowing blue light surrounding your shoes and, magically, the inside of your own foot's bones—and you could even see your toes wiggle. This machine tried to show parents that the new shoes had plenty of room for the child's toes and would not stunt their growth. Later, it was discovered that these X-ray machines, called "fluoroscopes," were not all that wonderful. They were used for only a few years, then banned in 1941 because it was discovered that exposure to X-rays was potentially dangerous and might cause cancer.

Uncle Max explained that as soon as you bought new shoes, it was imperative to have them shined. Why did brand new shoes have to be shined? I wondered. Apparently, this initial shine would impart to them a marvelous protective coating that would make them last much longer than normal. To this day, whenever I buy new shoes, I polish them before wearing them outside our home.

Outdoor shoeshine stands were a common sight in New York in

1939, but as I had never seen one before, I was thrilled to climb up into a high, specially designed chair, place my newly acquired shoes on a purposefully designed metal stand, and watch a young man painting, brushing, wetting, polishing, and waxing my new shoes, which looked fine to me before this elaborate process was undertaken. I did not immediately notice that the young man doing all this shining had very dark skin. This was the first black person I had ever seen.

We could not stay long in New York. We had a big wedding in Cleveland to get ready for.

Uncle Max insisted that shoeshines for all newly bought shoes were compulsory.

23

R & R

Father had not decided where the family should eventually settle down, and he decided to remain flexible. So, temporarily, our home in Cleveland was a comfortable apartment at the Hotel Sovereign, at the edge of Rockefeller Park. For an active and adventurous six-year-old, the park was full of new places to explore, and as we moved there in November, the added attraction was real snow, just outside our front door. Soon, both Mark and I were enrolled in nearby schools.

Father was busy exploring business opportunities, conducting albeit much reduced foreign exchange transactions, and importing and trading goods from China. Shanghai was not yet directly involved in any armed conflicts, so he was able to act as an America-based agent for Mother's China-based brother-in-law, a textile merchant.

Mark and I took full advantage of our new environment. The discovery of a completely new circle of relatives in Cleveland meant introductory visits, teas, dinners, and other social get-acquainted encounters. I found a few female cousins my age and after getting over the awkwardness of a language barrier, we eventually found some areas of mutual interests.

Cleveland in 1939 bore little resemblance to Brussels. I remember Mother often referring to it privately as "derevinia," the somewhat derogatory Russian word meaning the countryside or woods. For many people in Cleveland, Europe was a little-known and ill-defined group of countries, far away, that were continually in some form of conflict with one another, be it militarily, politically, or socially. This lack of even the most basic familiarity was to cause some concern among the family, specifically in relation to the upcoming wedding, which was to be a formal affair. Accordingly, Aunt Lisa was deputized to visit Mother to ensure that she and the rest of us would be appropriately dressed for the big wedding and not be an embarrassment. It would not do to have new cousins from Europe turn up in unacceptable attire. Mother assured my aunt that there would be no problem, and it was not necessary to loan her special clothing or jewelry for the occasion. Needless to say, Mother's entrance—in her latest Parisian floor-length haute couture gown, exquisite jewelry, long white gloves, and stunning white fur wrap—not only turned heads at the wedding but was the talk of the town for days afterwards. Father looked as if he was ready to go to the palace to meet the King, and Mark and I were smartly dressed with shiny black shoes, long trousers, velvet jackets, and matching ties.

Going south for the winter was common practice for all those in Cleveland who needed respite from the typically cold and snowy winters, especially as the north wind blew in over Lake Erie. Father did not need much persuading, but he had no automobile. Later in December, for $912.11, he bought a black Buick Roadmaster. With gasoline at eighteen cents per gallon, a two-day trip to Florida was a bargain. Uncle Max came with us to share the driving and make sure we did not get lost on the way south.

Our new Buick was ready for a family trip to the south.

Our first stop was Washington, D.C. We visited all of the important sights and had a very hasty American history lesson. I was disappointed to learn that the United States had no king, and when I saw the president's home, the White House, I thought how much nicer to have a palace to live in, like King Leopold, than a sprawling, two-story white house sitting on a rather undistinguished grass lawn.

Our next indoctrination into life in America was the Howard Johnson Motor Motel. The idea of being able to park your car practically in your bedroom was a great novelty for even the most experienced European traveler. There was no porter to carry your luggage. You could leave your bags in the car if you so wished. You did not even have to call in the morning to ask for your car because it was there waiting for you, just outside your bedroom door.

Unlike European roads, the American highways were practically overrun with billboards, sign posts, and fluorescent signs inviting one to shop, eat, or sleep, and there were frequent instructions, reminders, and admonitions about traffic regulations, hazards, and even weather conditions. These signs rapidly became part of our English vocabulary lessons, as we wended our way farther and farther south.

The stop after Washington was St. Augustine, Florida. After the pomp of Washington, it was hardly auspicious. However, the city was famous since it was here that the famous Spanish explorer Ponce de Leon had discovered the fountain of youth. No one knew for sure that it worked. On the other hand, no one could say for sure that it did not. Everyone drank some of the water. I categorically refused to drink any. "I am young enough!" I shouted. "I don't want to be younger. It took me so long to get to this age. Do they have a fountain for getting older?" I asked.

Our final destination was the White House Hotel in Miami Beach, Florida. The hotel was directly on the beach, and it was a short walk to the water. Having been accustomed to ice-cold seawater in Knokke, when I discovered that the ocean here was actually warm, I assumed that in Miami Beach, the sea was being artificially heated so that people could swim any time during the day.

My new party outfit for Miami Beach, in front of the White House Hotel

Although we had only been in America for a few months, the "Americanization" of the Strajevsky family was proceeding at a rapid rate. Everyone wore either moccasins or sneakers, both of which hardly existed in Europe. Mark seemed to have lost his heavy woolen socks altogether, and it did not take Mother long to learn how to walk on "wedgies."

It did not take long for us all to blend into the background and dress and act like most Americans.

Without beach instructors in Miami in 1940, we had to make up our own beach entertainment.

I am sure that I expected Miami to be an American version of Nice, France, but the only resemblance was the vegetation. Instead of lovely shiny rocks along the shore, there was beautiful golden sand. There were no hot dog or hamburger kiosks at every corner in Nice. Nobody rode bicycles in Miami; they took cars everywhere. And you did not have to carry your own beach chairs to the beach, as they were already on the beach waiting for you.

News of the escalation of the war in Europe did not appear to have reached Miami. As we took full advantage of the sunshine, sea, and beach, the future of our family—those we had left behind in Belgium—became uncertain and the source of great stress for both Father and Mother.

A few months later, in May 1940, the Germans invaded Belgium.

24

Becoming an American

After living in the Hotel Sovereign for months, Father decided that he should find something more permanent for the family. So it was in early 1941 that 2225 North St. James Parkway, in Cleveland Heights, became the first proper house that I ever lived in—with its own garage and back garden. Father rented, rather than bought, the house since our future plans had not been fixed yet. The immigrant mentality also meant one had to remain flexible because one was never certain what tomorrow would bring.

My uncle Max and most of our American relatives lived in Cleveland, so it seemed like an obvious and natural choice for us to begin settling down. Our relatives there were mostly in the furniture

Our new home in Cleveland came complete with front and back garden, garage, and even a basement.

business, so it did not take too long to furnish our three-bedroom house. And shortly after we moved in, the large wooden crate arrived from Belgium with some of our personal items, including paintings, some silverware, various pieces of crystal, and our ever-present loyal two ceramic horses.

I was determined to become an "American" as quickly as possible. Although I am sure I had no idea what was practically involved, I embarked on this mission very seriously. As a result, I developed an all-embracing passion for the Native American Indian, particularly his culture, history, traditions, and lifestyle. I cannot remember why I developed this passion or who suggested it to me. Perhaps it was because the local Major League baseball team was the Cleveland

Indians.

I quickly collected all the information I could find about the two most important local tribes, who were the Algonquins and the Iroquois, and their heroes soon became my heroes. Although World War II had already started and was the topic for every family dinner, I think I was more interested in the wars that the Indians had fought.

My appetite extended to being sent to a sleep-away, Indian-style summer camp called "Camp HI." I learned to ride bareback, use a bow and arrow, carve totem polls, make feather headdresses, wear beaded moccasins, sing Indian songs, and do some basic Indian dances. Mark attended the same camp to look after his little brother. I am sure he was not too happy there since he had no interest whatsoever in Indians and even less about cowboys.

The food I remember at Camp HI was not great, but on every visitors' weekend, the family—my parents, Uncle Max, my cousins Anya and Moulia—would arrive from Cleveland loaded with familiar food to keep us from "starving." There was a plentiful supply of fresh rye bread, corned beef, pickles, various pirogs, chopped liver, egg salad, and a vast selection of other familiar Russian foods. Lunch was usually served on a folding card table with a proper tablecloth and real china. It was not surprising that most of my fellow tepee campers did not recognize the food laid out on the groaning portable table. Somewhere, of course, there was an ice bucket with the mandatory bottle or two of freezing-cold vodka, without which it would have been impossible to have a truly Russian picnic.

Sleeping arrangements at Camp HI were in fairly primitive

*Cousin Moulia, Uncle Max, Mother, and Cousin Anya
always came to weekend open camp days with the car
loaded with non-Indian goodies.*

tepees, and at the outside washing facilities the water always seemed
frigid. It could not have been too bad because many years later, in
August 1945, after we moved to New York, I remember going back
to Camp HI again as a camper, this time with my close friends Peter
Schapiro and Jimmy Blier. I find it hard to believe that some parts of
the camp are still operating today. (Perhaps I should arrange a Camp
HI reunion!)

I can't remember if we had real Native Americans as counselors,
but I was certain at the time that they all were genuine Indians. Some
adopted Indian-sounding names and we were often referred to as
"braves." On most evenings, after dinner we would end up around
a campfire, where we were treated to Indian sagas and legends, and
taught Indian dances and songs. One of my greatest treasures which

I was allowed to bring home was not the standard linked belt or key chain lanyard but an ankle bracelet with bells used for dancing.

Of all the myriad camp activities—sports, swimming, arts and crafts, hiking, riding, canoeing—perhaps the one that remains most firmly engrained in my memory to this day is the ritual of visiting Chief Hi Hi's "grave." This visit was actually the most common form of punishment for various misdemeanors. The grave was probably near the center of camp and not far from our tepee, but for us it seemed to be miles away, through a dense forest with many scary animals prowling around and Indian spirits hiding behind most trees.

Punishments were meted out in fifteen-minute increments, depending on the severity of the transgression. One was led to the

Chief Hi Hi may have been just a legend for some but to those of us who had to visit and sit by his grave, especially on moonless nights, there was no question that he was still amongst us.

gravesite late at night, in the dark, to an opening in the forest with a large, distinctive rock, around which were seats made from slices of "ancient trees," each representing some heroic feat of a legendary Indian brave. There was never any physical punishment. All one had to do was take a seat near the stone and sit still for the designated time period—completely alone—hearing the cacophony of animal sounds and, of course, the deep breathing of Chief Hi Hi. If you were found guilty of a major transgression, the chief would come out of his grave and make you promise not to misbehave ever again. (Alberta thinks educational psychologists should have closed the camp down immediately for scaring innocent little children who remember the incident seventy years later.)

I have a permanent reminder of my first summer at Camp HI. I never quite got the hang of horseback riding, especially bareback riding. It was halfway through an Indian sports festival, during a relay horse race, that I fell rather badly off my trusty steed and broke my nose. I was collected and quickly rushed to the camp "medicine man," who somehow mended my nose, basically by twisting it back into its original position. It was only years later that I had the courage to inform the family.

25

I Want to Go Home, NOW!

In Cleveland, my parents had no problem deciding to which school I should go—there was only one in our neighborhood. Roxboro Elementary was just a few blocks from our new home and there was no other school nearby. I am not certain whether my parents visited Roxboro before they enrolled me, but on the appointed day my mother proudly took me in hand and walked me to my new school. It was nothing like my school in Brussels. The long, two-story building seemed to go on forever, and the grounds around the school were so huge that I imagined every child had his or her own separate playground, complete with jungle gyms, swings, seesaws, climbing posts, and slides.

After only a few months in America, spent mostly with my Russian-speaking relatives, I must have barely been able to express myself in English. I was assured by everyone that this would be no handicap since I would pick up the language quickly. Mother said she had arranged for me to be in a class with a teacher who spoke French. Well, once I was brought to the classroom and assigned a desk, I soon discovered that that was, at best, an exaggeration. My new teacher's French might have allowed her to order breakfast and find the railroad station but not much more. I think that, rather than she helping me learn English, I helped her learn French. After a few hours, I thought that maybe I should go to the principal's office and see if I could be moved to a class with a teacher who spoke Russian.

While the classroom was itself a revelation, the really big shock came during the first playground break in the morning. What I first thought was an air raid drill alarm actually turned out to be a signal for all work to stop immediately and for the entire school to stampede out the door and into the playground. Not wanting to be left behind on my first day in school, I followed the crowd.

It became readily apparent to me, once outside, that I was not dressed for the occasion. Short white trousers, a matching jacket, long white socks, and a well-starched shirt with some sort of frilly front were not exactly the school's style. I did refuse the white gloves. Even if someone had told Mother what children wore to school in America, I am sure she would not have believed it.

In the playground that first day, I had my first exposure to school life. Standing around with a group of classmates, as best I can remember the conversation went something like this.

"Hey, kid, why are you dressed like you're going to church?" someone asked, certainly not expecting an answer.

"I go to school for first day," I replied, using what limited vocabulary I had at the time.

"Where do you live anyway?"

"I was born in Belgium."

"So, are you Jewish or something?"

"I am an American!" I responded most proudly.

What happened next was not clear. Someone must have pushed me down on the ground because my carefully ironed and newly washed clothes soon looked as if I had been rolling in the mud.

It is perhaps not surprising that when I got home from my first day at school, I asked my mother, "Can we go back home to Brussels

Anyone with long trousers had to stand in the last row.

221

now?" My first day's school costume was relegated to the give-away clothing box, destined eventually for the Russian War Relief clothing sacks.

In fact, I remained enrolled at Roxboro until November 30, 1942, at which point the whole family moved to New York City.

26

My First Best Friend

David Rubinstein lived a few houses down the street from us in Cleveland. He was my age and in my class at school, and we would walk to and from school together as often as we could. David spent a lot of time in our house, especially in our kitchen, which was always the first stop on the way home from school.

Mrs. Rubinstein apparently was worried about her son because he was unusually skinny for his age, which was seven or eight. As David's mother saw I had no such problem, it was natural that she would one day ask me what I was eating that made me so healthy. I responded by describing an array of Russian delicacies that surely sounded most strange to Mrs. Rubinstein. Blinchiki, pirog, syrniki, plemeni, beef strogonoff, kissel, tvorog, and vatrushka were not obvious menus items for most Americans. In any case, she was interested enough to encourage David to try to mimic some of my eating habits, so after-school snacks in our kitchen soon became a sacred daily ritual.

One day as we were walking home from school, David asked me if I would like to be his best friend. While I am sure that at this point my English was not good enough to understand fully what responsibilities I would be taking upon myself by agreeing, of course I said, "I would be happy to be your best friend." Unfortunately, when we left Cleveland a few years later, I lost touch with him.

After a while Mother and Father decided that while David was an excellent influence on me, he had little interest in any physical activity,

Waiting for David outside our house.

preferring more cerebral and intellectual pursuits. It was time to get professional help. Two athletic skills were selected—swimming and tennis—clearly skills you could not learn in a shtetl. While my father's English was excellent, my mother's was still in the upward stage of the learning cycle. She obviously also must have had difficulty with abbreviations and logos because she chose to enroll me in classes for both sports at the YWCA (Young Women's Christian Association) rather than the YMCA (Young Men's Christian Association). I think I went once or twice a week and, not surprisingly, was the only male in either class. By the time the mistake was discovered, the classes were almost finished and I was ready for Wimbledon and the Olympics. My tennis skills never improved much after those wonderful lessons.

One of many distractions for me as a young boy growing up in a new country was the vacant lot behind our home and that of our neighbors, the Hartzmarks. Today, of course, a vacant lot in a popular suburban area would be unheard of. But our vacant lot was the epicenter for a great variety of different community activities.

In the winter, we would build up a snow wall around its perimeter and fill the lot with water that quickly froze, turning the area into a combination ice rink and hockey stadium. In the spring, we played baseball there. In the fall, a homemade backboard and hoop, nailed to a tree, was all that was needed to play basketball. I am sure we also played football, although I must have been too small to participate. And all year round, it was perfect for kick the can, hide and seek, dodge ball, and running bases. It was also a good place to hide on Halloween night after perpetrating a number of devious "tricks" on neighbors who refused to provide the requisite "treats."

Several times a year the lot was turned into a kind of community charity marketplace, where people sold their unwanted or surplus articles to their neighbors to raise money for a charity. The following year, the same unwanted things appeared again and no doubt were repurchased by their original owners. Those who had nothing to sell or trade had to resort to creating some simple games of chance, like throwing ring quoits or putting out candles with a water pistol, for which prizes had to be offered.

Of all the sports, baseball was clearly my favorite. And Bob Feller, the star pitcher of the Cleveland Indians, became my idol, role model, and star pin-up. Everyone knew exactly how many strikeouts he had to his credit, in addition to his ERA, BK, CG, IRA, and various other important statistics. I had so many pin-ups of Bob Feller that there was hardly an uncluttered bit of wall space left in my bedroom. Thanks to my neighbor Lee Hartzmark, baseball soon became my all-embracing passion. The biggest thrill of all was when I was invited to become the bat boy for the local team, which was a precursor of today's Little League.

Thanks to Google and the Internet, I recently caught up with Lee in New York (after more than seventy years) and have written to thank him for teaching me all about baseball and how to be a "real" American. Lee lives in Cleveland and Boca Raton, Florida. Also, I just located David Rubenstein, and to my astonishment, found that he has been living in England for almost forty years!

I was always ready to help Uncle Max, as he prepared to start his round of visits to his various "stops."

One Saturday morning, Uncle Max arrived at our home on North St. James Street and asked Mother if she could spare me for a few hours because he needed my help. As far as I can remember, there was no further information about the nature of the help an eight-year-old was expected to provide.

It turned out that Max had a most unusual occupation. He made prearranged visits to bars, cafes, diners, and restaurants throughout the city, not to eat or drink there, but to collect the coins that had accumulated in their jukeboxes and pinball machines. I later learned that he was also responsible for the repair, maintenance, and upgrading of the machines.

Max had a carefully laid-out route for each day of the week and was expected at each stop he made. His routine was fairly straightforward. After greeting the manager, he would go directly to the music box or pinball machine, using his special key to unlock the small receptacle where coins were collected, and then proceed to count the coins and mark down the amount collected. Typically, I later learned, the local manager or owner would get to keep 40 percent of the takings while Max would keep the rest. My job at each stop was to test the pinball machines to see if they were working correctly and report back to my boss, Uncle Max. From time to time, I was also allowed to help stack the coins, usually nickels, so that Uncle Max would have an easier time counting them.

Needless to say I waited anxiously every Saturday to see if this was one of the days Uncle Max needed my help. Years later, I learned that Max's unusual occupation was somehow associated with his years as a professional boxer. I was never clear about the precise nature of the connection.

When Max died many years later and I was by then considered to be a responsible adult, I was asked to help in sorting out certain matters related to his estate. As a bachelor, he had had an uncomplicated lifestyle. He did not own any property and, apart from his car, he had only basic possessions, which we donated to a local charity.

During the course of this process, I was curious about how we should proceed to dispose of his only real asset, which I concluded was his route. We readily found the names and addresses of the stops he made, together with some indication of the amounts collected from each stop. I considered this a saleable asset, and since Mother was the sole beneficiary of his last will and testimony, it was worth trying to add it to the estate. Eventually I found a name and telephone number that looked like Max's main contact. I phoned, introduced myself, and made an appointment to meet the man. The contact was a Marlon Brando look-a-like straight out of *The Godfather* films.

After exchanges of regrets and agreeing what a great guy Uncle Max was, I broached the subject of possible arrangements to sell Max's route.

"I am sure Uncle Max would have liked to leave his sister some money," I politely suggested.

"Look, you a nice young boy," my host patiently explained. "Your uncle waz very h'nest, hardworking, and kind. Go home and remember him that way. Take care Momma. Leave our business to us. Kapish?"

This brief exchange, which ended with a wry smile from my host, was enough for me to realize that my mission was going to be a lost cause. Since I felt it was not worth risking either one or both of my knees being shot up, I decided to make a polite but hasty retreat.

I did not come back from Max's funeral empty-handed, however.

As a war veteran, Max was entitled to an official military ceremony, which included draping the coffin with an oversized American flag. Before the coffin was lowered, the flag was collected carefully, folded into a regulation-size triangle, and handed to me as the closest next-of-kin representative.

27

Ration Books, Tin Cans, and Model Airplanes

Almost all of my recollections of the first few years of World War II are from my father's daily updates, or briefings, on the military and geopolitical situation in Europe and the rest of the world. Every evening meal would begin with a detailed news report about what was happening around the world and its implications for us and our friends and family still in Europe.

These sessions were far from a monologue, as we were expected to have questions and reactions to the day's events. A secondary source of world news was the astonishing photo essays in *Life* and

Look magazines, both of which arrived in the mail weekly. It was perhaps the happy memory of these evening meals that encouraged me to arrange my work schedule throughout my working life to assiduously avoid scheduling dinnertime business meetings if at all possible. During all of the years of my career, I would be surprised if, when I was in London, I had more than two or three "business dinners" in any single year.

After Pearl Harbor, December 7, 1941, America entered the war. Very soon, it was not possible to walk into a shop to buy as much sugar, butter, cheese, or meat as you might have wanted. You had to present your personal ration book, full of coupons that specified exactly how much of each rationed product you were allowed to purchase. The same was true for other rationed items, such as gasoline, tires, nylon stockings, and rubber shoes. As soon as the war began, it became clear that certain strategically critical materials would no longer be available, especially those coming from territories occupied by the Japanese. Two of the most common goods so impacted were sugar and tin from the Malaysian peninsula. The misnamed "tin can" was actually a steel can with a thin layer of tin inside to preserve the contents. These cans were the biggest non-military consumer of tin. Other uses of tin were in certain wrappers and packaging, primarily for chewing gum, candy, and toothpaste. It was in fact, the shortage of tin for toothpaste packaging that prompted my father to invest in a tooth-powder factory, a decision with disastrous consequences.

Being just eight years old and a dutiful son, I willingly signed over my ration cards to my mother. I don't recall ever being hungry during

232

Mother created a handsome Victory garden in our backyard.

those wartime years. While vegetables were not being rationed all over the country, "V for Victory" gardens began to spring up. We at 2225 North St. James Parkway were not going to risk being called unpatriotic, so Mother bought some seeds and started her own garden, too. I am sure she had very little prior experience in gardening, but she embraced enthusiastically the idea and gave it her full attention.

Children all over the country were soon mobilized to collect tin foil for the war effort. First, every patriotic child started his own tin foil ball. The foil of chewing gum wrappers was carefully separated from the paper layer and added to one's ball of tin foil. A child's patriotism was commonly acknowledged to be directly proportional to the size of his or her tin foil ball. While the tin foil itself was very thin, it was not uncommon to have a ball the size of a large orange and, surprisingly, as heavy.

In addition to tin foil, there was a nationwide drive to collect flattened tin cans. Once the can was emptied, you would carefully open the unopened bottom, put it on the ground, and flatten it by jumping on it. Collection points for cleaned and flattened tin cans sprang up everywhere. At one point, entrance to the Saturday matinee for children was free on presentation of ten flattened cans.

But while I was collecting tin foil and flattening tin cans, Mark was involved in a much more cerebral and fascinating home-front war effort: making model spotter planes. In modern warfare, where aircraft plays a major role, a key factor for success is the ability to identify quickly and accurately enemy aircraft and distinguish it from that of your own and your allies. In World War II, as many as sixty different aircraft needed to be identified at great distances. Waiting for the airplane to get close enough to read its identifying markings and insignias was not recommended.

Training Army, Navy, and civilian personnel in plane spotting was undertaken by the government, which hung exact model replicas of planes in a poorly lit room and had instructors point out major distinguishing characteristics for each plane.

To prepare for this, at the start of the war, the government announced that it urgently needed 500,000 model aircraft for this important training function, and a nationwide network of teenage model builders was created to accomplish this task. School superintendents throughout the country were issued plans and instructions for making the models, all to the same scale, 1:72. It was crucial that the finished model be a near-perfect replica of the real plane. Details such as landing gear, propeller shape and location, cockpit features, and wing and tail flaps were not usually required. Completed models were carefully examined for accuracy and, once approved, dipped into a vat of jet-black matt paint ready for identification classes.

Mark was one of many students in the Cleveland Heights High School who volunteered to construct model airplanes. Each model builder was supplied with a pre-packaged kit that included a template, a set of plans, sandpaper, and seven pieces of wood, roughly cut to represent the two halves of the fuselage, two wings, the tail, and the two ailerons. Before gluing the parts together, each of the roughly cut elements had to be meticulously sanded down to coincide with the outline dimensions as shown in the plans, and checked with the appropriate template, which showed the accuracy of the sanding and where adjustments were required.

I watched as Mark unwrapped his first model kit. It would not be an exaggeration to say that my brother, preferring more sophisticated pursuits, was not a naturally gifted craftsman. Faced with the problem of matching the roughly cut wooden parts to the shapes in the plans he decided to subcontract to me again, this time having me do the more detailed sanding work. He had no trouble gluing the pieces together. We soon developed a type of production line, and very quickly my brother's reputation for building models became well known throughout the school.

I am sure I was too young to have been given my own kit, but perhaps I helped some anti-aircraft gunner distinguish a Stuka from an ME 109, or a Zero from a Sally.

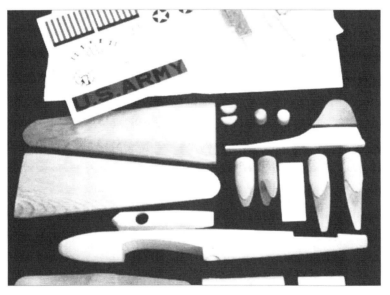

A typical pre-cut model plane kit

28

An Abbreviated Musical Career

What do the following have in common?

    Jascha Heifetz

    David Oistrakh

    Nathan Milstein

    Isaac Stern

    Henri Strajevsky

Well, they all had Russian parents. Correct. In fact, two of them were born in the same city in Russia—Odessa.

They all immigrated to the United States. Correct.

They all played the violin by the time they were seven years old. Correct.

But only one stopped playing when he was eight. This is the story of a great career that almost was.

It was my good fortune, when growing up in Cleveland, to have David Rubinstein as a neighbor, classmate, and first best friend, as I mentioned earlier. David was distantly related to Arthur Rubinstein, and my mother must have taken this as some sort of sign that I should learn to play a musical instrument.

Once we were settled in Cleveland, my parents were amazed at how quickly I became integrated into the process of becoming an American and how speedily I seemed to manage to learn the language, even though at home we still spoke only French and Russian. Unfamiliar leisure activities, especially sports, soon became an integral part of my normal routine—baseball, basketball, football, and ice hockey hardly existed in Belgium. I soon became acquainted with and vigorously participated in whatever sport was being played. However, it was decided that my repertoire of after-school and leisure interests lacked a cultural dimension. Clearly, seven-year-olds cannot live by sports alone. And so it was that one day my mother asked David's father, who was a highly respected musician and conductor with the Cleveland Philharmonic, for help in finding an appropriate music teacher for her young, rapidly Americanizing, culture-starved son. Since we had no piano in our house, violin was chosen, although as a pianist my mother was frustrated that I had to start my musical career with an instrument she herself could not help me learn.

In due course I was introduced to my venerable music teacher, who soon became known as Dr. Zo Zo. Being myself a recent immigrant it was assumed that I would be most comfortable taking lessons from another immigrant. Zo Zo was not his real name, of course, but most of his sentences would begin with "Zo, zo…." I am certain that at the beginning of our acquaintance he was convinced that I had unique talent, with perfect pitch and an instant love affair with my three-quarter-size violin. But after the first few lessons, he realized just how wrong he was.

My weekly lessons were anticipated with about as much enthusiasm as the daily spoonful of cod liver oil that my mother insisted was a vital part of every pre-teenager's daily diet, lest his growth would be stunted and he be perpetually ill. I soon negotiated the suggested practice of an hour per day to something more manageable—a half-hour per day and not on weekends or holidays. I convinced myself that time spent making terrible noises with tightly stretched, unbleached, white Siberian horse hairs was no substitute for almost any outdoor game.

The turning point in my musical career was when my mother decided that I should soon have my world premier solo concert. This was not to be a concert in the Cleveland Municipal Auditorium, but for me it was an equally daunting event. I was to perform in front of the whole family and friends at a holiday dinner. My accompanist was to be my dear cousin Anya Zelles, who was coerced into this overly ambitious project. Frankly, I do not recall if, in fact, the concert ever took place. If it did, it has been totally wiped from my memory bank.

After about a year, Dr. Zo Zo approached Mother with a heartfelt request. "Zo, zo, my dear Madame Strage, may I humbly suggest zat

*I doubt Menuhin had to practice as much as I did for
my concert debut, accompanied by Anya Zelles.*

you are vaysting your money and my time by continuing to try and
teach Genri ze violin."

I am sure this did not surprise my mother because she had
prepared a careful response. "Professor, we all need to be patient.
Henri is a slow learner."

"Ze problem is threefold, Madame. He has no interest, no talent,
and no incentive."

Mother's second plan of attack was unassailable. "We will stop
the lessons when he finishes the music book you have given him to
learn. When he is able to play the last composition in his book, I agree
we will stop."

At my next lesson with Dr. Zo Zo, to my astonishment he skipped at least 120 pages, turned to the last score in my music book, and announced, "Today ve vill commenze to learn ze *Barcarolle*, my favorite piece of music."

Barcarolle, a folk song from the opera *Tales of Hoffman* by Jacques Offenbach, is the only piece of violin music I can still play on the violin today!

29

Remembrance of Food Past, with Apologies to Marcel Proust

We all reflect often on our poor memories. "I can't remember his name" or "I just don't remember being there" or "I just can't place the face." The curious thing is that you seldom hear someone reflect on a food or dish that has slipped from someone's memory and cannot be recalled. Proust wrote many pages describing his memories of eating a simple madeleine he once had in his youth. I have similar memorable gastronomic experiences.

ZAKUSKI

A typical Russian meal was a multi-course encounter. Meals would begin slowly with zakuski, which would have been sufficient for an entire meal. The great variety of zakuski would be followed by a delicious soup, which then would be followed by a huge main course, and the meal would be concluded almost certainly with at least two or three high-calorie desserts, all washed down with ice-cold, natural or bison-grass flavored (zubrowka) vodka. And somewhere nearby there was always a generous supply of black bread and unsalted butter.

It would be a gross error to suggest that zakuski are just hors d'oeuvres—appetizers or snacks. Zakuski are essentially an array of small bits of specially prepared foods, accompanied with vodka, usually set out on the table before people arrive. The tradition of zakuski originated in country houses on vast estates in Russia to which guests typically came over long distances on bad roads, often in subzero temperatures. People might arrive at any hour—often unexpected and usually hungry. Zakuski offered a practical way to give visitors some sustenance and keep them in good spirits until a formal dinner could be prepared.

In time, zakuski grew increasingly lavish, with more and more varieties of dishes. No wonder those unfamiliar with the custom often mistook zakuski for the main meal and could not believe that soup and the main course were to follow.

Zakuski are similar to an overture of an opera. At all festive parties, special occasion dinners, or celebrations, one would not be surprised to find as many as twelve different dishes laid out on the table before the guests sat down. It was customary, maybe even mandatory, for guests to serve themselves zakuski. You were never asked if you wanted seconds; you were simply expected to take them yourself. If someone did not take a reasonably sized second portion, they might be asked if perhaps they were ill.

Each family's zakuski was unique to that particular household. And, of course, each recipe was exclusive, never written down, typically handed down verbally from mother to daughter, sometimes even to daughters-in-law. Preparing zakuski was not a trivial matter. I can remember my mother starting the process early in the morning, or even the day before an event. The catalogue of the most common dishes would span several pages. Everything from caviar to sturgeon, sliced tongue to chopped eggs, and beetroot salad to an array of differently prepared eggplant dishes would be served.

Several special preparations are still very fresh in my mind, such as *Сельдь* (herring). In our home, herring was an indispensable staple part of any zakuski table. You had to have at least one and usually two different herring preparations on the table. In whatever form it was served, however, there had to be a bowl of fresh sour cream (smetana), an ample supply of fresh dark pumpernickel bread, and some small boiled spring potatoes, unpeeled and liberally sprinkled with dill.

Simple herring fillets were swimming in mustard, onion, or sour cream. One of my favorites was herring in sour cream with chopped onion, apples, and a little bit of lemon. Yogurt was often substituted for sour cream, but in either case, marinating the herring in the refrigerator for at least five hours before serving was essential. For good measure, garlic was usually added to the fillets.

The other very common herring zakuski was chopped herring. Today, one would drop into the blender herring, onion, apples, eggs, and pickles. In the past, that simple approach would have been considered cheating. Every ingredient had to be handled in its own distinctive mode.

At home, the preparation of herring was often a collective family enterprise. My favorite job in the kitchen was operating the cast iron, manual food grinder, which was attached to a portable kitchen step-stool so that I could reach it comfortably and not take up valuable kitchen table or countertop property. I was sure it was the most important and prestigious function, and I took my responsibilities seriously indeed. One day, which I recall vividly, the herring that was passed to me for grinding still had its head and tail attached. Up to that day, the herring I received was just a plain raw slice of fish without head or tail, and mashing it up in the meat grinder was just a necessary step in its preparation. When I saw that I was actually mashing and chopping a real fish, I had second thoughts about how much fun this process was, especially when it was suggested that I should chop off the dead fish's head and tail first so that they would not get mixed up with the rest of the fish. I am sure that the question that went through my mind was, how can I be sure the fish is actually dead?

Herring in tomato sauce with pickles, and herring in curry sauce also found its way to our table from time to time. One dish that Father loved and nobody else would even taste was pickled pig's knuckles (actually it is the knee of the pig), embalmed in what looked like chicken soup-flavored Jell-O. The "Jell-O," which was actually aspic, acted as a preservative and so, alas, once prepared one could expect to see it on the menu for a whole week or more. A popular variation of this dish was using the pig's head instead of the knee. Fortunately, this particular variant never made it to our table, as far as I can remember.

There was a special herring-like fish that was also very popular and very, very salty—anchovies. Isa was in charge of taking the salt out of the anchovies. His expertise in this function was a legend and I remember how, when he came to visit us in London, he would desalt the anchovies by carefully washing each little fish in milk. If you do not believe me, try it.

SOUP'S ON

No self-respecting household with even the barest hint of Russian ancestry or heritage would be without a dedicated borscht pot that could easily serve a family of twenty. While it would blasphemous to use this pot for anything but borscht, it has been known to be used in an emergency as an ice bucket, beer cooler, sangria mixer, chicken-stock production facility, and for temporary cut-flower storage.

I am sure that every family has its own unique borscht recipe. Perhaps the only common ingredient was beetroot, which gives the soup its characteristic red color. Carrots, onions, potatoes, garlic, and

247

even celery are the usual suspects, but variations abound, not only in different regions of the former Soviet Union but also in countries as distant as China and Cuba. Other borscht additives were hard-boiled eggs, sausage, and even chicken.

A final mandatory touch was the addition of sour cream, which was floated on top of the hot soup and gradually stirred in by a much-practiced clockwise movement of one's spoon. In Poland, heavy cream was used instead of sour cream, and in some countries, yogurt. In all countries, though, the result was to change the dark red color of the beets to a more appealing pink liquid. The production of the evening's borscht would begin directly after breakfast and the soup would simmer on the stove for the whole day. Two days' supply was the minimum volume prepared, and borscht on the second day was always better than on the first.

In our home a crucial ingredient in borscht was flanken, better known as brisket. Its primary function might seem to be giving the borscht a realistic meat flavor, and after the soup course, the flanken was served in the same soup bowl and became the main course. I remember it was one of my father's favorite menus. And after Alberta and I were married, my mother made certain that Alberta knew her unique recipe. My father always insisted that the main course, the meat, be served in the soup bowls and that the strongest possible horseradish be available in plentiful quantities. In London, I frequently had to struggle to hold onto my soup dish when I had finished and was waiting for the meat course. Alberta was brought up to believe that the soup bowl was for soup and the dinner plate was for the main course.

For six months of the year, borscht was served hot. Then somehow, without any formal agreement, beginning on June 1 in households around the world, borscht was served cold, with ice cubes added to maintain the right temperature—and with spinach or sorrel, whichever was fresher and more plentiful, instead of beets as the main ingredient. This summer-only soup was also called "green borscht" (schav). I must say it was not one of my favorites.

CHEESE, ANYONE?

The Russian menu typically did not feature a separate cheese course, but when our family arrived in America, I have clear memories of my father developing an insatiable appetite for a very distinctive-smelling processed cheese from Wisconsin called Limburger. "Distinctive" is a polite way of saying "smelly." In fact, one of the few times I recall Mother and Father saying strong words to each other was on the subject of precisely where the Limburger should be housed. Mother flatly refused to let Father keep it in the kitchen refrigerator, as the smell would almost instantly migrate to every other product being stored. It was summarily relegated to a windowsill, where it could do little harm. When we lived in a large apartment in New York, on the ninth floor, the "safe house" for the malodorous Limburger was also the kitchen windowsill, but its home there was short-lived—the neighbors soon complained. Perhaps Limburger had something to do with the limited tourist traffic to Wisconsin.

BEEF STROGANOFF

On special occasions, the dish usually prepared was beef stroganoff, served traditionally in our home with crispy thin potato straws. The first time Alberta prepared it in London was on the occasion of a certain amount of disbelief on the part of our local greengrocer, Mr. Cranley. My mother's recipe called for equal weights of meat and mushrooms, and massive amounts of soured cream. Mushrooms were typically sold in small quantities in a straw punnet. When Alberta casually asked for three pounds of mushrooms, the reply came, "Do you operate a restaurant, Madame?" And by the way, when we first arrived in London in the early 1960s, if the cream became soured, the local grocer would just throw it away and never try to sell it to customers. Like borscht, there were many variations on the basic stroganoff theme. Rice occasionally replaced the shoestring potatoes. And the meat might be chicken.

KISSEL

"Well, to me, kissel looks and tastes like just plain old Jell-O."

"Not exactly," I retorted. "Kissel is essentially a fruit soup that can be served either hot or cold."

"Whatever you call it …."

A festive meal would not be complete without at least one dessert. While kissel was perhaps my favorite, there were many other options on the dessert menu. Pastilla, baked apple, syrniki, kugel, halvah, rugelach, and cooked mixed fruit compote were the ones I remember best.

THE RUSSIAN NATIONAL FOOD

One Russian delicacy can truly be called a historic national dish and has been served for over eight hundred years, since Alexander Nevsky discovered and popularized it in 1239. It is uniquely versatile. You can find it in appetizers, main courses, and desserts. It can be served hot or cold, by itself or with anything from onions and bacon to cottage cheese, pumpkin seeds, or cloudberries. It not only is a food but during its long life has been found to have a host of other unexpected uses in different walks of life, from medicine to furniture and house construction.

Most Russian children began eating this as soon as they could consume solid food. It was always in plentiful supply; inexpensive; ensured regular body functions; stimulated the brain cells; strengthened the hormonal system; helped maintain the active flow of digestive juices; and probably, although I am not sure, increased one's sex drive.

As children got older and required a more sophisticated diet, this food was served with a large variety of sides, such as eggs, cottage cheese, onions, bacon, corn, and spinach. For those who craved a more modern diet, this magic food was served with tofu, alfalfa, bean sprouts, black beans, and many other so-called natural foods that are "good for you."

In the Russian army, this became a secret weapon. While U.S. soldiers had to make due with K-rations and Spam, every Russian soldier carried a plentiful supply of this food, which could be consumed hot or cold, with milk or coffee, and needed no special container or refrigeration. It is alleged but never proven that the army developed a special formulation permitting soldiers to take it intravenously.

Adults desperate to relive their youth discovered still more creative ways to consume this food. They stuffed it into whatever fruit or vegetable they could hollow out. Tomatoes, green peppers, aubergines, marrows, and pumpkins were the favorite choices. I am reliably told that it goes well with apples, pears, and various fruity puddings. And a favorite form was made with semolina. It found its way as an ingredient in place of fruit preserves in two other classic Russian dishes—vareniki and piroshky. In time, even more creative uses for this food were discovered, e.g. in ravioli (pelmeni), sushi, stir-fried in place of rice, as a pizza topping—and the uses grew and grew.

So, growing up as I did in a Russian household, this food was almost considered a staple similar to bread. What did this food do for me?

NOTHING.

I tried it once. I hated it on sight, in whatever form it was dished up. I could not bear the smell, texture, or taste, and when I tried it, bits of it got stuck between my teeth, only to be dislodged by rinsing with sulphuric acid. Its smell was so powerful that even when disguised or embedded in some dish I loved dearly, I was instantly repulsed.

What is it?

KASHA!

Yum! Yum! Where is my fork?

30

The Letter That Changed Our Lives

You may well wonder how a one-page letter from the American Dental Association has found its way into a prominent place in our family archives. This letter has an unusually important role in our family history. It not only changed our family's life, but was more than likely a major factor in my father's untimely death at age forty-four.

While the rest of the family was busy trying to integrate itself seamlessly into its new environment, Father was concentrating on finding gainful employment. Since joining his uncles in the furniture business was not an acceptable option for him, he decided to try to rebuild a trading enterprise based on his well-established worldwide network of banking and commercial contacts. It was a bad time to create such a venture, despite having a substantial sum of money available for investment. The uncertain world political situation, the undependable transportation network, and poor communication made any form of international trade or legitimate funds transfer essentially impossible. Father's files paint a depressing canvas of painful and, in most cases fruitless leads, false starts, broken promises, and lost opportunities. At one moment, he even considered buying a wine and spirits franchise. Because he was officially classified as a Resident Alien, many opportunities were simply not open to him.

Finally, he found what he felt would be an exceptional opportunity. America was soon to be put on war footing and a lot of materials destined in peacetime for consumer goods were diverted for military or defense uses. Toothpaste in aluminum tubes was soon replaced on the shelves of stores with tooth powder in cardboard containers. Plastics were not on the scene yet.

Overnight, instead of squeezing toothpaste directly onto toothbrushes, people found themselves putting a small amount of tooth powder into their palms, adding some water, and making a type of paste, which they then carefully folded into their toothbrushes. Demand for tooth powder exploded.

A certain gentleman approached my father one day with a proposition to manufacture tooth powder to meet the growing demand. As a dentist himself, Dr. Graver assured him that he had formulated an exceptionally effective tooth powder for which he had exclusive patent rights, in addition to the coveted and required the ADA (American Dental Association) seal of approval. Father invested a large part of his nest egg into this venture and bought a second-hand factory in Cleveland to produce and package the miracle tooth powder.

I remember my excitement at going to the factory on Saturdays to watch all of the machinery in the factory mix, fill, label, and pack tooth powder in a never-ending symphony of turning wheels and gears, with mechanical arms pushing and pulling the product through seemingly endless steps of the semi-automated assembly line. After several months of production, growing sales, and national recognition, everything pointed to an outstanding success.

Then the letter arrived. It was a letter from the ADA and Father discovered, to his horror, that Dr. Graver was not a dentist at all, had no patent rights, and had falsified the ADA seal of approval on the design of the tooth powder containers.

The factory had to stop production. The formula, once tested, did not meet the ADA requirements. Dr. Graver disappeared, leaving my father with a worthless factory, a warehouse full of useless powder and containers, and huge debts. Father was devastated. The land of opportunity had become a land of con men, and he was soon left with a much-depleted personal bank statement. Father prided himself that throughout his life he had been scrupulously honest; this reputation had helped him build up his business in Brussels. He would never believe that in American business, morality was a variable principle. He looked for but never found Dr. Graver.

This was the event that triggered our move to New York City. Father was not running away, but he felt he needed to leave Cleveland and get on with finding another business. New York had been his original preference when we arrived in the United States. In New York he believed he would have better opportunities, with a circle of friends from Europe who were involved in a wide variety of businesses.

Things did not turn out as he hoped. International communication was hopelessly unpredictable. Foreign trade transactions, the basis of his expertise, were now exclusively based on military supply needs. The best he was able to do was to import trivial, low-cost surplus products and materials that had accumulated in obscure warehouses, with only a limited demand at the lowest possible prices.

In the end, he was reduced to becoming a salesman trying to dispose, literally, of cheap products, such as indifferent costume jewelry from China, cheap perfumes from South America, kewpie dolls made in the Far East, and reject china and silverware that no one wanted. I remember some of these products well because Father's only warehouse was a closet in our New York City apartment.

Yes, my father was overweight. Like most men of his generation, he smoked regularly. But I also know that he must have been horrendously depressed, under immense personal daily stress, and faced with terrible, seemingly irreversible, frustration. I believe all of these circumstances were major contributors to his sudden premature death.

That is how a one-page letter about tooth powder changed our lives.

AMERICAN DENTAL ASSOCIATION

COUNCIL ON DENTAL THERAPEUTICS

PLEASE ADDRESS REPLY TO
COUNCIL ON DENTAL
THERAPEUTICS

222 EAST SUPERIOR STREET, CHICAGO
March 3, 1943.

L. PIERCE ANTHONY, D.D.S.
Editor, Journal of the American
Dental Association, Chicago, Ill.,
Ex-officio.

J. HOWARD BROWN, Ph.D.,
Sc.D.
Associate Professor of Bacteriology, Johns Hopkins University,
Baltimore, Md.

EDWARD C. DOBBS, D.D.S.
Associate Professor of Pharmacology and Therapeutics, University of Maryland, School of
Dentistry, Baltimore, Md.

PAUL J. HANZLIK, M.D.
Vice-Chairman of the Council,
Professor of Pharmacology, Stanford University School of Medicine, San Francisco, Calif.

THOMAS J. HILL, D.D.S.
Professor of Clinical Oral Pathology and Therapeutics, Western
Reserve University School of
Dentistry, Cleveland, Ohio

MILAN A. LOGAN, Ph.D.
Professor of Biochemistry, University of Cincinnati, School of
Medicine, Cincinnati, Ohio

ARNO B. LUCKHARDT, M.D.,
Ph.D., Sc.D., LL.D.
Professor of Physiology, University of Chicago, Chicago, Ill.

HARRY LYONS, D.D.S.
Professor of Periodontia and
Oral Pathology, Medical College of Virginia, School of
Dentistry, Richmond, Va.

VICTOR C. MYERS, Ph.D., Sc.D.
Professor of Biochemistry, Western Reserve University, Schools
of Medicine and Dentistry, Cleveland, Ohio.

FLOYD D. OSTRANDER, D.D.S.,
M.S.
Assistant Professor of Dentistry
(in charge of materia medica
and therapeutics), School of
Dentistry, University of Michigan, Ann Arbor, Michigan.

HARRY B. PINNEY, D.D.S.
Secretary, American Dental Association, Chicago, Ill., Ex-officio.

HAROLD S. SMITH, D.D.S.
Chairman of the Council, 180 N.
Michigan Ave., Chicago, Ill.

DONALD A. WALLACE, Ph.D.
Secretary of the Council, Director, A.D.A. Bureau of Chemistry, Chicago, Ill.

Grasco Products, Inc.
West 2nd and Nobel Court
Cleveland, Ohio

Attention: Dr. C. J. Graver

Gentlemen:

    According to our records no reply has been received to our letters of November 23, 1942 and January 26, 1943, which embodied a request for information concerning Graver's Tooth Powder.

    Unless a reply is received to this communication within ten days, it will be necessary for the referee to recommend to the Council that your dentifrice be deleted from the list of Accepted Dental Remedies.

        Very truly yours,

        Donald A. Wallace

        Donald A. Wallace, Secretary
        COUNCIL ON DENTAL THERAPEUTICS

DAW:ED

The letter that changed our lives

PART IV
THE BRONX IS UP AND
THE BATTERY'S DOWN

The first big bite of the Apple. Every visitor must see New York City from the top of the Empire State Building. Left to right, Henry, Ronald Reider, Stephen Weiner, Phillip Weismuller, Peter Schapiro, Marshall Megginson. The tour guide stands behind the group. February 1944

Introduction
Filing Cabinets for People

How important is one's environment in personal development? In my case, I believe it was critically significant.

The family's move from Cleveland to New York in November 1942 was a seminal event in my life. I cannot recall if anyone tried to explain to me why we were moving, and why we were doing so in the middle of the school semester. I hated leaving Cleveland. I could not understand why we had to leave our wonderful house, beautiful garden, many friends and neighbors, lovely relatives, and my beloved Cleveland Indians to move to dark, overcrowded, friendless, and chaotic New York.

Moving into Apartment 9D on the ninth floor at 131 Riverside Drive was another big change for all of us. In retrospect, on the positive side, it expanded my horizons and opened countless doors to opportunities and experiences that Cleveland would never have been able to provide. It gave me a wider variety of opportunities and activities than I could have imagined or, at first, comprehended. On the negative side, all of our backyard sports activities were relegated either to the street or to one of several nearby public parks.

Being introduced to new friends from a wide variety of backgrounds and experiences quickly helped fill the void left by moving. My parents, who must have become accustomed to moving, and for whom trauma had always been a part of life, accepted the reality of the move and proceeded stoically to face the many challenging tasks that presented themselves—finding accommodations and schools, developing a network of new friends, and continuing to try to manage a stress-free household. The biggest and most complex challenge was certainly for my father. Once again, he was forced to start looking for a means of making a living and supporting the family. Once again, he was worrying about how his young family would adjust to a new and unfamiliar environment. In addition, he had to adjust to the bitter disappointment of losing much of his life's savings.

No one could know that he would only live for two more years.

31

How I Was Almost Expelled from Fifth Grade

The second school I attended in the United States proved to be a great success, especially compared to the first school. Public School 9 (P.S. 9) was practically on our doorstep, at 82nd Street and West End Avenue. It could not have been more than a ten-minute walk from our apartment, which was on Riverside Drive and 85th Street.

By the time of our move, I had become a fully qualified A-1 Yankee Doodle American kid. No white gloves, frilly shirts, long knee socks for me. I played a reasonable game of marbles, occasionally won at penny pitching, and religiously read *Superman* comics. When allowed, I listened to *The Lone Ranger, Ellery Queen,* Jack Armstrong, Henry Aldrich, *The Shadow,* and *Fibber McGee & Molly* on the radio. If I had been especially good, I was even allowed to go to the Saturday afternoon double feature at the local RKO movie theatre, where the ticket price was twenty-five cents. Those without sufficient funds would go to the theatre and try to walk in backwards, and when challenged for a ticket would announce that they were just leaving.

Unlike the new, modern Roxboro school in Cleveland, which had two floors and vast grassy playing fields adjacent to it, P.S. 9 had been built in the 1890s in ecclesiastical English Gothic style, with five floors, and it used West End Avenue as its playing field. Another unique feature of the building was that most of the floors consisted of wide-open spaces with moveable floor-to-ceiling partitions that were attached to fixed railings. This allowed the teachers to adjust the room size to fit the size of the class and any planned activities.

Because everyone in the school lived in the same neighborhood, one's social pattern was largely dictated by religion and local geography. Geography was a factor because you always walk to and from school with your friends who lived nearby. Religion was significant because the local synagogue or church became a magnet for many after-school and weekend social activities, as well as obligatory religious classes. Peter Schapiro lived around the corner on 86th Street; Jimmy Blier's apartment was on Broadway and 83rd Street, and Steve Wiener was the farthest away, on Central Park West and 77th Street.

A unique feature of our social structure, even at the ripe old age of nine or ten, was that girls played an integral part in many of our activities. For example, Patsy Fingerhood, Sondra Kantor, Wilma Schnitmann, and Sara Taylor were all equal partners in our "gang."

School was not particularly challenging in the fifth grade. Between classes and after-school clubs, we wrote and distributed a mimeographed class newspaper filled with gossip and announcements of special events. The school produced a formally printed, annual literary magazine, *The Jasper Journal*, to which anyone could contribute their bon mots. The array of extracurricular school activities included choral groups, dramatic clubs, and elective current events workshops, frequently with guest speakers.

The classic American two-seater school desk is probably still in use today.

The standard school desk was a two-seater bench with a hinged double desktop that lifted up and revealed a small open space for notebooks and writing implements. Our fifth grade classroom was arranged alphabetically and I usually found myself sharing a desk with Sara Taylor. Sara was a very bright student and it seemed to me that she seldom needed to pay much attention to what was going on in class, but she still managed to do extremely well. She was also a voracious reader and was never without a book. One day during a lull in the classroom, Sara opened her side of the desk, took out a book, and began reading. I could not see what she was reading, but she was clearly totally engrossed and enjoying it immensely. On this particular occasion, the teacher became quite annoyed that Sara was not paying attention and instead was reading from a book that, she assumed, was on her lap.

"What are you reading, Sara?" Mrs. Collins demanded, as she left her perch in the front of the classroom and approached our desk. "Would you like to share it with the rest of the class?"

"I'm not reading, Mrs. Collins." Sara politely and untruthfully explained. "My head was down because I have a headache."

Mrs. Collins knew she was reading and decided to make an example of her. Quick-thinking Sara was petrified that Mrs. Collins would not approve of her choice of literature, and surreptitiously lifted the desktop just a bit and slid her book onto my side of our desk.

If Mrs. Collins was surprised not to find a book in Sara's lap, she did not show it. Without showing any emotion she exclaimed, "Open your desk, Sara, please."

What she saw shook her up a bit. "Henry! What are you doing reading *Studs Lonigan*? This is not suitable for a fifth grader!"

I was so traumatized at this point that I became speechless. For me to suggest it was Sara's book was unlikely to be believable, and I was not too worried about having to take a note home with the details of my transgressions. I was certain Mother would not have known anything about Studs Lonigan or its author, James Farrell. My silence clearly confirmed my guilt.

I did, in fact, have to take a note home from the teacher but I was not expelled. Apart from having the novel confiscated, I think my only punishment was some form of detention, such as having to come to school a half-hour early for a whole week.

I still have not had a chance to read the book. Mrs. Collins kept Sara's copy. I will have to check if there's a copy on eBay.

P.S. 9 came back into my life in January 2007, when my dear friend Maury Allen, a distinguished and nationally recognized sports writer and radio commentator, invited me to participate in his weekly radio broadcast. Maury was the author of several books about Mickey Mantle and his weekly radio sports show came from "Mickey Mantle's Restaurant" in midtown Manhattan. Often when I was in New York, Maury would invite me to be a guest on his program and take telephone call-in questions about English sports.

Maury would usually send a note ahead of my visit suggesting the subject about which we might talk. On this particular occasion, he wrote that I should be prepared to discuss cricket. When I arrived,

I was prepared to deliver a comprehensive exposé on the British national sport, about which I knew very little. On the air that evening, Maury started by asking me if would I like to make some comments about the upcoming Wimbledon tennis tournament.

Having prepared to talk about cricket, I was dumbfounded and speechless. Janet, Maury's wife, was in the restaurant that evening and saved me by going to a nearby pay phone and anonymously phoning the radio station, and specifically asking if Maury's guest might explain the finer points of cricket.

On the same day, Maury had another guest, Barry Daub, whom I had never met. Barry had just been named the new principal of a soon-to-be-opened school for special education known as P.S. M811. Maury invited Barry on the radio show because the school was to be called the Mickey Mantle School, and Maury was keen that his listeners hear why a New York City public school came to be named after his favorite baseball player, even if he did play for the New York Yankees. (Maury was a devoted Brooklyn Dodgers fan.) Barry's description of the school sounded familiar to me. You can imagine my amazement when it turned out that the new P.S. M811 was, in fact, the old P.S. 9. Barry was so excited about meeting a P.S. 9 old boy that he cordially invited me to be a special guest at the new school's official opening ceremony the following week.

Perhaps of interest to Trivial Pursuit fans is the fact that Public School 9 enjoys the rare distinction of being one of only a few schools in the United States on the National Register of Historic Places. This award had nothing to do with my being a student there.

In 1889 a letter to the mayor of New York was published in *The New York Times*, citing some grim conditions at P.S. 9: "There is no visible plaster in the entire building. The wooden staircases and wood-lined stairways are only twenty-nine inches wide. Large stoves and stovepipes beneath the stairs and elsewhere used for warming the building are dangerously close to the woodwork. The passages are thirty inches wide. The building is devoid of any means of escape from the rear and devoid of any fire escapes. Means of egress from the building is insufficient," the letter said.

The following year, in 1890, that building was demolished and a few years later the Board of Education erected what was considered a modern school building on the same site. This was to be "my" P.S. 9.

There was a popular legend in the school that Danny Kaye was once a student there.

No self-respecting street kid would go anywhere without at least one in his pocket.

32

My Most Valuable Possession

Walking along New York streets recently brought back memories of the wide variety of street games that everyone played. For most of us, the street was our habitual playground and hangout. How did we ever manage to survive without TVs, iPods, iPhones, Facebook, Game Boy, and texting?

Ask any person who grew up in Manhattan in the 1940s what his most valuable possession was and he will immediately answer, "My Spaldeen." The Spaldeen has been called by some "the Rosetta stone of urban childhood fun." It was a small pink tennis-like ball without the fuzz, indestructible, costing two bits (for those under sixty, that was twenty-five cents), and an absolutely essential part of one's personal arsenal of recreational possessions.

The variety of games one could play with a Spaldeen was limitless. Perhaps the most popular street game was "stoop ball." Just as in Amsterdam, where the word originated, a stoop is a set of stairs leading to the front door of a typical New York City brownstone. However, it was more than just a way into one's house. In New York, it actually was part of the house, just like any other "room." In Amsterdam, it was primarily a way to raise the main living spaces in houses located in parts of the city that were frequently subject to flooding. In addition to one's Spaldeen, all that was needed was a stoop, hence the name.

There were three major variations of stoop ball. On the West Side of Manhattan, the most popular variation was called "bounces" and was based on the rules of baseball. It required a minimum of two players and there was no upper limit. Usually two of us would begin playing and as others passed by, they were just added to one side or another. There were no uniforms, no special shoes, and no organized teams. Rules varied depending on which street you were playing on and whatever permanent street hardware was nearby. There were no bats, no bases, and no runners.

West 85th Street was a stoop-ball heaven because between Riverside Drive and West End Avenue there were perhaps twenty brownstone houses with appropriate stoops. The idea was to throw the ball as hard as you could against a corner of the steps as fast as possible. If you managed to connect directly at the leading edge of the stoop, the ball would typically travel in a trajectory that might reach the other side of the street and even hit the building opposite, hopefully avoiding a window—but not always. Any contact of the ball below that point usually meant a smaller trajectory into the street. In the unusual event of a window being broken, the plan was for everyone playing to run in a different direction and if caught, to plead ignorance. "I didn't even know there was a game going on, Sir! I was running to the library to get there before it closes."

If someone had chalk, lines would be drawn on the street, but a small sharp stone was usually a satisfactory substitute. The ball had to go into the street. If caught on the fly without a bounce, the thrower, or batter, was automatically out. Should it bounce first on the sidewalk, or be hit into an area designated as outside the playing field, the batter was also out. If the ball was caught after one bounce, it was considered a single. Two bounces meant a double. And so forth. A home run usually required one to hit the building opposite. After this the normal rules of baseball would apply—three outs per inning, nine innings per game, a dropped ball was an error and an automatic single, and so forth. Available physical landmarks, such as garbage (rubbish) cans, lampposts, and fire hydrants, usually designated foul lines.

If there should be a car about to park in the street opposite home plate, our playing field, or stoop, we would ask the driver of the car just to move down or up the street so that it was not blocking our field. In the exceptional case when the driver would not move, we would move to a new field and rechalk the boundaries. In really tough neighborhoods, failure to move a car blocking the pitch might be punishable by a flattened tire or worse.

If we ran out of stoops, we would revert to a variation of the classic game that became known as "curb ball." In this variation, the ball was thrown at the curb edge of the street and steps were not necessary. This was a little more difficult and the most popular variation was a form of base running. Once the ball hit the curb, you had to run and reach the other side of the street without being tagged out. Running bases organized between sewer covers was another option.

In streets without stoops or curbs, a more elaborate variation of baseball—"stick ball"—became popular. First, four bases were designated either by a verbal agreement or tradition (for example, the fire hydrant is first base) or by drawing each base with chalk on the street. A broom or mop handle served as a bat, which is why the game was commonly called stick ball.

There were two well-established variations. In the most popular version, the pitcher would pitch the Spaldeen on a bounce towards the home plate, where the batter would try to hit the ball with his stick. In this sense, it was not unlike cricket. Home plate was often a sewer cover, which was always in the center of the street. Second base was the next sewer cover. Your prowess was measured by the number of sewer covers you could hit the ball past. An exceptionally good batter was awarded the exalted title of "three-sewer man." I never made it.

"Punch ball," also known as "slap ball," was a variation of stick ball that did not require a stick. The batter tossed the ball up or bounced it, and then punched it either with his fist or an open palm, and tried to get to first base before a fielder threw the ball to the first baseman and tagged him out. If there were not enough players, one could, with prior agreement, throw the ball directly at the runner. If you hit him before he reached first base, he was also considered out. This alternative was often rewarded with appropriate black-and-blue bruises.

Stick ball was not without its hazards. There was always the possibility of hitting a foul ball and breaking a window. That was automatically designated as a time-out or a game called "on account of weather" to allow time for everyone to run for cover and disappear.

Secondly, there was the danger from police action. While there was no law as far as I know against stick ball, people did complain about the noise and the inevitable hold-up of traffic while a pitch was completed. The police response was draconian. They would stop the game and break the bat in half. A far worse punishment was reserved for a serial offender. The police would grab one of the players and threaten to "book 'em." I was caught only once, and the police drove me far away from our familiar neighborhood and left me to find my way home. I don't remember my parents ever filing a complaint.

Next to various baseball-oriented games, the most popular ball games were played against a wall. First, there was a type of hand ball where the boundaries were conveniently permanent—the edges of the paving stones that seemed always to be the same size—four foot square. The server had to hit the ball so that it would bounce into the adjacent paving square. The receiver would return the serve against the wall and play would continue until someone missed. The really good players eventually would substitute a very hard, small black ball for the spongy pink Spaldeen. For this game, a glove was useful but hardly ever available. Anyway, tough guys don't use gloves.

There were as many variations of hand ball as there were walls on which it was played. One of our favorite pitches was a corner of a building on West End Avenue and 83rd Street. Here, balls could be hit against two adjacent walls, greatly increasing the possible variations. At some point, I recall dozens of purposely built hand ball courts being created at Riverside Park.

"Kings" was the second most popular hand ball game that allowed several players to compete. Abutting pavement squares were designated as ace, king, queen, jack, and so forth, one for each player. The person in the ace box served with the palm of his hand and the ball was supposed to bounce first in his ace box, then hit the wall and then bounce into any other box. The player in the box had to return the ball by first bouncing it in his own box and then sending it up or down the wall into another wall. If he missed, he went to the end of line and got a "k." When someone lost five times consecutively, he got "k-i-n-g-s" and was out. Top players mastered control of the ball with curves, slices, drop shots, and "butter" spins.

What did we do if no one had a ball? A popular option to baseball or wall games was called "Johnny on the pony." A group is divided into two teams. Each team selects a "post," who takes up a position with his back against a wall. The rest of his team bends over and forms a line facing him—basically as a type of saddle. The first player from the second team, standing some twenty feet away, runs and jumps as far forward towards the post as he can, landing on the backs of the crouching team members. The second player follows and this continues until all the players are "on the pony" or the first team collapses.

Some of the other popular outdoor games in our neighborhood were Mumbley-peg, Ring-a-levio, War, Penny-pitching, and Freeze, and as the players became more affluent, basketballs, footballs, soccer balls, and even sometimes tennis racquets began to appear.

What if it were raining or too dark?

There were indoor pastimes as well. If it was raining, or dark, or no one was around with whom to compete, there were hobbies with which to occupy one's time—stamp collecting, making scrapbooks, photography, coin collecting, listening to music, or perhaps reading.

The opportunities for inventing variations of the classic games grew exponentially. And, of course, each neighborhood, or sometimes even a street, would boast its own innovations.

No one was ever bored!

33

The Best Way to Throw a Knife?

Next to one's Spaldeen, the most important not-to-be-without possession when growing up in New York was one's penknife. This was not a hunting knife, nor was it a seven-inch switchblade, or an equally sinister Bowie knife, nor a Swiss army knife armed with screwdrivers, pliers, hacksaws, cherry pickers, fruit knives, magnifying glasses, or surgeon's scalpel just in case one had to perform an emergency tracheotomy. Rather, it was a very simple, usually single-blade, garden-variety pocket knife with no bells and whistles.

Knife games had to be played where there was reasonable soft soil or short grass, so the playing field was no longer one's street but rather a neighborhood park. We had two choices—Riverside Park, which was across the street from our apartment house and meant simply crossing the street, or Central Park, which was at least a twenty-minute walk.

You can imagine which became the more popular venue.

There were essentially two games, although I am certain that there are probably many variations.

Mumbley-peg was a game of skill involving fifteen or more progressively difficult trick tosses. To be counted, your knife had to stick in the ground deep enough to put at least two fingers between the knife handle and the ground. One started with a classic throw, which required the knife to execute a half-turn in the air before hitting the ground. The first two throws were made from an open fist—first from the right hand and then the left. If your throw did not stick in the ground at an appropriate angle, you lost you turn and had to wait for the other players to go. After the open-hand throw, the knife was tossed from a closed fist with the sharp point resting just behind the knuckles of one's up-turned hand.

From here on, the starting position of the knife became increasingly more difficult. Soon one had to start with the knife balanced on the tip of each finger—the knife had to flip up and do a 270-degree turn. The variations of these post-graduate positions were always left to local customs, and each throw acquired its own name, which often had little to do with the nature of the throw itself. I recall such colorful descriptions as "cherry trees," "round the world," "over the fence," "Pike's Peak," and even "apples and pears." Some names are best forgotten.

Another popular game we played was called "territories." The first player would draw a territory on the pitch. A circle was at first the most popular shape but eventually the size and shape were no longer critical factors. The second player would divide the territory, using straight lines, so that the number of territories was equal to the number of players. Each player would select an area as his home base. Then each player would throw his knife into the playing area and draw a line from one edge of the dividing line to the perimeter, adding to his original area accordingly. He would place his mark in one of the new areas, thus capturing some of his opponent's land. This was a game of high drama and, of course, required great strategic intelligence. Once a player was left with territory that was smaller than the size of his hand, he lost.

A favorite question that Boy Scout leaders used to pose to the younger Cub Scouts was, "What's the best way to throw a knife?" The answer was, "You should never throw knives any way."

34

Publish or Perish

For as far back as I can remember, I was intrigued with anything mechanical or electrical with movable parts. I would sit spellbound in my father's Brussels office exploring the various machinations of his hand-cranked mechanical calculator.

It is not surprising, then, that my curiosity was aroused when I first watched my father use his portable Olivetti typewriter, in our apartment in New York. After a suitable period of apprenticeship and a carefully planned practical examination to test my skills at changing the awkward black-and-red ribbon, I was allowed to test drive the Olivetti, and soon afterwards was on my first solo test run. I was ten years old.

After an initial rush of adrenalin, it became apparent that the actual uses of my new typing skills were limited. There were no school assignments, letters to send, papers to write, or book reports to prepare. But one day Peter, who was now my best friend, and I decided that since we had access to an ancient portable typewriter we would write, publish, and distribute our very own newspaper.

It was an ambitious and audacious undertaking because we had no idea how we would print the newspaper. It would be a few more decades before Xerox machines would make their debut. We had no funds, no reporters, no access to news services, no photographers, and certainly no experience or knowledge of anything even remotely journalistic. As I said, it was a bold move! The enterprise was further handicapped because English was not my mother tongue, nor was it Peter's.

Despite all this, we persevered and in the fall of 1944, Number 1, Volume 1 of *The Voice*, a five-page monthly newspaper, was launched on a totally unprepared market—our classmates and friends. We divided the editorial tasks between the two of us. In addition to summaries of local, national, and international news, *The Voice* had several feature sections, including movie reviews written by Steve Weiner, radio suggestions, quizzes, and something we called "Believe It or Else." My brother, although six years older and not in our class, appeared on the masthead, responsible simply for "stories." Our printing press was, of course, the trusty Olivetti typewriter and an ample supply of carbon paper, which allowed us to publish four copies at a time. We spent many of our evenings typing. Without a lot

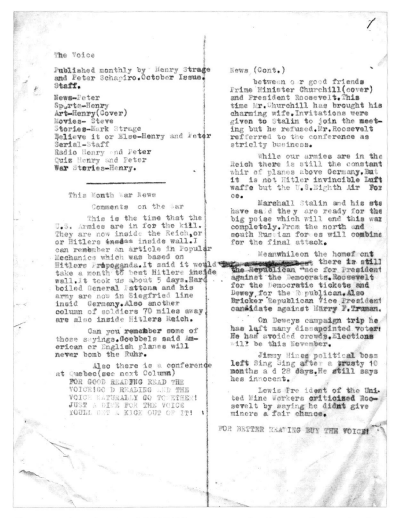

Our own, hand-printed VOICE newspaper had no predetermined publishing schedule, as publication date was dependent on whoever had access to a typewriter.

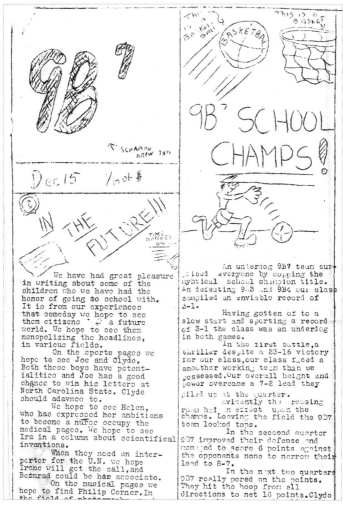

9B7, our next newspaper for our class in Joan of Arc Junior High School, was printed, had a bigger audience, and was published twice a month.

of market research, we set the cover price at one dime, which was ten cents. Our logo read:

FOR GOOD READING READ *THE VOICE*

GOOD READING AND *THE VOICE* NATURALLY GO TOGETHER

JUST A DIME FOR *THE VOICE*! YOU'LL GET A KICK OUT OF IT!

We certainly did not establish any circulation records, but for each new edition, we attracted guest contributors anxious to see their bylines in print. I have no record of how many issues were actually published, but miraculously three or four complete editions have survived intact.

Our editorial partnership continued when we went to Joan of Arc Junior High School. Now, as hardened newspaper proprietors and journalists, we applied our skills and experience to *9B7* ("*9B7*" was the designated identification of our class) and produced a weekly newspaper that was mimeographed, rather than typed with carbon copies, thank goodness! This would become a much more ambitious project than *The Voice*, with a bigger staff, more pages, and a "guaranteed" circulation. The cover price remained the same—ten cents.

As our audience—and we ourselves—were now much more mature, we had a lot more to report on and write about. The need to provide a synopsis of world news and sports practically disappeared and in its place were interviews with teachers and classmates, class sports, news of various social functions, as well as exposés and some amateur attempts at humor. Some editions were similar to *HELLO* magazine, without photographs. Of course, when it came close to graduation, there was news about the secondary schools that various classmates would be attending, as well as the inevitable popularity poll.

Our new logo was: ALL THE CLASS NEWS THAT'S FIT TO PRINT.

This period of Peter's and my journalistic experience coincided with our curiosity and interest in the activities of the United Nations Security Council, which met at Lake Success on Long Island. This was the first home of the United Nations, before it moved to its new building in midtown Manhattan. Lake Success was a few subway stops from Manhattan and the visitors' gallery never seemed to be full, so we were frequent spectators. If we went on a weekend, we would pack lunch for ourselves and hear sessions of the Security Council. While I suppose we appreciated little of the geo-political implications of what

The staff of our Bronx High School of Science 1951 class yearbook included several of our original journalistic partners.

we were hearing, I somehow knew that I was watching history being made. I remember hearing Abba Eban many times representing Israel after the United Nations voted for Israel's independence.

Peter and I spent many days in the visitors' gallery, and I think it was at around this time that we both decided we absolutely wanted to become foreign correspondents. I remember one day going to the visitors' gallery and actually meeting real reporters, who told us that the key skill we needed to become successful journalists was shorthand. Later, when the opportunity presented itself at a local community center, we both took an after-school course in Pitman shorthand. A small problem was that the lady instructor in the course was from the Deep South and so we learned Southern-accented shorthand. Many years later, I recall impressing my secretary when I challenged her to a shorthand race using my somewhat dated, very rusty basic skills.

Peter and I joined forces again several years later at Bronx High School, when we were co-editors of the high school yearbook, which thankfully was formally printed and bound, and had a massive twenty-person staff and some semi-professional oversight from a faculty member.

Later, when I was in college, I seemed naturally to drift once again into journalistic activities. The most challenging turned out to be my year as editor-in-chief of *TECH NEWS*, the Worcester Polytechnic Institute college newspaper, and in my senior year serving as co-editor of the yearbook. Being editor of the college newspaper is not without its risks, as I found out. In several editorials, I challenged the wisdom of there being a paucity of liberal arts subjects in the university curriculum. My enthusiasm seems to have raised questions about the future of my financial aid scholarship there.

My final and rather unexpected editorial challenge was in 1953, when I was dragooned into editing a yearbook journal of our battalion's activities in the Army Officers Candidate Training program in Alabama.

35

The Day My Father Died

Although I was probably forty years younger when my father died than when my mother passed away, my memories of his death are clearer and more vivid than they are of my mother's passing.

It was a normal school day. As usual I walked the few blocks from my elementary school, P.S. 9, on 82nd Street and West End Avenue, to our apartment on 85th Street and Riverside Drive. As I got into our elevator, Johnny, the so-called "elevator boy," in a calm monotone told me that my father had died earlier that day.

"Someone is at home," Johnny said, "and will tell you what happened."

Death was something that happened to other people in wars.

It was when soldiers were shooting at each other. When bombs fell on innocent civilians. When cars crashed on highways. Or when the good cops got the bad guys. There was no war in New York City. What could Johnny be talking about? Perhaps my father was ill. That was all I could just about understand.

The door to our apartment was open, and as I walked in I could tell that something had, in fact, happened. Usually when I got home, Mother greeted me with a big hug and plied me with milk and cookies or something else that was usually sticky and sweet. On this occasion, she was not there. Instead, I could hear unfamiliar voices coming from the sitting rooms.

Someone, I cannot remember exactly who, saw me and came over to greet me.

"What happened to my father?" I asked.

I do not remember the precise response, but it was something to suggest that he had become very sick during the morning, fell unconscious, was taken to the hospital, and never woke up. What an inadequate description of the last hours of a beloved parent's life!

In May 1945, I was eleven years old, and death and its implications were something I knew nothing about. Why should I?

I asked someone I did not recognize if Mother was all right, and was assured that she was with friends and would be all right, but was not at home at that moment.

The next thing I remember is permanently and indelibly etched into my memory bank in great detail. I was dressed up, or least had changed from my school clothes, and was driven to a building on

Amsterdam Avenue and 76th Street, which I later learned was the Park West Riverside Chapel. I was ushered into a small room on the ground floor, where I saw Mother for the first time that afternoon. She looked awful. She immediately came to me and hugged me as hard as she could. She told me that everything would be all right—of course, it wouldn't be—and then asked if I had had something to eat when I was home. I am sure Mark was there as well, but I don't really remember.

Unlike Cleveland, where we had lots of relatives, the only family we had in New York was Lazarus Joseph, his sister Frances, and Sam Halperin. The next day Max, Mother's brother from Cleveland, arrived with Sam Zelles, cousin Moulia, and another cousin.

In this small room, a few of our family's friends were sitting in small groups and chatting in very low tones. In the center of the room, on a platform with large brass wheels, was a huge, shiny, black box— Father's coffin. The coffin was half open and I could see Father's face. Everyone assures me to this day that this could not have happened. It is not part of Jewish custom to have an open coffin on display and I must have dreamt or imagined it. I did not.

Perhaps the funeral home did not know at that point that we were Jewish. This is really the only possible explanation I can imagine. But it was, after all, a Jewish funeral home. The term "home" in this context remains in my mind to this day as a ridiculous description of the functions carried out in such an establishment.

The finality of death is almost impossible to explain to an eleven-year-old. I was sure that the person lying in the coffin could not be my father. It was someone else. I have very little memory of the next few days and only vague images of the funeral service or the burial in Baron Hirsch Cemetery on Staten Island. I am sure that I had somehow talked myself into believing that soon this whole affair would turn out to be a mistake, a bad dream, and my father would get well and reappear as if nothing had happened.

For years afterwards, when I would see a person walking on the street, sitting on a bench in the park, or on a bus or subway who even remotely resembled my father, I would pause and for a brief moment pray that this look-alike would, in fact, be my father and that he would rush over to me, grab me in his arms, and hug me ever so tightly.

It took many years for me to get over this feeling.

36

My Waistcoat

Actually, the waistcoat never fit.
It was far too big for me but
a well-placed strap and buckle meant
I could gather all the extra material in the back
and it seemed to fit just right.
Styles in waistcoats haven't changed much.
Even after eighty years it always looks elegant,
always in style, always matching the shirt, tie, and jacket
in perfect harmony.
I didn't really know him very well.
We were both too young to realize how
few years we would have together.
Somehow when I wear his waistcoat I feel
he is nearby,
watching, anxious to help,
curious to know how am I getting on.
His love of life,

his passion,
his personality,
his gentleness,
all seem somehow effortlessly to seep
through the fading fabric and are
ingested into every pore of my body.
Perhaps that is why people who knew him always said,
"You're just like your father."

Still in style

*Historic tapestry—a copy of an early eighteenth-century
print of sailors aboard the HMS* Victory

37

Restoring a Lost Art

The photograph of a rare one-off embroidery has never before been seen in public or on the Internet. This unique tapestry, which proudly hangs under glass in London, depicts a scene from an early Victorian drawing of two HMS *Victory* sailors toasting their good fortune. The unusual work, made up of over 4,500 individual stitches and more than thirty-five separate color threads, is an outstanding example of post-war workmanship in New York City.

Art weaving, one of the oldest forms of artistic expression, has been traced back to early Egyptian times. It is a skill representing and demanding many highly developed talents and skills—artistic, mechanical, manual dexterity, cultural awareness, color sense, patience, and thoughtful concentration.

It is not surprising, therefore, that it was a subject that highly advanced schools in the 1950s decided to add to their curriculum. One such "advanced" school was Joan of Arc Junior High School in Manhattan. It was a school that prided itself on combining high academic standards, creative teaching techniques, and a unique core curriculum. It also prided itself on its ethnic diversity and human rights considerations.

The legendary principal, Dr. Stella Sweeting, who died a few years ago at age 101, was unique among principals in the New York City school system. She seemed to have the power and authority to hire and fire teachers as well as to introduce and teach subjects that were not taught in any other schools. I remember that it would not be unusual to meet her first thing in the morning as you arrived at the school's main entrance. If you were not wearing the compulsory necktie, she would "rent" you one for the day and give the proceeds to the United Nations Children's Fund.

Dr. Sweeting was keen on making certain that the girls in her school had the same opportunities as the boys. As a result, all girls were required to take woodworking classes, as well as mechanical drawing, and something called "metalworking." My mother was polite about the tin-can sugar scoop I had patiently fashioned in metalworking class, although it disappeared from sight after several months of living on the bottom shelf of the kitchen closet.

The boys had to take their chances in classes for cooking, sewing, and apartment basics. The school had created a model apartment complete with beds, dining room tables, kitchen, and bathroom. The idea was that we should know the basic chores associated with maintaining an apartment. Making beds was easy. Setting a table for a dinner party was slightly more complicated. But surely the last straw was learning how to polish the tarnished silver our teacher, Mrs. Moore, brought from her own apartment.

The experiment in rotating the traditional roles of the sexes took a major setback when one girl sawed off a bit of her finger. But although my tin-can sugar scoop is long gone, my priceless embroidery hangs proudly in our home as a reminder of times past.

38

Maybe I Should Have Been a Lawyer

On a sunny fall day in 1948, two budding entrepreneurs, both of them immigrants, met in a Riverside Drive apartment in New York City to cement in place their first official partnership contract. Unfortunately, there were no witnesses present to proofread the documents. The contract was discovered only this year (2014) amidst a decaying collection of old newspapers and magazines. While there were many typos and misspellings, including the name of one of the principals, the underlying spirit of the document has been preserved and the partnership has endured. Alas, the major purpose of the agreement—"to make money"—has only partially been accomplished.

This is how it all started.

Andy Meisels, one of our classmates, was selling and delivering *The New York Times* to students and staff at Joan of Arc Junior High School every weekday morning. It appeared he had cornered the market at school and was collecting a lot of money for what seemed like little effort. He was not interested in a merger, and my friend and classmate Gerard Smetana and I had no resources with which to engineer a takeover, but Andy was happy to hire us as subcontractors to do the actually deliveries. We each got paid $1.25 per week, which came in the form of a check from *The New York Times* office.

We thought, after a while, about starting a competitive delivery service for the same newspaper but that clearly made no sense. Then Gerard hit upon a great idea. Why not sell the competing daily newspaper in New York, the *New York Herald Tribune*, to the students? It had one big competitive edge—it had comic strips.

Gerard went to visit the *Tribune*'s educational department in Times Square, and very soon we became the sole distributors of the *New York Herald Tribune* at Joan of Arc Junior High School. We quickly struck a deal with the local "HT" distributor. Every morning, he would deliver to the front door of the school as many copies of the *Tribune* as we had sold for that day. Our job would be to distribute them to the students before school started. As I recall we charged the students two bits (twenty-five cents) a week or a nickel (five cents) a copy. We had to buy the papers from the distributor for three cents.

I3I Riverside Drive

New York,24,N.Y.

Sep$tember,17,1947

To Whom It May Concern;

This is to painly show that the undersigned Henry
Strage and Gerard Semtana have as of today, the 17 th. day
of the month of September gone in to a partnership. Their
many purpoes is to make money. They expect to do this by
selling in School the New York Hearld Tirbune . They agree
to share all the work equally , and as a wesult to divide
equally the amount of money they together may make , besides
that they agree to share any expense that come up. No decisions
may be made by one many with out the others approval. No
other person or persons will enter this organazation .

Any thing which possibilly left out of this written
agresment may be at once added.

Respectfully.

Signed and agreed upon ....Henry Strage
Signed and agreed upon ....Gerard Setana
n

Every new business start-up needed to have a properly signed contract.

The brains behind the enterprise (Gerard)

The brawn (Henry)

307

This represented a 66 percent margin on costs. It seemed like a good deal, even though we had to pay in advance with no refunds. We basically had no fixed or operating costs, so all we needed to do was plan how to spend the money.

There were some down sides however. Some we foresaw. Others appeared as the venture got underway.

First, we had to come to school early enough to deliver all of the papers before classes began. That seemed like a small price to pay.

Second, we had to develop a carefully considered marketing strategy to beat the competition—*The New York Times*—and Andy was a smart guy. We took advantage of our dedicated school radio station, WJOA, which was the first radio station in a New York public school. We made frequent advertising announcements about our special offers, such as discounts and competitions. We even had our advertisements broadcast in several different languages.

Finally, we had to develop a financial control and audit system to (a) collect the money ahead of time; (b) provide credit in case someone did not have a quarter handy when we came around to collect the money; and (c) operate a mini banking system in case we were providing credit to someone.

We enjoyed two big competitive advantages. The *Tribune* was much more geared to the school education market, and every week or two they produced a highly popular and readable school supplement on a topic of current interest or controversy. And if a teacher required students to read a particular supplement, we were laughing all the way to the bank.

For a while things were going well. In addition to the advantage of the comics and the supplements, we invented a "discount" for monthly subscriptions—$1 per month. We never worked out if this was a profit-maker or a loss leader. The notion of return on capital had not yet entered our vocabulary. In due course, *The New York Times* realized that they, too, had to produce educational supplements if they were to stay competitive.

Our usual routine was to come to the school to collect our pile of *Tribunes*, mark each with the room to which it should be delivered, and then walk around dropping copies in each classroom. One day, the pile of our papers was missing. After a desperate search, we found our *Tribunes* at an entrance that was far from where they were usually left. To this day, Gerard and I suspect it was Andy up to some dirty tricks. After that we had to come to school earlier to make certain the distributor actually handed the papers to one of us, rather than just dropping them on the sidewalk and then having them mysteriously moved to some other location.

My newspaper delivery career ended when I left to go to The Bronx High School of Science. Gerard was cleverer. He continued in the business through Stuyvesant High School, City College, and even University of Michigan Law School. Meanwhile, Andy Meisels continued with journalism right up to the end.

ANDREW MEISELS, NEWSMAN, DEAD

By Jere Hester

Wednesday, April 16, 1997, 2:02 a.m.: Andrew Meisels, a novelist and veteran journalist who brought to life the epic of war and peace in the Mideast for *Daily News* readers, has died, his family said yesterday.

Meisels, who passed away hours after becoming ill Monday at his Tel Aviv home, was 64. The cause of death was not immediately known, said his oldest daughter, Tami.

Friends, family, and colleagues were shocked by the sudden death of a man who loved life and the news.

"Andy was a knowledgeable, hardworking, dedicated journalist," said the *News* National Editor, Diane Goldie. "We could call him day or night, and he would be on top of the story. He was a true pro and always a gentleman."

Meisels, who was born in Budapest, immigrated with his family in 1939 to the Bronx. They later moved to Manhattan, where Meisels attended City College.

In the late 1950s, Meisels joined The Associated Press and worked in New Jersey. He immigrated to Israel in 1963, toiling variously for the *Jerusalem Post*, Israeli radio, and ABC-TV and radio. Meisels' voice and byline were familiar to New Yorkers, who heard his reports for AP Radio and read the stories he wrote for the *News* over the past dozen years.

In a memorable dispatch filed during the 1991 Gulf War, Meisels offered a gripping first-person account of an Iraqi missile raid on Tel Aviv.

"I have been under attack before. I covered the 1967 Six-Day War and the 1973 war. I was in Lebanon when Israel invaded that country," he wrote in the January 18, 1991 edition of the *News*. "That was terrifying, but this was at home, in my living room, with my wife and daughters. This was different."

Colleagues recalled Meisels as a kind, giving man who was passionate about his work. "He was totally committed to the profession of journalism," said Jay Bushinsky, Mideast bureau chief for WINS radio and a long-time friend of Meisels. "Every story he prepared was punctiliously accurate, and he was a stickler for details."

Meisels is survived by his mother, Margaret; a sister, Marianne, and daughters Tami, Ruthie and Judy. His wife, Martha, died two years ago. Meisels was to be buried today in Tel Aviv.

Practically the entire 9B7 class of 1948 at Joan of Arc went on to university.

Park Central Florist on 86th Street and Columbus Avenue, where Gerard and I worked as delivery boys for many years.

39

Flower Power—My First Job

Despite existing child labor laws in the United States, I began working when I was thirteen years old. In the high-rise world of the Upper West Side of Manhattan in the late 1940s, and in the absence of DHL, FedEx, and similar professional distribution services, delivery of packages, food, newspapers, and small parcels opened the door for enterprising youths to become delivery boys.

Dmitri Sokolos, one of my classmates at Joan of Arc Junior High School, one day suggested that if we really wanted to earn some serious spending money, Gerard and I should look into becoming delivery boys for a flower shop. Dmitri's parents owned a flower shop on 86th Street near Columbus Avenue, and he explained that delivering flowers was far more attractive than delivering groceries or newspapers. Flowers were lighter, you didn't need to get up in the early morning, and tips, which were the major source of revenue, were much better.

On Columbus Avenue, around the corner from Dmitri's flower shop, there was a smaller but busy flower shop called Park Central Florist. It was owned and operated by a charming Japanese couple, George and Kim Yuzawa. Collecting all the courage available to thirteen-year-olds, one day Gerard and I offered our services to Park Central Florist. George said he would be delighted to give us a try.

Delivering flowers in Manhattan was a continuous adventure full of daily dramas and challenges. Perhaps someone will write a TV sitcom based on the flower delivery business. Unlike groceries or newspapers, you were unlikely to make a delivery to the same address more than once. In addition, in most cases the people to whom you were delivering flowers were not expecting any deliveries, so sometimes getting them to open their doors, especially in crime-ridden areas, involved impresssive powers of persuasion coupled with extreme skills in diplomacy.

Manhattan on the West Side is like a human Grand Canyon, consisting of enormous concrete filing cabinets for people. For a flower delivery boy, the only advantage—if you were lucky—over other delivery services is that you could make multiple deliveries in a single location, ergo less traveling and more tips. One usually had to negotiate entry into the building with an ageless doorman who only trusted nuns and rabbis. If the doorman told you he would take the flowers "up" himself, there was, of course, no chance of getting a tip. Those apartment houses were in the "avoid at all costs" classification.

Let me describe an oft-repeated scenario. After convincing the apartment house doorman that I was just delivering flowers and not trying to break into any apartment, I would ring the bell of Apartment 17A.

"Yes, who is it?"

"Good afternoon. Park Central Florist, delivery."

"I don't expect any flowers."

"Are you Mrs. Schwartz?

"Who wants to know?"

"Madame, I have a bunch of flowers for Mrs. Gloria Schwartz. If that is you, please open the door so I can deliver these flowers!"

"Who are the flowers from?"

"Would you like me to open the sealed envelope with your name on it to find out who the flowers are from?"

"Open my mail? Do no such thing! I'll call the police."

"Please, don't call the police. Would you like me to come back tomorrow?"

"No, leave the flowers on the door mat."

"I can't do that, Madam, I need you to sign the receipt so that I can show I actually delivered the flowers to you."

"What kind of flowers are they?"

"Mrs. Schwartz, please open the door."

"How did you know my name?"

Mrs. Schwartz would finally open her door, take the flowers, and give me twenty-five cents.

Let me explain the underlying economics of flower delivery. Essentially the shop provided free delivery within a three-mile radius of the store, although sometimes this rule was interpreted rather loosely. As delivery boys, we relied entirely on tips. One could never be sure if you would get a tip or how much it would be. So it was in one's interest to make as many deliveries as you could during the time you were working and, of course, always smiling.

Flower deliveries, I discovered, fell into one of four categories:

Cut flowers to an individual or family.

A potted plant, usually in some type of terra cotta pot.

Cut flowers to a funeral home, cemetery, or banqueting room.

Bouquets to a person living in a hotel.

In the last two categories, tips were most unusual. At least, I never got any. Delivering a potted plant was a mega drag because the pots were usually very heavy, which meant you could only deliver a single item per trip. Cut flowers to individuals were the best option. You could generally handle three different addresses at one time and the weight was generally modest.

But there were dangers.

As the senior delivery boy, Gerard, who was older than me, was in charge of deciding who delivered which order. I remember one afternoon when I drew the short straw. Not only was the location a long subway ride away, but it was a funeral arrangement. This meant no tips. And on top of these negatives, the location turned out to be a scary Buddhist temple that looked like a scene from a Charlie Chan horror movie. I remember this one well.

There was a massive door that opened mysteriously as I approached, and closed equally mysteriously after I got inside. The interior appeared to be one gigantic room, at least an entire square block in size, windowless, dark, with a powerful smell of what I later learned was incense, not dope. The only person to be seen was an ancient, wizard-looking man who must have been 124 years old sitting cross-legged in the middle of this vast room. He was either in deep meditation or dead. When I approached to ask him where to put the flowers I had brought, he looked up and through me as if I were not there at all. And he certainly was not interested in my flowers or in signing my receipt. I tried to find someone who would speak to me. There was no one. And then the only person in the room, the man who had been meditating, suddenly disappeared in a cloud of white smoke.

What was even more frightening is that when I turned to leave, I could not find the door I had entered—it seemed that all of the walls were covered with doors and I had no idea which one I had come through. Near where I stood trying to collect my thoughts was a massive wall painting of a young man who appeared to be praying to have his life spared from the almost certain decapitation that seemed imminent. I quickly decided that since the flowers were going to someone who was already dead they would not mind if I just left the arrangement neatly laid out on the floor. After trying several "doors," I finally found one that moved, and left as quickly as I could, elated to get back into a hot, crowded, friendly subway train and be on my way home. After that, Gerard and I would flip a coin to see who would get the short straw whenever there was a delivery to a Buddhist temple.

After we stopped working with them, Gerard and I would stop by and say hello to George and Kim whenever we were in the neighborhood. If there were customers in the shop at the time, George would smile and proudly introduce us as his "boys." George was particularly thrilled when, on one occasion, I appeared in my smart Army lieutenant's uniform. Many years later, Gerard helped George's daughter get a job in Chicago.

Park Central Florist closed in 1982, but we remained friends with Kim and George for fifty years after our employment there.

40

How a Drosophila and Gregor Mendel Changed My Life

I went to The Bronx High School of Science, which was part of the New York City public school system and hence free, but entry was based on a three-hour entrance examination which, they said, only a fifth of all those applying passed. To this day, I am amazed that I passed it.

To turn out well-rounded students, as not everyone there would go into science or medicine, we were encouraged to participate in various extracurricular activities. Besides the obvious sports teams, one could join the chess club, math team, debating society, biology society, drama club, radio station, any of about fifteen different musical groups, and there were many, many other options.

As I had no particular leaning to any of the groups, I decided to try to join one in which a rather attractive young lady I fancied was already an active member. Benita Levine's interest was in biology and heredity and so she had joined the Drosophila Squad. A drosophila is a common fruit fly, which, because of its short period of gestation and easily identifiable mutations, became the insect of choice for studies of heredity. Although tiny, one could easily identify different eye color, wing size, or body shape of selected specimens.

Unfortunately, by the time I got around to applying to join the squad, there were no vacancies and my romantic motives were stymied. However, situated in the next laboratory was the Histology Society. I had no idea why a history group would have a laboratory, but it was geographically in the right place so I signed up.

The focus of the Histology Society was not about history at all but was about making slides of human or animal tissues in order to study and compare basic characteristics such as color, shape, structure, size, and opaqueness. How was this done? Briefly, a selected tissue sample of the organ to be examined was saturated with wax, stained with a mixture of complex dyes, and fixed into a microtome, where it was sliced as thinly as possible—perhaps a few microns—floated on water, and then transferred to a slide, where it was dried and made ready for microscopic examination.

How did Mendel get involved?

Benita was doing complicated experiments with drosophila to

test some of Mendel's theories. She not only wanted to see the obvious physical changes in different generations of flies but also hoped to examine changes in the insects' chromosomes, which were extra large (thankfully) in the salivary glands and hence easy to extract. In due course, my job in the Histology Society was to take Benita's drosophila chromosomes and prepare slides for her microscopic examinations and analyses. Obviously this would be a most romantic arrangement—or so it seemed.

While it was not part of my master plan, I became intrigued with the effects that different types of stains or dyes have on the ability to "read" chromosome slides, and this became the basis of a project of mine that the school entered into the nationwide Westinghouse Science Talent Search competition. While I did not win top prize, it was considered a good effort, as I was a runner-up.

Problems in the lab arose during holidays and summer breaks, when certain experiments could not simply be suspended or delayed but had to be looked after. This was the case with the drosophila breeding experiments one Christmas vacation. The little drosophila

The common fruit fly is a popular candidate for many different scientific experiments, especially in regard to heredity.

flies were kept in small glass milk containers that were usually covered with cotton. The flies were chloroformed and placed in carefully labeled jars, to which was added some honey-soaked paper to create an environment where they could thrive and multiply every five or six weeks.

At a crucial point, it became necessary for someone to volunteer to take about thirty of these incubators home over the Christmas holidays, as the school building would be closed. All they needed was to be kept in a dark warm place. The back of a clothes closet was ideal. I agreed to help.

The thirty milk containers were clandestinely and very carefully moved to my closet in our apartment. This solution was perfect, except that several weeks into the holiday, I went to look at how the experiment was progressing and was shocked to find that the back of the closet was empty. After hours of searching for the jars, I decided to ask my mother if perhaps she had moved them while she was straightening out my closet. To my everlasting horror, she explained that she thought there had been an insect infestation in my closet, which she had to clean out before it got worse and spread to the rest of the apartment and attacked all our clothing. She had disposed of all the "vermin."

What a way to end a romance!

The extract below is taken from a recent Bronx High School of Science curriculum booklet.

(Five periods per week—Special Permission; application not required—Fills the Lab Science Requirement for seniors—3rd, 4th, 5th or 6th major, Pre-requisite: AP Biology). This course follows the sequence of genetic discoveries. It begins with the "dance of the chromosomes" during mitosis and meiosis. A natural progression is made from meiosis to the identification of Mendel's unit characters, the genes. Correlating genes with chromosomes leads to the construction of genetic maps. A discussion of chromosome mutations sheds light on how map accuracy has been improved. Chromosome and gene mutations will be studied with special emphasis on human applications. Laboratory experiences involve breeding mutant Drosophila in order to discover Mendel's classic laws of inheritance. The course will then apply the principles of classic Mendelian genetics to current molecular genetics and techniques. The molecular nature of the gene and gene regulation will be studied in detail. In a genetic engineering lab, students will isolate, transform DNA from bacterial cells. Students will analyze transgenic animals to localize gene expression and protein function. Finally, students will isolate and analyze chromosome structure. State of the art advances will be introduced through field trips and guest speakers.

They don't mention that someone needs to take the "mutant Drosophila" home for the holidays!

There was never a shortage of ideas for informal weekend outings around New York.

41

Growing Up in New York City

How many hours a day does the average teenager today spend on the computer, iPad, iPhone, or watching TV?

It is hard to believe the answer—five hours—and that is the average! This includes texting, watching YouTube, emailing, Twittering, monitoring Facebook, staring at mindless films, watching sporting events, soap operas, etc. I suppose it also assumes some of these connections are made during school time.

One of my lovely grandchildren asked me how we managed to grow up without all of these "mod cons." "How did you ever spend your time without going mad?" one asked.

Well, somehow we did. The only device we did have was a radio or, as it was known then in some countries, the "wireless." Some very rich folks even had something called "television"—black-and-white only, of course.

How did we fill the days after sleeping, eating and attending school?

OPTIONS GALORE

It was not difficult to keep occupied, challenged, and intellectually active in New York City. In Manhattan, almost everyone lived in high-rise apartment houses. As a result, one's social network was typically around the corner or down the street. No one had a car. Public transportation was plentiful, safe, and affordable. I can recall when a subway ride was five cents.

In addition to the usual after-school activities, there were public-sponsored activities in most city parks, libraries, and special museums. The city also managed to offer specially focused youth-centered cultural activities, ranging from Saturday morning children's concerts to special museum visits and activity centers. I remember going to the New York City Center on 55th Street on many Saturday mornings to attend children's concerts conducted by the distinguished Leopold Stokowski. All of these concerts ended with everyone singing the famous Neapolitan song "Funiculi Funicula."

Public sporting events, organized competitions, and informal community sports meant that everyone could participate in or watch various sports. In the winter, ice-skating races on the frozen lake in

Central Park were always popular. In spring, summer, and autumn, the baseball and football fields were always full, as were the hand ball courts and the few tennis courts in the city.

Informal groups of friends would often plan weekend outings to various local places of interest. Usually these were all-day affairs, with a picnic thrown in. I clearly remember some of the places we visited—The Cloisters, Coney Island, the Statue of Liberty, Orchard Beach, the Bronx Zoo, Ellis Island, Chinatown, Hester Street, the botanical gardens in Brooklyn and the Bronx, and around-Manhattan boat trips. Those were the times when the subways were all considered completely safe, and our parents allowed us to travel anywhere in the city without worrying much.

New York museums had a wide range of special programs for children. The Museum of Natural History on 81st Street and Columbus Avenue was my local museum. For several weeks, I was recruited to work here, or more correctly, observe the workings of the scientists in the paleontology department. Each summer, the museum would sponsor expeditions to various sites in the far west of the United States to bring back huge rock slabs that contained thousands of tiny bone fragments. Every piece of bone had to be delicately pried free from the rocks in which it had been embedded for millions of years, and then, like a gigantic three-dimensional puzzle, all the pieces had to be put together to recreate (hopefully) the original skeleton. I was most impressed at how the paleontologists could look at a tiny bone fragment and immediately identify precisely the exact part of the skeleton to which it belonged.

I worked with a group of professionals on a project that later became known as the "pocketbook dinosaur" because of its unusually small size. While the experts worked with picks, hammers, and chisels, I was only allowed to use special brushes to clear away the debris and allow the next layer of rock to be removed by the experts. I did a lot of sweeping up, too. "My" pocketbook dinosaur was eventually put together and became part of one of the permanent displays in the museum's dinosaur wing. I have visited it several times.

VIVE L'ENTREPRENEUR!

I doubt if Mother acknowledged or even recognized the concept of an allowance or spending money. And the notion of getting paid for making one's bed in the morning or helping in the kitchen was a totally foreign, almost subversive, concept that was banned. While certainly not a born entrepreneur, I did manage to earn some spending money, probably more than I needed.

Several times each winter, New York was blanketed with several feet of snow. This was an opportunity for enterprising youths to earn a few dollars for each automobile we dug out of the snow so that its owner could safely drive it out. There was always a problem of what to do with the snow we were able to remove from around our client's car, however. We soon figured out that by assiduously moving snow to the area of another car, one whose owner had not yet expressed an interest in our snow removal services, we increased our chances of being hired.

Snow removal was never going to be a reliable source of income. In my case, selling newspapers in schools and delivering flowers provided a much more predictable source of revenue.

HOBBIES

Somehow between work, sports, social activities, and community programs, everyone found time for leisure activities. For many, this meant learning and practicing a musical instrument. Having retired early in my career as a promising but indifferent violinist, I found other diversions. Most of these activities fell into the category of collecting things.

Stamps   Stamps were perhaps the most common collecting hobby. It was more than a solitary activity because trading stamps was an integral part of the process. We all had our own *Scott's Catalogue* of prices and a trading book of extra stamps, or "doubles." I managed a very active trading account because I had a good supply of stamps from China and Finland.

Coins   Coins were perhaps the next most popular collectible. Instead of stamp albums, one displayed a coin collection on cardboard "pages" with slip-in spaces for coins. I am sure my "boards" of buffalo nickels and Lincoln pennies still are hiding somewhere in my archives. Coins proved less challenging than stamps because of their limited range, since one was, for practical reasons, limited to U.S. currency.

Magazines The other popular collectible items were magazines. Just like stamps, there was always a small market for certain magazines that people needed to "complete a set." Sam Klein had a complete set of *Superman* and *Batman* comics, of which he was justifiably proud. My taste in magazine collection was slightly up-market. I collected science fiction magazines in general and *Amazing Science Fiction* monthlies specifically. Magazine collections were not popular with mothers. They not only took up closet space, but Mother was convinced that old magazines were a fertile breeding ground for all sorts of common beetles, especially cockroaches.

The most unique collector's items were signed copies of *Time* magazine covers. Whenever the magazine cover was of a single person, we would carefully separate the cover from the rest of the magazine and send it to the person on the cover with a polite request for him or her to sign and return it in an enclosed, self-addressed, and stamped envelope. I think I still have a few of these carefully preserved.

Baseball Cards   Some in our gang collected baseball and other sports cards, for which there was an active market—and which were also used in a common street contest called "flipping." Contestants would choose one of their baseball cards and flip or drop it on the pavement. The other would then do the same, announcing before he dropped his card, "Odds" or "Match." If he said, "Match" and both cards were face up, he would win and take his opponent's card.

Photo Albums and Scrap Books　　　In the absence of television, the field of photojournalism thrived, especially during the time of war. Weekly oversized photo-based magazines were the way we were all able to see, rather than just read about, the horrors of war. *Life* and *Look* were the two most popular weekly magazines, but newspapers often had an abundance of photographs to support the written word. After the war, my brother Mark became the picture/photo editor of a magazine called *Pageant*.

In April 1944, the Dachau concentration camp was liberated and the world saw for the first time photos of the barely alive inmates, of the masses of corpses inhumanely piled, and of the harmless-looking but deadly gas chambers. At first I just began to cut out the photos I wanted to save. Then someone, Father I suppose, suggested that I save the newspaper photos in a more permanent manner and bought me some inexpensive blank photo albums and paper glue. I did not need to label any of the photographs because each printed photo came with its own detailed caption. Perhaps my interest was connected to Father's anxiety that many of his family had perished in similar concentration camps. Regrettably, he passed away before I had finished my album.

Several of these albums have survived.

Model Airplanes   Before the introduction of plastic model planes, tanks, and cars, almost all model building was based on balsa wood. The most popular models were balsa-framed, tissue-covered, rubber-band-propelled flying models. Everything you needed was in the box—or so it said. You actually also had to find (a) a bread board, (b) wax paper, (c) straight pins, (d) special balsa wood glue, (e) nail polish varnish, (f) sand paper, and (g) some of Father's used single-edged razor blades. I do not remember if any of my models were able to fly. But they made useful decorations hung from the ceiling of one's room.

Reading   Without doubt, the most popular children's books when I was growing up in New York were those featuring the Hardy Boys. The Boys were two teen-aged would-be detective brothers. Their mysteries and adventures were recounted in more than one hundred books. Once you had finished one Hardy Boys book, you tried to find someone with whom you could trade it for one that you had not yet read. The girls' counterpart was a series of Nancy Drew books. When someone discovered that the girls' adventure stories were equally readable, the book exchange market greatly increased. I recall reading such titles as *Nancy Drew and the Mystery of the Empty Well* and many others.

In time, one's taste matured. Sherlock Holmes was the obvious replacement for the Hardy Boys. Until we moved to London, I thought Holmes was a real detective. Somewhere along the line, science fiction became popular and short story authors like Isaac Asimov,

Van Vogtand, and Eric Russell became household names. *Amazing Science Fiction* monthly became essential reading. Influenced by Mark, I soon also discovered Joseph Conrad, O. Henry, Rider Haggard, and Charles Dickens. Richard Halliburton's travel adventure books were, of course, essential reading and still occupy a special place on my book shelves.

It was only after being mesmerized by Dr. Zagorsky's Great Books course at Bronx Science that I began to dip into the more erudite classics. I read many of those books again twenty-five years later, at a two-week seminar at the Aspen Institute of Humanistic Studies.

I never thought of reading as a hobby or leisure-time activity. It became, somehow, a part of one's normal routine. Post-bedtime reading with a flashlight under the covers worked for a while until Mother confiscated the batteries.

CULTURE HOUNDS

Movies were unquestionably the main formal entertainment. I think the cost of admission on Saturday afternoon, which was the only time we were allowed into movies without adults, was a quarter (twenty-five cents). At most movie theatres you would be able to enjoy a double feature plus a short episode of some popular adventure series—perhaps Tom Mix or *The Lone Ranger*. I never remember going to the movies in the evening. A social high spot was going to the Saturday afternoon movie on a "date."

Another attraction that Gerard and I discovered was the Saturday afternoon matinee at the Metropolitan Opera. Standing-room tickets were reasonable at $1.25. After several visits, we discovered that the best standing-room places were usually in the rear of the orchestra seats. If we were lucky, friendly ushers would take pity on us and after the first act would direct us to seats that were not occupied.

I can only remember being taken to one live theatre. My mother must have decided that my education was not complete without seeing at least one live Yiddish Theater performance even though I neither spoke nor understood the language. Mother chose well because I remember the occasion clearly. I saw and mostly heard the famous Molly Picon, a sort of Yiddish Judy Garland. I remember her name came up again many years later when I saw her play Yente the matchmaker in *Fiddler on the Roof*.

Yiddish Theater, whether it was drama, musical, satire, or comedy, was a most popular form of entertainment in New York and still exists today. At Camp Cejwin, a summer camp I attended in my teens, a highlight of the amateur theater production was a Yiddish musical. I vaguely remember the words of one Yiddish song—"Rozhinkes mit Mandelen" ("Raisins with Almonds")—that I had to learn as part of the cast of a Yiddish Biblical operetta, *Shulamith*.

ORGANIZED PROGRAMS

I specifically recall being involved in two formal programs. I would guess that the idea to help the Russian War Relief (RWR) came from some of our Russian family friends. It was sometime in 1943

334

or 1944 that RWR became very active in New York City. They had a shopfront on Broadway, to which people were invited to bring their surplus clothing so that it could be sent to Russia, which was suffering badly as a result of the relentless and seemingly never-ending advance of German troops. Several of us volunteered to help collect clothing from people in the neighborhood who agreed to donate their things for the drive. We were given a list of names and addresses and some large sacks, and off we went. In addition to clothing, we were given lots of kisses for agreeing to help such a worthy cause. Occasionally, we were also offered tea and sukariki. It was only years later that we discovered that RWR was actually a front for the Communist party. As far as I know, RWR was never mentioned in my CV or on my ROTC application.

One day, Gerard and I decided we should make a contribution to the community, and our chosen project was to set up a local Boy Scout troop. Gerard's local synagogue on 86th Street was to be the new home for Troop 657 and the notorious Flaming Arrow patrol, aka the FA's, or Farstunkena Armpits! First we awarded ourselves the rank of Eagle Scout, the highest rank possible. That was a requirement for holding a leadership role. To dress up our uniforms and make us look even more important, we awarded each other various merit badges—not so many that it would raise questions but enough to impress the parents who signed up their children.

Scout meetings were held every other Thursday in the ballroom of the synagogue and we planned at least one overnight "hike" to the Scout center at Ten Mile River Camp. Besides the usual exercise programs, we taught knot tying and first aid. For other subjects, we had access to a shopping list of specialist volunteers who came to our Thursday meetings. Most of the time was spent doing some simple exercises, learning to march in a straight line, and arranging various competitive activities such as relay games, dodge ball, or Simon Says. My early pre-teen love affair with Indians, their history, customs, and crafts, was a useful bonus. I taught all the FA's how to make lanyards, key chains, and bracelets. I cannot remember if we ever trained our successor, but after a year we both felt we had done our bit. Our swan song was a weekend Scout Jamboree for Scout leaders of all five boroughs in New York City at Ten Mile River Camp. We then bestowed on each other official honorable discharges from the service.

COMMUNITY HQ

Whether or not they were religious or not, almost all Jewish neighborhood kids regarded B'nai Jeshurun as community headquarters. Unfortunately, apart from Ping-Pong tables, it did not have any athletic facilities; it shared various indoor and outdoor sports facilities with other local institutions and the public parks.

By the time they were teens, I suspect, every young New Yorker had been exposed to *Robert's Rules of Order*. This little book spelled out the basic immutable rules for creating, organizing, managing, administering, and conducting any form of organization, club, or society. Clubs typically were created within the aegis of a neutral institution, usually a school or religious organization. It only took two to form a club and so it is not surprising that at B'nai Jeshurun (BJ) we had groups or clubs devoted to chess, bridge, Ping-Pong, musical performances, singing, baseball, football, basketball, and dancing plus many others.

The group that I remember best was the Community Youth Council. It was essentially an umbrella organization for all youth activities at BJ, created to encourage activities, plan joint events, manage the event calendar, and provide liaison functions with other informal clusters of local youth clubs, both Jewish and non-Jewish. As with all formal organized clubs, we had formal meetings. Before there was any discussion, there was a roll call, minutes of the previous meeting were approved as is or corrected, and excuses for absences were noted. In case you find all of this extraordinary, I have kept one of the minute books. Joan Gottlieb was the official secretary because of her beautiful penmanship, and someone called "Michael" was the treasurer. I seemed to have been president during the period covered by the minute book I rescued. Judging by the minutes, we spent most of our time planning the details of a big May Day ball. We also had a successful softball team that played other local synagogue teams, and a basketball team.

New York was a very special place in which to grow up.

My original, first stamp album is still, today, a treasure chest of historical, geographic, political, cultural, and scientific information. Unfortunately, I have not been successful in attracting any of our grandchildren to stamp collecting.

42

Twenty Million and Counting

What is the most popular hobby in the world?

No, it is not gardening, fishing, or sailing. It is stamp collecting. In America alone, there are at least twenty million people who collect, trade, and exchange stamps.

Stamp collecting was also perhaps the most common hobby among my New York City circle of friends. Stamps provided not only a great way to "travel" around the world without leaving one's room but were a great learning device. The history of most everything is documented in stamps. In addition, as most collectors were also "traders" of stamps, the exchange of stamps gave one an initial live encounter with the world of commerce, value estimating, and negotiation.

My collection began when I "rescued" letters from far-off countries that my parents received from friends and relatives. Most came from China and Europe, but occasionally there was a letter from South America or Australia. There was an art to removing a stamp from a letter, which was not particularly difficult but required some patience and skill.

The objective was to remove the stamp from the envelope, where it appeared to be permanently fixed. The first step is to set the envelope and stamp afloat in a bowl of hot water, which somehow worked better and faster than cold water. After a little time, the water would dissolve the glue, and the stamp would drift off the envelope and float to the top of the water, usually rolled up, but hopefully still intact. After carefully lifting the stamp out of the water, one would put it on an ink blotter and wait for the blotter to absorb the water. If the stamp curled up at the edges, it needed to be "ironed" by putting it into a heavy book and pressed. I recall hovering over the incoming mail every day to insure that potentially valuable envelopes from exotic lands didn't somehow end up in the trash bin or be irreparably torn by careless hands, anxious to see what was inside.

Blank stamp albums were available in many sizes and shapes. My first album was rather skimpy, but most of the world's countries and major colonies were represented. (I have kept it all these years in case someone wants to look at it.) Then all that was needed was a package of stamp hinges. About half of my stamps at this early stage were from China and so extra pages were needed for that section of the album. I soon discovered I had many duplicate stamps. This was my introduction to trading and what I much later learned was popularly called "street smarts."

How much was a 60-Yuan blue stamp with a Chinese country scene worth in the open street market of West End Avenue in New York in 1947? Could I trade one Cape Verde 6-pence stamp with a picture of King Albert for a Chinese 30-Yuan stamp? Perhaps an Austrian 10-mark 1930 stamp with Prince Metternich would be a fairer trade? These and similar issues were soon resolved when someone produced a secondhand copy of *Scott's Catalogue* of world stamps. Here the value of every known stamp was listed both in mint or used condition. So at last there was some basis for honest negotiation.

As my interest grew, I bought two additional pieces of equipment, which every serious collector needed. First was a magnifying glass that lets you look at the stamp in some detail and, most importantly, to ensure that there were no rips or holes, as a torn stamp was absolutely useless. Then, a pair of custom stamp tweezers, which were important to handle your stamps with, since it would not do to get your grimy fingerprints on your precious property.

Once the supply of stamps from family and friends ran out, the search began for other sources. There were readily available mixed assortments of stamps that came in large envelopes with clear windows. You could buy them, as I recall, in quantities of fifty, one hundred, or even two hundred stamps. Most were worth very little but provided a rich trove of stamps to begin filling up your own book or

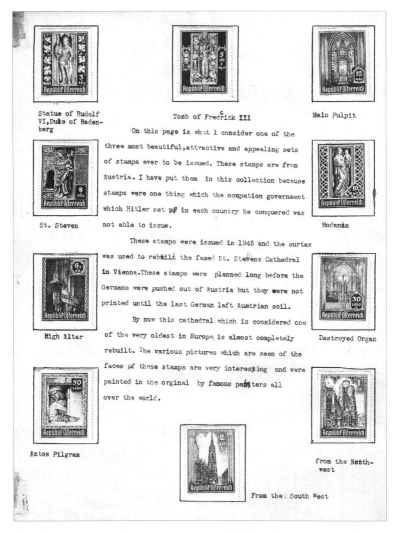

Statue of Rudolf
VI,Duke of Baden-
berg

Tomb of Fredrick III

Main Pulpit

St. Steven

On this page is what 1 consider one of the three most beautiful,attractive and appealing sets of stamps ever to be issued. These stamps are from Austria. I have put them in this collection because stamps were one thing which the occupation government which Hitler set up in each country he conquered was not able to issue.

Modania

These stamps were issued in 1945 and the surtax was used to rebuilt the famed St. Stevens Cathedral in Vienna.These stamps were planned long before the Germans were pushed out of Austria but they were not printed until the last German left Austrian soil.

High Altar

By now this cathedral which is considered one of the very oldest in Europe is almost completely rebuilt. The various pictures which are seen of the faces of these stamps are very interesting and were painted in the orginal by famous painters all over the world.

Destroyed Organ

Antos Pilgram

From the South West

from the North-
west

Simple commemorative stamps gave useful insights into national cultural values and morals.

your "stock book." One always searched for a special priceless stamp that somehow got mixed up with all the others but I, at least, never found one. If one was particularly interested in a specific country, one could find country-specific stamps available in the same style of large envelopes.

At some point, I was ready to graduate to a more serious stamp album. I still have this larger album and a few other specialty albums, with many hundreds of stamps, in my stamp library. When the children reached the age when I thought they might have some interest in stamps, I offered each of them my precious collection. Each of them in turn rejected my offer. Geoffrey actually tried, but his idea of putting stamps into the album was by using Superglue. While none of my grandchildren show interest in my collection, perhaps among the great-grandchildren there will be at least one interested.

MORE STAMP SOURCES

Of the many different sources of stamps that came my way, two stand out as being very special to me. In 1946, in lieu of being drafted, Mark enlisted in the Army and took up a special arrangement that allowed college students to go into the Army for one year, in return for which the universities granted them a year's college credit towards a degree.

Given his language skills—Russian and French—Mark was quickly assigned to an intelligence unit in Germany, where he was busy interrogating German POWs (prisoners of war) and chasing some of Hitler's cronies. His unit was particularly active in looking for Martin Bormann. Knowing my interest in stamp collecting, he frequently sent me parcels of German post-war stamps.

As part of the German propaganda campaign, Hitler had arranged for the printing of a vast number of attractive stamps that purported to commemorate Nazi achievements in the arts, sciences, and economy. After the war, each of the three Occupation forces printed their own stamps for use in their respective Occupied sectors. The stamps Mark sent me soon found their way into my album, while the duplicates were proudly displayed in my stock book. Later, they became the basis for a special school project.

I cannot remember exactly what the assignment was, but I decided to write a report on "The History of Germany Through Stamps." It turned out to be a fascinating project and a unique learning experience for me. Like so many countries, Germany had been using stamps to mark special events and honor their heroes for decades. These landmarks provided me with the basis for writing a history of modern Germany. Fortunately, despite my appalling typing and spelling, my teachers found the "history" creatively conceived and marvelously executed.

Another unexpected source of stamps came from the Philippines. Fima and Isa spent the years from 1941 to 1945 interned in a Japanese compound in the Philippines. While this was not a concentration camp in the European sense of the word, they and their fellow prisoners were restricted for all four years to a ghetto in Manila.

When it was clear that General Douglas MacArthur was finally

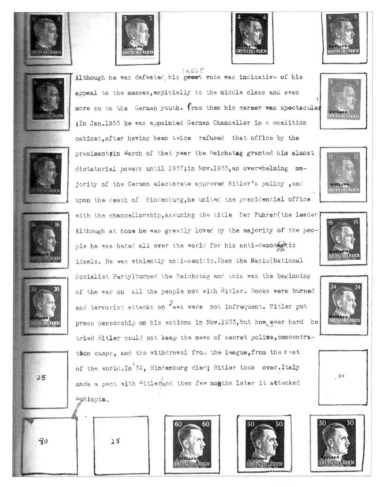

Although he was defeated, his great vote was indicative of his
appeal to the masses, espicially to the middle class and even
more so to the German youth. From then his career was spectacular
;In Jan.1933 he was appointed German Chancellor in a coalition
cabinet, after having been twice refused that office by the
presisent;in March of that year the Reichstag granted him almost
dictatorial powers until 1937;in Nov.1933,an overwhelming majority of the German electorate approved Hitler's policy ,and
upon the death of Hindenburg,he united the presidential office
with the chancellorship,assuming the title Der Fuhrer(the leader)
Although at home he was greatly loved by the majority of the people he was hated all over the world for his anti-democratic
ideals. He was violently anti-semitic.Then the Nazis(National
Socialist Party)burned the Reichstag and this was the beginning
of the war on all the people not with Hitler. Books were burned
and terrorist attacks on Jews were not infrequent. Hitler put
press censorship on his actions in Nov.1933,but how ever hard he
tried Hitler could not keep the news of secret police,concentra-
tion camps, and the withdrawal from the league,from the rest
of the world.In 34, Hindenburg died; Hitler took over.Italy
made a pact with Hitler and then few months later it attacked
Ethiopia.

Collecting and organizing stamps around a specific historical
event provided an extraordinary learning experience.

345

going to return to Manila, among the many celebrations to commemorate this day was the issuing by the government of many Victory Day stamps. Fima and Isa saw this an opportunity to make some money.

A letter sent on the day a new stamp was issued, referred to as a "first-day cover," had collectors' value. There are many collectors worldwide of these philatelic oddities. Fima and Isa decided that first-day covers celebrating the liberation of the Philippines could, in time, be worth a fortune. So they set about addressing and stamping several hundred specially printed envelopes with the new stamps and sent them to themselves, friends, and family. In time all of these letters were bequeathed to me. It was a real treasure trove I was creating. Could it pay for my college education? Buy me a new car?

Alas, that did not come to pass. Isa and Fima's idea was not unique and, indeed, several thousand first-day covers were issued on Independence Day. They are currently available on eBay for about $3. (Sorry, Stanley and Michael!)

At some point during the last few years of high school, I decided to concentrate my collection on early United States stamps. I invested in a special album, learned how to put stamps into specially prepared clear sleeves, bought a collection of tweezers, and joined the unique fraternity of dedicated stamp collectors. I was surprised to learn, when I recently checked stamp prices in *Scotts*, that my U.S. collection is worth more than a thousand dollars.

VERY RARE first-day cover—300 envelopes still available

Monopoly absorbed the attention of three of our most sophisticated grandchildren—Misha, Sonya, and Katya.

43

Bored Games

Rain, poor light, cold weather, or sports injuries were all reasons for moving the gang indoors. Indoor games, while clearly less physical than the outdoor variety, were certainly as competitive and varied. They usually fell into one of three categories—cards, board games, or other.

Most card games were played on the floor—tables were introduced later, when more serious games became popular and light refreshments were introduced, usually milk and cookies. We divided games into those that required some skill and those that were just as much fun but essentially mindless. Mindless games included Go Gish, Old Maid, Slap Jack, and something we used to call "Snap." When the idea of skill as opposed to chance was introduced, the games became more sophisticated. Games included, for example, Hearts, Concentration, I Doubt You, Crazy Eights, and Popocatepetl. Why was a card game named after a volcano in Mexico?

Mark and I often played cards with Mother and Father. The game of choice was a Russian classic called Pousa or Durok, which as best I can recall meant "pot belly" or "dummy." It was a mixture of Hearts and Old Maid—with a generous mixture of Memory, Gin Rummy, and Mahjong, all thrown in together—and was played by four people. When we began playing cards with our children, this was one of their favorite games. Another classic that could be played by all ages was Spoons.

Remember?

You placed one less teaspoon at the center of the table than there were players. Everyone was dealt four cards. The idea was to be the first to get four-of-a-kind in his hand. The dealer would pick a card, and then either take it into his hand or pass it, or another card, face down to the next player, who could either keep that card or pass it along. When a card came back to the dealer he would put it in a "spent" pile and take the next card from the top of the deck. As soon as someone had four-of-a-kind, he was allowed to take a spoon, usually trying to do so when no one was looking. All the other players then had to make a mad dash for the other spoons. The person left without a spoon lost that round and became an "S." It was a good idea not to have anything on the table when you were playing, as the rush for spoons would often get fairly hectic.

In the evening and on weekends, while the adults played Gin Rummy or Canasta with high stakes, the younger set concentrated on bridge, poker, and blackjack.

I cannot remember exactly when, how, or why bridge was introduced into our young lives and became popular among our group. I suppose it seemed very grown up, required more skill than Slap Jack or Crazy Eights, and was always played on an "adult" folding card table. In time, to make it more interesting, a financial incentive was introduced, but only when my mother was not around. We started playing more seriously when I got to Bronx Science, as my circle of friends expanded to include a more intellectual crowd. Bronx Science, as you would expect, not only had several bridge clubs and frequent tournaments but inter-school bridge challenges as well.

When I arrived as a freshman at WPI, I started to play bridge until an upper classmate, Dan Furman, and later a fraternity brother, Michael Zucker, both urged me to give up playing bridge until I graduated. "You can keep playing if you want, but I guarantee it will result in your graduating with a much lower overall average." I stopped, and have not played since.

I had a basic idea about counting points, conventions, or slams. But we did have one unusual convention, which came to be called "the Schneebaugh convention" after its founder, Bernard. It went like this. Once the cards were dealt out, Bernard would look quickly at his cards and if he did not think they were very good, he would announce, "Misdeal, I only have twelve cards."

His partner would quickly respond, "Yeah, I have fourteen," and then Bernard would throw his cards face up into the center of the table, which was, of course, followed by Bernard's partner doing the same thing. The Schneebaugh convention seems humorous today but at the time, it caused a great deal of drama and stress, as you can imagine.

Somehow card playing today, like reading, is no longer fashionable.

Once we each had some pocket money, Poker and Blackjack became very popular, usually played with coins—mostly pennies. Mother took a dim view of children playing for money in her house. She implemented her point of view in a most dramatic way. If she caught us playing for money, even pennies, she would come in and either tip the table so that all of the money would end up mixed together on the floor, or just come over and scramble all of our individual piles of money together in the center of the table. Predictably, very few Poker or Blackjack games were played at 131 Riverside Drive. Friendlier, more hospitable home-based "gaming casinos" were found.

Chess and checkers were, of course, also popular and frequently played. When magnetic boards became available, the subway ride to and from school became a common venue for both of them. Very quickly the chess players became divided between pros and others. The pros, like Sam Klein, memorized all of the classic opening moves, were familiar with all of the classic offensive and defensive moves, and followed international tournaments with the same gusto as most of us followed the World Series. The variations of the standard chess game were almost without limit. "Handicap chess" meant the strong player would play without one or more pieces. "Speed chess" was played with a time limit for every move. "Suicide chess," "bughouse," and "crazy horse" were other variations that became popular, especially in the school lunchroom. Checkers, too, had its own variations, the most popular of which was "sheep-and-fox." The biggest challenge was when someone introduced a Go board.

Unlike card games, chess, checkers, and most other popular games required some sort of board, dice, cards, and other equipment. Monopoly was, and still today is, without doubt, the most popular board game. The official rules, while clearly written, were hardly ever followed without some modifications. Instead, a complex series of local rules or conventions sprang up and everyone who had a board would insist on playing with his specific rules. Sometimes property cards were dealt out. According to some rules, house and hotel shortages were impossible, but in Sam's apartment, for instance, the number was strictly enforced. When we played at Peter's apartment, houses could be bought from other players. But at Stephen's, once all of the properties were owned, no property could be sold until all monopolies were created. Gerard would insist on being the banker or wouldn't let us play. And Marshall distributed twice the regulation amount of cash at the start. In my version, I would set a time limit, usually with an alarm clock, and when it rang, the game was over and the player with the most money and property won. And remember, there was always an argument about how to value property you owned and had mortgaged.

Today you can play Monopoly on-line on the Internet and there are even worldwide tournaments you can enter. And, of course, it is available in most languages, and variations include properties related to golf, war, history, baseball, and politics—there is a variation that uses a circular board rather than the conventional square format. Most recently an electronic version came out that eliminates the handling of money with individual electronic purses.

Luck-driven or not, it is still played in our home. Can you tell who is winning?

After Monopoly the most popular board games were Risk, Scrabble, Battleships, Cluedo, Sorry, and Territories.

44

Summertime and the Living Is Easy

For most middle-class Jewish families, it was practically mandatory to escape from the searing heat of New York City in July and August. The choice of where to go was a function of one's budget, history, and what other family friends did. For some, the decision was easy since each summer was essentially a repeat of the previous summer—the same camp, the same summerhouse, and the same camping trip. Travel any real distance away from home was a treat reserved for the uber rich. Europe was not a viable travel location because the war had just ended, and later, well into the 1950s, it was not viable because of the post-war economic instability and reconstruction. Everywhere else was simply considered GI—geographically incompatible. My summer experiences were limited and consisted of first attending, and later working in, various summer camps. Later I was to have more creative experiences.

THE YEAR 1944, GREENER FELDER, OUR LAST SUMMER WITH FATHER

Greener Felder day camp kept campers busy from sun up to sunset.

After many classic beach holidays, it was decided that mountains and lakes should replace sand and sea. The Bagins, New York friends who were also from Brussels, strongly recommended a family camp called Greener Felder. The camp was a reasonable driving distance from the city, somewhere in the mountains of northern New Jersey near the New York State border.

The camp consisted of a collection of essentially family cabins. Some were single-family stand-alone cabins, others were attached but had separate entrances. Families would rent a cabin for the whole summer or by the month. There was also a so-called "big house" with motel-type rooms for those who came for shorter periods of time and a cafeteria for those who chose not to cook for themselves. Equally important as the nourishment was the opportunity to socialize and catch up on "news."

Our cabin had two bedrooms, and a large sitting room with a dining table at one end. There was a small kitchen because most meals were taken in the public cafeteria-style dining room. This obviously must have been a big plus for the mothers, who had a two-month reprieve from the normal kitchen chores. I don't remember much about the food, other than that it was fairly hearty and hefty German Jewish cuisine. When Father came back to the camp on weekends after being away in New York during the week, he invariably brought back several shopping bags of essentials that were always a great welcome treat and a respite from the public food.

Camp life consisted of different activity centers, a variety of sports, hiking, community entertainment, and a pleasant lakefront for swimming and watercrafts. Most of the children were enrolled in a formal day camp complete with counselors, sports lessons and competitions, a hobby center, and an entertainment program. We met after breakfast in pre-assigned age groups and followed a well worked-out schedule of activities. For me at least, it was a great improvement from the previous summer at the beach.

1945, FATHER NO LONGER WITH US

After Father died in May, it was decided that it would best for me to be sent to a sleep-away camp during the summer. I am sure that I was never asked. Given the enormous family upset, the consensus was that it would be best if I were spared the process of adjusting to family life under the new circumstances. In addition there was little I could do to contribute to the depressing process of closing down Father's affairs. Camp HI was a fail-safe choice since I had been there before. It was close to Cleveland and our family in Cleveland. Mark did not come this time, but Jimmy Blier and Peter joined me.

I remember that summer well. One day at the beginning of August, just after lunch, the entire camp population was summoned to an unusual assembly. The camp director announced in a somber tone that the American Air Force had just dropped a massive new atomic bomb on the Japanese city of Hiroshima. No one knew that the bombing would not only almost completely demolish the city but also kill 160,000 people. The justification for this appalling bombing was the hope that it would accelerate the ending of the war in the

Pacific. In fact, the Japanese a few days later did surrender unconditionally. While, of course, I could not possibly appreciate at the time the significance of an atomic weapon of this magnitude, the implication that it would end the terrible war was a conclusion that was certainly not lost on an eleven-year-boy.

1946, FAR ROCKAWAY BEACH

In 1946, influenced, I suspect, by our history in Belgium of going to the seaside, my mother decided to rent a modest bungalow in Far Rockaway, which was one of the last stops on the New York City subway line and hence accessible, and if necessary even commutable during the work week. There was a sandy beach, salt water, mild surf, a large Jewish community, and no car fumes. Everything was in place for a typical normal healthy and relaxing summer. It also was relatively inexpensive.

The beach was very different from Knokke, which I remembered well. Here the beach was always crowded and noisy. But that was well compensated-for by the fact that the water was always warm. In Knokke all of our beach equipment chairs, umbrellas, towels, shovels, and pails were locked away in our own private cabana at the edge of the beach. In Rockaway, each day we had to transport (schlep) all our gear from our bungalow, and find and stake out our own territory on the beach, much as early settlers in the West did. The best place was not too close to the sea, in case the tide came in, but not too far from the water, so that you could be watched for safety. It was also useful to

A day after fishing, not catching, in the sea at Far Rockaway. Mother was the cheerleader, Mark was in charge of operations, and Mr. Maisel, a family friend, was keeping score.

choose an area that was unlikely to be a meeting place for those who insisted on listening to ear-shattering music from a "ghetto blaster."

I actually always hated the sand and still do. After a few weeks, every piece of clothing one owned was sufficiently sandy to make it uncomfortable to wear. At our summer home, what ideally should have been a sand-free zone became practically an extension of the beach, if not because of human contamination than by means of the sea breezes which, while providing a respite from the usual sultry weather, always managed to carry more than its share of fine sand that inserted itself into every nook and cranny, and onto every flat surface and everyone.

By 1946 Fima and Isa had immigrated to the U.S. from their internment in Manila and were living with us in our Riverside apartment. They often spent the weekend with us. I don't remember having lunch on the beach since our bungalow was close enough to the beach to eat at home. Apart from fishing, strolling on the boardwalk, and visiting the local amusement park, the variety of activities was certainly limited. We did a lot of fishing but very little catching. Surfboards, wind surfers, wave runners, Frisbees, kayak, and volleyball had yet to arrive on the beach.

We were indeed "deprived."

1949 IT'S BETTER THAN WALKING

"From the misty beaches of Oregon we will traverse by bicycle numerous mountain ranges, wooded forests, amber waves of grain, endless cow pastures and barren plains as we cross the continent to the boardwalk in Coney Island, ride through the Canadian Rockies, Oregon, California, Washington, Idaho, Montana, North Dakota, Minnesota, Wisconsin, Michigan, and along the Great Lakes to Niagara Falls."

This advertisement in the Sunday newspapers caught my attention in 1948 as I was musing about how to spend my next summer holiday. Having just celebrated my fifteenth birthday and feeling very grownup, I decided that it was time for a solo adventure. No more family holidays.

While the description of the tour sounded amazing, in practical terms it seemed unlikely to become a reality for me. For a start, I did not own a bicycle. A small problem that I dismissed after looking at the Secondhand Bicycles section in the same newspaper. With no idea of the cost of such a trip, I decided I might have to work more hours to supplement my shrinking savings bank account. The advertisement gave no indication of any age or experience requirements.

The biggest hurdle and the most problematic, I decided, was getting agreement from my mother to go across country on a bicycle that I did not have, for two months with a group of people I did not know, and in a part of America that was totally unfamiliar. To my everlasting surprise, my mother did not seem the least bit concerned, and urged me to collect more information about what kind of group was sponsoring the trip, the costs involved, and a variety of details such as which hotels we would stay at, what would we do for food, was a doctor coming along, and so on.

My enthusiasm for the trip grew exponentially with the volume of details I was able to collect. I learned:

the trip would take sixty days during July and August;

the tour would be led by a mature married couple just out of law school;

the organizer was the American Youth Hostel Association, a reputable institution that operated hostels around the country;

this would be the first time an "across America by bicycle tour" would be arranged and as such it was experimental.

There was, however, another potentially insurmountable hurdle.

362

As space was limited, interested persons were invited to complete a long questionnaire, provide a written essay on why they should be selected, and describe what special skills they were planning to bring to the group. All of this would be followed by face-to-face interviews to ensure that the group would be made up of people who were likely to be compatible, in good physical condition, and able to cope with unexpected situations.

I decided there was no sense being concerned about parental approval, cost, and equipment until I had in fact passed the admission test barrier. It turned out that I was not an obvious choice. Apart from being the youngest applicant, the absence of any cycling experience was certain to be a knockout factor.

Miraculously, in February, after a painless interview and closer examination of my very limited credentials, I received an acceptance letter from the organizers. Please would I send a small deposit to hold my place, and select from the enclosed list possible special areas or skill sets that I would be willing to take responsibility for on the trip.

At this junction and before sending in a deposit, some of the details of the trip began to unfold. I suspect these details were designed to separate those who were committed from those who were unsure. There were no hotels. All overnight stays would be either in Youth Hostels, which were limited, or "camping out under the stars" so bring a warm sleeping bag. The group would prepare all meals themselves—no restaurants were on the schedule. Appropriate cooking utensils would be purchased and distributed to individuals. There would be no back-up or support vehicles, so all clothing, baggage, and equipment would be carried by each individual in their bicycle saddlebags. There would be no doctor on the trip but two of the possible travellers were pre-med students who would take special first aid courses beforehand. It was impossible and totally impractical to provide a detailed trip itinerary since a lot would depend on the effective speed of the slowest cyclist in the group. For planning purposes it would be safe to assume each day would involve twenty-five to thirty-five miles of cycling, rain or shine.

These details increased my excitement about the trip. I think my Mother was less impressed and may even have had second thoughts.

Among the special areas of suggested designated skills that I recall were first aid, budget management, food preparation (broken down by breakfast, lunch, and dinner), commissary, communications, purchasing, mechanical and repair support, security, safety, and map reading. Less attractive tasks, such as cleaning up after meals, were to be shared on a rotation basis.

I volunteered for the mechanical and repair brigade. And was promptly designated as the lead Sturmey-Archer maintenance technician. I must admit that at this point I had no idea what equipment I was to be in charge of maintaining. I soon found out. Every bicycle on the trip had to be equipped with a three-speed Sturmey-Archer gear shift. This was the latest "must have" feature for all serious bikers. Alternatives were acceptable by special permission only.

I discovered more about this essential piece of equipment after it was arranged for me to spend three afternoons at a specially prepared bicycle maintenance course somewhere in Brooklyn. From the outside, the gear looks harmless. About the size of a fist, it sits on the back wheel with a sturdy wire connection to a shift device on the handlebars. However, inside the harmless steel housing there are perhaps seventy-two parts in all shapes and sizes, each with its own dedicated function. For three bewildering afternoons, I watched closely as the experts tried to explain first, how to maintain the gears so that they would function properly and then, how to replace cracked or broken parts should the gear stop functioning altogether, which I was assured was not often.

My graduation certificate was proudly presented to me on the last day, along with a massive, unreadable operating and repair manual, a selection of replacement parts for the most common faulty elements, and two cans of special designed oil to make sure nothing went wrong. I later discovered that others volunteering for the maintenance detail had less complex assignments, such as tire changes, spoke repair, wheel balancing, lights, brakes, and seat and handlebar adjustments.

Our trip was a sensational adventure and the memories of it were indelibly etched into my ever-expanding memory bank. Highlights include riding our bikes in the Calgary Rodeo opening parade, cycling downhill from Yellowstone National Park for sixty miles without peddling, waking up in Jasper National Park with our milk bottles frozen and cracked, travelling for a week in the multipurpose Canadian Railroad Rolling Hostel, with its own kitchen, sleeping in railroad stations, church halls, community centers, and museums, and, of course, seeing the most beautiful sights in both Canada and the far west of the United States.

For two months, our AYH group of twenty-five intrepid
cyclists made their way across the United States
carrying our kitchen and sleep essentials on our bikes.

It was our good fortune that no one got sick on the trip, there were no major accidents, very few burst tires, no bent spokes, and most important for me not a single gear repair was required.

The sequel to the trip actually happened three months after we returned. While cycling in Manhattan on East 54th Street I collided with a taxi and was thrown off my bike. The taxi stopped and the driver came to where I had landed on the street to ask if I were all right. At that time I had no pains, all my bones seemed to be intact, and apart from some bruises I was, as I said to the driver, "fine." That was not the case with my bicycle, with a twisted front wheel that made riding it totally impossible.

I dusted myself off and proceeded to walk the bicycle home to 85th Street. It did not take much convincing by those at home that

I needed a rest from the trauma. I lay down and woke up two days later. I don't recall asking about the condition of the bike. And the taxi driver never called to find out how I was feeling.

Three thousand miles without an accident or a flat tire.

45

Is There a Rabbi in the House?

Having gone every morning for a whole year to synagogue to say Kaddish for my father, I became familiar with our local synagogue, B'nai Jeshurun, its activities, its teachers and principals, as well as the senior, much-loved rabbi, Israel Goldstein.

Apart from the very active social life in the synagogue, I did continue to go to Hebrew schools two afternoons a week and to the more popular Sunday morning classes, which were primarily about history and customs. Eventually there were no more classes for me to take.

So, in June 1950, our beloved Rabbi Israel Goldstein decided I should be enrolled in the Jewish Theological Seminary National

Leadership Training Program. As only one person from each congregation was selected, I was ecstatic, and refusing was not an option. This program would not make me a rabbi but it was designed to prepare students for significant responsible leadership roles in the community, initially at the local level but eventually in a much wider national arena as well. If the candidate later chose to continue his education at the seminary to become a rabbi, it was considered a bonus—several of my classmates did. Being a student, even part time, at the Jewish Theological Seminary (JTS) in New York City did not mean I was beginning my rabbinic studies. Nevertheless, if I became interested I would have had a head start.

An important milestone in developing community leadership skills

Classes at the seminary were held two afternoons a week, and there were additional sessions on two Sundays every month. Special field trips and events were also on the program that one was expected to attend. The seminary was on 123rd Street and Broadway, and so only a short ride from home.

The classes were all in English, although I soon discovered that I was one of the few people in my class who could not speak reasonable Hebrew. One half of the course work was devoted to religious subjects taught by faculty of the seminary. The other half was about the history, culture, and structure of the Jewish community both in America and elsewhere, and the format typically was not lectures but, essentially, seminars or workshops dealing with contemporary local, national, and international issues. The general sense of the discussions was to have the students discover the most significant aspects of subjects for themselves and discuss them with their peers.

There were several lessons I took away with me from my time at the seminary. Tolerance and the need to empathize with people who do not necessarily agree with you on all matters were important messages I learned, and a principle which I hope I still practice. Just because people do not agree with you does not mean that you cannot respect their point of view. This helped me to understand, but not necessarily accept, for example, much of Jewish Orthodoxy. Unfortunately, too often my tolerance was not reciprocal.

Just as important but perhaps less philosophical, I learned that Jewish laws, rituals, conventions, practice, and instructions are all open to interpretation and appropriate adjustment to fit the real world and one's own role in it. While it was essential to understand how and why the laws of keeping the Sabbath were initially conceived, one could adjust them to fit one's existing views and still be Jewish.

I found a letter I wrote just after returning from a workshop in Washington DC:

Personal reflections after a thought-provoking seminar weekend of training

I never imagined that not far into the future, I would have the occasion to put some of my religious learning to practical use. Gerard Smetana, Maury Allen, and Marty Hanfling urged me to work with them at Camp Harlee Mitchell in Pennsylvania, where they all had been waiters for several summers. I was invited to meet the camp director, "Uncle" Eddie Mitchell, who sadly told me that all of the positions for waiters had already been filled. When he noticed on my application that I had been studying at the JTS, he asked if I might be interested in another position at the camp that was open, so I could be with my buddies. I had visions of getting a job behind the scene doing dishes or peeling vegetables, but to my surprise, he asked if I felt I could handle the job of camp rabbi. He took my hesitation and surprise at the offer as a positive sign. "All you will need to do is to lead two services on Friday nights, one for the children before dinner and a fuller service for the older campers and guests after dinner."

"That's it?" I quizzically responded. "I don't have to teach Hebrew or anything like that?"

Uncle Eddie was not forthcoming when I asked him, "What happened to the rabbi you had last year?" I imagined some modern form of rabbinical inquisition, organized by hordes of mutinous campers more interested in basketball than praying. In any case, the rabbinic route seemed to be the only plausible avenue for employment that summer at Camp Harlee Mitchell, so I agreed. He then explained that in addition to my religious obligations, I would also be responsible for a small bunk of four or five young campers, and would be expected to teach tennis most afternoons and be available for miscellaneous functions as required.

Surprisingly, my combination rabbi, tennis instructor, and bunk counselor assignment worked well until the third week. My waiter colleagues decided I was having it too easy and so decided to picket my Friday night services. They chose a curious approach. Sitting together in the rear of the converted "prayer" hall cum basketball court, they waited until I started to deliver my Friday night sermon. Then quietly they started a continuous low level clapping, and chanted, "We want our money back; the rabbi is a goy!" The hall that evening seems to have had more than the usual number of parents as guests. The camp director happened to be present and was not amused. He had them evicted from the hall despite their pleading for religious tolerance, freedom of speech, and the rights of assembly.

One of my extracurricular activities turned out to be arranging American Indian campfires on Wednesday nights. Fortunately, I discovered that I was able to adopt some of my experience from Camp HI to a traditional camp environment. When one Wednesday the usually harmless flame hoop dance somehow got out of control, only the quick reflexes of some of the onlookers prevented what could have been a major disaster. Needless to say, flaming hoop dances were outlawed after that evening, as they had been years before at Camp HI.

Maury Allen and Gerard Smetana, having some time off with their sometimes spiritual leader. Left to right, *Maury, Gerard, and I*

PART V

HIGHER EDUCATION

You never stop learning—something.

Introduction
How Do Things Work?

A curious educational byproduct of World War II was that high schools in New York City introduced a January graduation. As a result, I graduated from the Bronx High School of Science in January 1951. I think this was the last time there was a midyear graduation class in any New York City high school. While it made little difference in most matters, it did create a problem with university admissions, procedures, and administration.

Most universities maintained the normal September matriculation schedule. The prospect of waiting nine months to start university was not very appealing, especially for those who were eighteen years old (I was actually only seventeen) and eligible for the draft. As the Korean War was still "work in progress," being drafted was a potentially life-threatening event. Attending university as a full-time student was considered suitable grounds for deferral.

The only advice my mother ever gave me about a career was to implore me to have a profession so I would have an opportunity to earn a living. I am sure this was a reaction to seeing so many men in her family, especially my father, struggle to earn a living and support their family without a profession to fall back on. Mother did not care which profession—law, medicine, engineering—as long as I had some qualifications. Being a businessman or entrepreneur was just not good enough for her.

I think I was always destined to become an engineer. I was

everlastingly curious about how and why things worked. And I enjoyed making things, whether it was helping Mark make model spotter planes during wartime, building rubber band airplanes with balsa wood and crepe paper, or trying to recreate the Eiffel tower with toothpicks. I always seemed to have at least one construction project not far from my desk.

A significant impetus to entering the field of engineering came in high school when I had a class in mechanical or technical drawing. We had to learn the discipline of preparing plans that visually communicate how something functions or is constructed. Although I did not realize it then, it emerged many years later that I seemed to have had a particular good grasp of spatial relations.

But I think it was my high school chemistry teacher, Dr. Joseph Harwell, who triggered my deep and serious interest in the world of chemistry and the many unexplored avenues that needed discovery. Every class session with "doc" became an unforgettable experience.

So chemical engineering was where I was headed.

46

Welcome to the Real World

I submitted my application to five universities—Massachusetts Institute of Technology (MIT), New York University (NYU), Rensselaer Polytechnic (RPI), Worcester Polytechnic Institute (WPI), and City College of New York (CCNY), and then began to contemplate what I could realistically do for nine months before university began in September. Since I was not yet eighteen, an all-expense-paid trip to Korea was not an issue. Before having to make any decisions, the Engineering School at NYU decided to offer a January admission class and I gladly accepted. If that turned out to be a bad decision, I felt I could always transfer in September to one of the other four schools that had accepted me. Of course, everything was dependent upon receiving some generous financial aid.

I must have been at NYU for about a week when I received a telephone call from WPI saying that they had decided at the last minute to admit a small class in January. Those entering would have to agree to go to summer school to make up the work they had missed so that they could join the rest of the class in September as sophomores. The best part of the news was that the school would, if I decided to accept, grant me a $400 per semester scholarship, which would cover my entire tuition fee.

Our class consisted of just twenty-six students. We quickly became a closely knit team and after the sophomore year began, we continued to share a special camaraderie that lasted until we all graduated. I am still in touch with several of my "Jan class" mates and one of them, Al Costantin, and I even accepted employment offers from the same company—Union Carbide in Bound Brook, New Jersey. Paul Alasso, and Walter Kirk are two other January classmates with whom I stay in contact to this day.

My first year, or actually nine months, at WPI was amazingly successful. There were several reasons. First, I understood very well that my scholarship would depend on achieving and maintaining a high academic standard. Second, my preparation at Bronx Science provided a unique foundation for undertaking college-level courses, especially since in several subjects, I had already covered the basics of much of the material. Finally, I had decided that I would, from the first day of class, strive to excel academically.

The decision to go to Worcester was clearly a "game changer" but it was not without much painful soul searching. At the time, leaving home to go to university was for me largely a dream. Mark had stayed home to go to Columbia University. Mother was home alone. Financially, it seemed almost impossible under the circumstances to leave home. And my best friends were staying in New York. Gerard went to CCNY and Peter started at Columbia, as did Stan Lubman.

Before the sophomore year began, all Jan-plan students had to have an interview with Dean Donald Downing to discuss their experience and outline their future plans. My interview turned out to be a life-changing experience.

"Boomer," as he was affectionately known on campus, listened attentively to my impressions, looked over my record, and made some suggestions about how I should approach the next three years of my life. His advice had a profound impact not only on my academic

One of my most memorable mentors, Dean Downing, at Worcester Polytechnic Institute, helped me establish a lifelong value system.

career but on my whole life. I felt so indebted to him that in my senior year, as managing editor of the university's yearbook, I arranged for the book to be dedicated to him.

"Henry, you have done extraordinarily well in your first year. Your grades are outstanding and your teachers with whom I spoke are most impressed with your dedication and conscientiousness. But you should be aware that there is more to a university education than attending class and achieving high grades."

At this point, my mind raced quickly through my last nine months trying to recall if I had somehow committed a major transgression or somehow broken the school rules. I was certain that I was about to be told my time at WPI was at an end.

"School is more than classrooms, textbooks, laboratories, and exams. You have a unique opportunity to explore the world, to join colleagues in activities you may never have a chance to experience after you leave, to learn to learn. You can develop new skills that are never taught in a classroom. You can interact with other students whom you would never get to meet. Am I making myself clear?"

Boomer's message was indeed clear. But as a seventeen-year-old, while the words seemed clear, the question of what exactly I should do differently was vague. Was I to let my academic achievements erode to make room for some non-educational activities? Could I seriously contemplate losing my scholarship and the chance to stay at WPI? What exactly does learning to learn mean in practical terms? How would I explain all of this back home?

My metamorphosis began a few days later. A poster on the

dormitory notice board was calling for students interested in playing varsity soccer to come to tryouts next Monday afternoon. While I had played soccer in high school, I knew I was not very good and it would be a colossal stretch of the imagination to think that I could possibly play on a university team. Surprisingly, although I had played for several years, I had never seen a professional team in action. With Boomer's thoughtful counsel still ringing fresh in my mind, I decided to sign up. One of the things that attracted me was that varsity players did get some special discounts on schoolbooks and supplies, and during the season, athletes were entitled to special high-protein diets, i.e. steaks and chops. This was a type of subsidy in lieu of an athletic scholarship, of which there were none at WPI.

In retrospect, I had two things going for me at soccer tryouts. First, if the ball was not moving and I could have a good long run up to it, I could hit the stationary ball further than any of the others trying out. Second, I was considered big for my age and could run quite fast—albeit not very far. Also, I was not afraid to push my weight around if necessary.

So, miraculously, I was selected for the team. I suspect the main reason I won a place on the squad was that I could be a substitute for the first string fullback. The fullback in question did not achieve the required academic levels, and so I managed to play three years of varsity soccer for WPI.

As classes began with many new courses, I was uneasy about having a large chunk of my discretionary time being decanted into soccer training and playing. I think we had Mondays off but

Fortunately for me (at left), our style of playing soccer required more brawn than skill. There is a good chance I might have actually missed the ball in this action.

otherwise we were expected on the pitch every afternoon from three until it got too dark to see the ball. Most of the games were played on Saturday afternoons. Thanks to the feisty coaching of Jim Geddes and Jim McKechnie, I began to learn how the game should be played, although it took me a few years to fully understand Coach Geddes' Scottish accent.

By Christmas of my sophomore year, when the season ended, I was happy to turn in my kit and hang up my cleats. As I was leaving the locker room for what I thought was the last time, one of my teammates announced, "Bye, guys, see you in February!" As far as I knew, there was no soccer season during the winter semester. I could not imagine that they would have a whole winter season of indoor training. When I sheepishly asked someone what was happening in February, he said, "Lacrosse season begins."

In fact, officially there was no lacrosse season, as it was just a sports club, not a fully recognized WPI team. Nevertheless, it was a way of keeping fit. The only major injury I had in all my years of playing at the varsity level in university was in a lacrosse game.

Someone once said that if you want something done, assign it to the busiest person in the group. I always felt this was an immutable law of human nature. I was indeed busy and somehow I began to accumulate an eclectic range of responsibilities and assignments on campus.

Did my academics suffer as a result of my apparently overzealous extracurricular activities? Of course, they did. I did not make Tau Beta Pi, the honorary engineering fraternity, nor did I graduate "laude" anything. Nevertheless, being selected by my classmates to give the graduation address and being elected to Skull, WPI's honorary society in recognition of extraordinary contributions to college life, were much more meaningful to me than getting a slightly higher grade for a paper or on an exam.

Henry Michael Strage
Chemical Engineer   *Hank*
AEΠ; Skull; ΠΔE; Who'sWho
Soccer. "W" 2. 3. 4; Tennis. 1-4; Tech
News, 1-4 Ed.-in-chief; Peddler, 2. 3. 4
Managing Ed.; Masque. 1, 2. 3 Student
Director, 4, Pres.; Debating Club, 1-4.
Pres.; Tech Council. 4; A.I.Ch.E., 4;
R.O.T.C., Captain, Battalion Staff (S-2);
Frat. Pres., 4.
131 Riverside Drive. New York 24, N. Y.

*I found it hard to say, "No." Consequently, I
had little time for sleeping.*

2 *The Evening Gazette* Worcester, Fri., June 18, 1954

WPI Seniors Urged To Benefit Mankind

Worcester Polytechnic Institute seniors were advised today to use the scientific method in which they have been trained to develop an objectivity which will benefit their fellow man.

Henry M. Strage, 20, of New York City, youngest member of his class, spoke at Class Day exercises in Alden Auditorium.

"Objectivity is a trait we, as engineers, can give as our contribution to our generation," he said.

"Happiness and success are goals of everyone," he said, "but success for yourself and security for your family are not enough.

"For the real complete measure of happiness lies in the contributions which you will make to the welfare and the progress of your fellow man.

Greatest Happiness

"If you can honestly say to yourself that you have helped to make this world a better place to live in . . . then indeed you will have found the greatest happiness than any soul can hope to achieve in this world.

"Let us subscribe to no principle or formula until it has been critically analyzed," he said. "Let no criticism be offered unless we have some alternative constructive suggestion."

David F. Gilbert of Broomall, Pa., permanent class president, was chairman of Class Day exercises.

Edwin Shivell 3d of Fall River gave the class history. Richard W. Lindquist of 33 Hapgood road presented the class gift to Dean Francis W. Roys, acting president.

Special Awards

Special awards were made by Edward J. Power Jr. of Quincy, president of Tech Council. Richard V. Olson of 2 Chalmers street was in charge of tradition tree and ivy planting ceremonies at Kaven Hall.

Rev. Walter Donald Kring

minister of First Unitarian Church, will speak at 8 tonight at baccalaureate exercises in Central Congregational Church. His topic will be "Why Scientists Mount the Pulpit."

Class reunions will be held tonight by the classes of 1899, 1904, 1915, 1929, 1945, 1946, 1947 and 1948.

Alumni Day program tomorrow will open with registration in Higgins Laboratories and campus open house until noon.

Corporation Meeting

The annual meeting of the corporation will be at 10 a. m. and the Alumni Association at 11.30 a. m. in Janet Earle Room of Alden Memorial.

Fifty-Year Associates will meet at noon in Janet Earle Room. Alumni will gather in front of Alumni Gymnasium for the traditional parade followed by dinner at 1 p. m. in Alden Auditorium.

Kaven Hall, the new civil engineering building, will be dedicated at 3.15 p. m. in the building's assembly hall.

Rev. Dr. Thomas Sherrard Roy, former minister of First Baptist Church, will give the invocation and benediction. Dean Roys will discuss "The Institute Erects a New Building." Arthur J. Knight, professor of civil engineering and superintendent of buildings and grounds will speak on "Reminiscences."

Alumni speakers are George Rich and Burton Marsh.

The 86th commencement will be at 3.30 p. m. Sunday in Worcester Memorial Auditorium.

The college will award 114 bachelor of science degrees, eight master of science degrees, one professional engineering degree and three honorary doctors of engineering degrees.

The Evening Gazette, June 18, 1954. I was humbled when my classmates voted me the Class Orator, which included making the valedictory address at graduation. (See photo on next page.)

389

AT WPI CLASS DAY

These seniors at Worcester Polytechnic Institute took part in the Class Day program today in Alden Auditorium. From left, Richard V. Olson of 12 Chalmers road, chairman of the tree and ivy committee; David F. Gilbert of Broomall, Pa., permanent class president; and Henry M. Strage of New York City, class orator.

The Evening Gazette *article, cont'd from previous page*

47

My Short Career in the Army Signal Corps

To suggest that I had a distinguished career in the U.S. Army would be an exaggeration of the truth. However, it was for me a great experience, most enjoyable, and full of exceptional adventures and incredible learning opportunities. Despite many unusual and unexpected events, when my obligatory period of active duty came to an end, I was invited to stay in the service as a career officer, with a promise of a worthwhile pension on retirement. It was not a difficult decision to decline regretfully the offer. What I was not aware of was that I had earned an extraordinarily scarce strategic MOS (Military

Occupational Specialty), one that almost caused me to be recalled into active duty during the Vietnam War.

My initial decision to embark upon a military career had been made, I must admit, not for patriotic reasons but rather for two pragmatic ones. I did not particularly want to go and be shot at in Korea, and I could use the money. Twenty-seven dollars a month was not much, but you did get free uniforms and, occasionally, special meals.

The Korean War had just started when I entered university, and at that time, all males between the ages of eighteen and twenty-six were required to register with the Selective Service System, known simply as "the draft." The system was also referred to as the Compulsory Military Service Act. Throughout the country, local draft boards met periodically and selected a certain number of draftees from among the young men who had registered in their district. These draftees had to report for active duty, typically for a period of two years. Among the many excuses that one could present to the board in order to be deferred, i.e. not be drafted, was that you were enrolled in a bona fide university and had passing grades.

As soon as I was able, in my sophomore year, without much fanfare, I joined the Reserve Officers' Training Corps (ROTC) unit at WPI. Each university with an ROTC unit was designated to be part of a specific specialized branch of the Army. Our unit at WPI was a Signal Corps unit. The objective of the Signal Corps was to provide and manage communications and information to support the command and control of the combined armed forces, whether in an active military zone or not.

We had to learn how to carry, mount, repair, maintain, and operate the basic military telephone system known to everyone as the ANGRY 9. Its real name was AN/GRC. You can buy a used version today from eBay.

Apart from weekly drill sessions during the school year, all ROTC candidates were required to attend classes in military subjects and pass basic physical examinations. Failure to do so or not to pass periodic exams on military subjects would usually result in your name being passed to your local draft board, with obvious consequences. I cannot remember anyone failing a military science course, but our unit was rather small.

Several times during the term, the entire corps, made up of several platoons, was obliged to participate in field exercises or maneuvers. My career in the Signal Corps got off to a catastrophic start during one of these field maneuvers.

Almost all military communications were designed to be portable, so the equipment was separated into packages that could be carried by an individual soldier. I was put in charge of setting up the switchboard that served as the center or hub of the communication system. I practiced setting it up several times in the classroom and thought I knew what I was doing or was supposed to do. This was not complicated per se but, unfortunately, no one told me that in the field it was crucial to ground the equipment. Without proper grounding, it was possible to give someone a nasty shock, with serious permanent consequences.

It was my extremely bad luck that Lt. Col. Harris, our commanding officer, decided on the day of our field maneuvers to visit the site of our exercise and make a phone call using the switchboard I had just connected so carefully, or so I thought. He plugged the designated telephone plug (male) from his phone into the corresponding socket (female) on my master switchboard. As he did so, several hundred volts (well, a lot anyway) went through his body and he was hurled some twenty feet across the field. I was sure I had electrocuted him and was already planning on what to put into my duffle bag for the trip to Korea.

I was somehow spared.

"Would you care to join the Naval Unit?" Colonel Harris enquired as he was brushing the dirt from his otherwise pristine uniform.

I suggested that this did not seem like a good idea since I was prone to seasickness.

"Could I respectfully suggest, sir," I replied humbly, "that I might be better suited for the Chemical Corps?"

Despite this unfortunate episode, I did complete the course and in my senior year proudly wore my second lieutenant gold bar.

No wonder I couldn't see anything. I'd left my glasses in my room.

48

Close Encounter with Procter and Gamble

The Chemical Engineering Department at WPI was proudly housed in a charmless four-story building, constructed in 1898, called Salisbury Hall. One of the perks of becoming a junior in the department was that each student was assigned a permanent desk space in what was euphemistically known as the "bullpen," which occupied about half of the ground floor. Actually it was a rather grim affair best described as an upmarket prison dining room with improved lighting. The desk was not, in fact, a desk but rather a basic kitchen-like table with a single drawer. But it was our home for the next two years. The only form of entertainment was an aging, three-legged Coca-Cola machine leaning against an inside wall.

Nevertheless, our bullpen had many advantages. First, it meant we did not have to drag our textbooks and notebooks to every different class. This is not a trivial advantage. No self-respecting "chem-eng" junior would be seen without at least his three bibles in hand.

The first was Perry's *Chemical Engineering Handbook*, all 1,942 pages of it. In it could be found such priceless information as Van Laar Constants for Binary Immiscible Systems (page 533); Physical Properties of Refractory Materials (page 1549); and, of course, the all-important Drag Coefficient and Related Functions for Spherical Particles (page 1019). The other bestseller was *Groggin's Unit Processes in Organic Synthesis*, and the collection was rounded off by the official ASME Steam Tables, showing the thermodynamic properties of water vapor, liquid, and solid.

The second advantage of the bullpen was it was very conducive for working in teams. As we were seated alphabetically, practically all of my team laboratory experiments and project assignments were conducted with Walt Stewart and Ed Shivell. The private offices of several of the department's professors opened up to the bullpen, so help was always at hand. The canteen and library were close by, as well as the so-called unit ops lab, where we spent many hours trying to figure out what actually happens inside the mass of pipes, tubes, vessels, and meters with which I was predestined to spend a significant portion of my working life.

Bob Wagner, our youngest professor and an engaging, friendly, enthusiastic teacher, was always available and willing to explore and explain the intricacies of chemical engineering. I am not sure why, but one day Bob called me into his office and challenged, or perhaps encouraged me to submit an idea for the school's annual Peel Prize competition. Mr. Peel donated $75 each year to the undergraduate who could present the best idea for a commercially viable engineering innovation. Why did Bob suggest I enter this competition? Perhaps because my responses to engineering problems in class seldom resembled the expected "school solution." This type of thinking was subsequently referred to as thinking "outside the box." I took Bob's challenge as a compliment, without having the vaguest idea about what my engineering innovation might be.

After producing a written paper, one was expected to make an oral presentation before three independent local engineering executives. What innovation should I present? Bob suggested I search my work experience and find a practical solution to an everyday problem. Unfortunately, my work experience consisted mainly of mowing lawns, washing dishes, playing rabbi at a children's camp, and doing odd jobs around campus. I found no practical and innovative ideas related to this particular array of jobs.

Finally, as the deadline approached, I concocted an idea that, while fairly mundane, had some commercial value, or so I thought. One of the odd part-time jobs I had at university was working in a local commercial laundry as a maintenance engineer—i.e. sweeper. In this laundry, I was intrigued to watch how the operators unceremoniously dumped washing detergent by the shovelful into the vast rotating drums. The basic process in commercial laundries was essentially identical to the way home laundries worked, except each batch of laundry would typically go through at least ten cycles of washing and rinsing rather than one cycle, and a variety of chemicals were added to help things along.

Perhaps, I thought, if they were able to measure the precise amount of detergent that was actually needed for each batch, they might save a few pennies. If they could add soap in amounts that were directly related to the volume of material to be washed and its degree of dirtiness, they would have a more efficient and cost-effective process. I am not sure Bob understood what I was talking about, since this was hardly chemical engineering, but he agreed that it might be a useful idea. And so I started to work on the project, building a small-scale demonstration and preparing my written submission.

How do you measure how dirty your laundry is?

I reasoned that if I could analyze the quality of water leaving the washing machine after the first rinse, I could develop a reasonable surrogate that would be an indicator of the dirt content of the load, and then could adjust as appropriate the exact amount of soap required to remove the rest of the dirt in the batch.

All I needed was a window in the exit pipe and a photoelectric cell to measure the density of the exiting water. Once calibrated, the cell and meter would indicate the quality and clarity of the water and relate it back to the weight of detergent and other chemicals, such as bleach, needed for the next step in the process, and some idea of the optimum length of time for the next cycle.

Dressed to present my soap-saving invention at the Peel Prize final presentation.

For the oral presentation, I had assembled four containers of water and a photoelectric cell attached to a simple meter. In each container, I simulated different amounts of dirt and demonstrated that each one gave a different reading on the photoelectric cell. While scientifically it was rather a bogus demonstration, it seemed to impress the judges. I won first prize and a first-page picture and story in the local newspaper.

The next day, after the winners were announced, Bob Wagner was delighted.

"I knew you could do it, Hank," he proudly proclaimed.

"I have a problem, Doc," I said. "I would like your advice."

"What is the problem?"

"Well, Prof," I explained, "this morning I had a long distance call from the development director of Procter and Gamble. He read about the detergent-saving device in the press and would like to see me about it."

"That is great news!" Bob announced. "But I would stall them for a while until you begin the patenting process and perhaps hear from some other interested detergent manufacturers."

"Why a patent?" I replied naively.

"P&G may feel the best place for your detergent-saving device is locked up in their vaults. You could hold out for a bigger price if your idea is already protected."

"Bob," I pleaded, "be realistic! My 'invention,' as you call it, is an idea without much experimental evidence or proof. While I did suggest at the presentation that the savings might be as much as 30 percent in detergent cost and hot water, and maybe even more when electricity consumption is taken into account, I have no practical evidence or basis for those numbers. Frankly, I was making up the numbers."

Bob was not impressed with my moral or intellectual dilemma. "Just work out the bugs, Hank, and do a patent search and we'll make an application for a patent as soon as you're ready."

The bugs that Professor Wagner alluded to were more like mega dinosaurs.

Why did I think there was any relationship between the transparency of the exit water stream and the dirt content of the clothing in the washing drum? Wouldn't the detergent foam mask any transparency and provide really questionable data? Would all "dirt" react in the same way with all detergents or did different types of grime or stain have different properties? Is all dirt created equal? Are some kinds more equal than others? Could you increase the effectiveness of a wash cycle by increasing the concentration of the detergent? What about the temperature of the water? Would changing the volume or weight of material being washed make a difference?

After looking at some related patent applications, I saw the work that would need to be done and decided to take the prize money and run. I wonder still, to this day, if P&G or anyone else decided to take my winning idea further.

Alberta assures me this was a lost opportunity. To prove it, she showed me a box of detergent with complicated instructions on *how* much detergent to use, *how* long to run the machine, and at what temperature the water should be. "These are all the critical parameters you identified fifty-nine years ago. Don't you have any more useful ideas? Back to your drawing board, Thomas!" she declared.

Fifty years later, I had the opportunity to bring up the subject of the Peel Prize once again at WPI. Alberta and I were looking for a creative way to help the school and celebrate my fifty years as an alumnus. The idea came to us that we might reinstate the tradition of the Peel Prize. Mr. Peel withdrew his prize a few years after I won it. Had he run out of funds, gone bankrupt, or just gotten bored with the competition? In any case, Alberta and I decided to replicate the idea of an annual prize for innovation and bring the competition up to date.

After a series of negotiations with the university, it was agreed that we could reintroduce a competition for an outstanding innovation by a WPI student. Since Peel had long disappeared without trace, the new competition would be known as the Alberta and Henry Strage Innovation Award. To avoid the possibility of bankruptcy or worse, we created an endowment to fund the award, thus making it permanent. We defined our objective in establishing the prize in a brief statement of purpose.

Objective: The objective of this competition is to encourage the development of student knowledge and practical experience in the translation of creative ideas into viable new projects or ventures, especially for those students who are interested in pursuing an entrepreneurial opportunity now or in the future. A panel of distinguished judges will consider commercial, social, and philanthropic ventures.

Since the competition's inception in 2005, three winners have translated their winning ideas into commercially viable enterprises.

Prize giving at the annual Strage Innovation competition in 2006 at WPI. Alberta is presenting first prize to Artur Janc, right, *whose winning innovation became the basis for a new high-tech venture.*

49

When Niagara Falls Fall

In 1953, after years of enjoying carefree summers of traveling or working in children's summer camps, I decided that it was time to get a serious job and get a practical taste of working as a chemical engineer.

Summer employment for engineering students was a well-established option. Many large American corporations had formal summer programs. These programs were set up to provide corporations a closer look at potential full-time employees. In many cases, the final exit interview for summer students coincided with an offer of full employment upon graduation.

E.I. du Pont de Nemours (DuPont), then the largest chemical

company in the world, became well known through its "Better things through better living through chemicals" PR campaign. DuPont had an insatiable appetite for new chemical engineers and the rumor was that it needed to hire 30 percent of all chemical engineering graduates just to keep up with its growth objectives.

I was recruited to work in its Niagara Falls plant for the 1953 summer.

Niagara Falls was hardly a city in which I would have selected to spend my summer, but landing a job with DuPont was considered a coup and not to be turned down lightly. On the positive side, the city was closer to New York than many of the company's other sites. It was close to both Cleveland and Toronto, where I had relatives to visit. With a major national tourist attraction in the city, there had to be at least a minimum amount of entertainment amenities.

Apart from the date I was expected to begin work, my letter of appointment spelled out such important details such as normal working hours, dress code, suggested arrangements of lodgings, and, of course, salary. The dress code presented some problems. We were expected to wear a suit and tie every day at work.

DuPont's plant in Niagara Falls was one of the largest chlorine producing plants in the world at the time. Chlorine was a nasty chemical, being the basis for everything from a popular chemical warfare gas to a major pesticide (DDT) and various types of cleaning materials, such as trichlorides and tetrachlorides. The plant made many of these, and you could smell the chlorine a mile away from the factory gate. Rachel Carson exposed the dangers of various chlorinated chemicals, including DDT, in her 1962 book, *Silent Spring*. That was the end of many chlorinated compounds.

The unfortunate byproduct of working in the plant is that the chlorine odor was daily impregnated into all of your clothing. My most practical mother, who I am certain had never come near a chemical factory, suggested I wear only washable clothing, so-called "hang and dry" nylon shirts and a summer-weight hang and dry suit to go along with it. I thanked her every day that summer for her wisdom. I never had a laundry bill. Every day when I returned to my apartment, I would run the shower and get under it with all my clothing on except my tie and shoes. First I washed and rinsed my jacket, took it off, and hung it on a hanger. I followed this with my nylon shirt, trousers, and underwear. By the morning, everything was dry, wrinkle-free, and ready to start another day.

I may not have been the best chemical engineer in the plant, but I suspect I was the cleanest and the best-smelling!

My wear-shower-soap-rinse-drip-dry-and-wear-again suit

A summer in a real chemical plant was a valuable learning experience, especially with respect to the need to solve engineering problems with common sense rather than reverting back to what was taught in the classroom. I was assigned as a junior chemical engineer to a rather gloomy section of the plant. The area supervisor to whom I had to report was not very excited about having a bunch of novice engineers assigned to him. A neat little sign behind his desk summarized his feeling:

GET THE F------- ENGINEERS OUT OF HERE

And, LET'S GET ON WITH PRODUCTION.

One day, I was asked to design and fit a flow meter on a small holding tank in our area of the plant. A flow meter, as its name implies, measures the actual volume of liquid passing through a tube or pipe. In this case, the pipe was carrying some reagent into the tank to speed up a reaction. After searching the equipment catalogue and the plant store's inventory, I decided which instrument would best suit the situation. Then I went to the drawing board and drew an appropriate self-standing L-beam pillar to hold my flow meter. Next, it was time to book the construction department, which would order the flow meter I had selected, arrange to build the pillar, and send a team to install it.

When the team arrived at the site of the tank, they asked to see where I wanted the meter placed. They took one look at my drawing, dismissed it, selected from the inventory a much simpler flow meter than the one I had so carefully selected, and attached it to the pipe in question with a simple metal belt-type strap. The whole operation took about an hour. It was an embarrassing but very useful lesson that I had never learned in university. One should always seek advice from those with experience.

After a month in the plant, I was rewarded by being moved to a top-secret research and development pilot plant. DuPont had developed a chlorine-based rocket fuel that was highly corrosive, inflammable, and explosive. The pilot plant was making small quantities of the fuel so that it could be tested with various engine parts to examine how they would stand up to high temperatures and pressures in a new, experimental engine. My role, as I recall, was essentially to collect data during the manufacturing process, prepare performance graphs, and write daily reports.

Because the process was not 100 percent tested and was potentially unstable, the pilot plant—about the size of a small two-story house—was surrounded on three sides with a thick explosion-proof barrier about fifty feet high. One side was left open so that should there be an explosion it could only go in one direction. One morning while having breakfast, I heard the morning radio news blurt out the news that overnight an explosion in a highly secret area of a nearby DuPont factory had unexpectedly occurred, fortunately without any casualties (except my temporary position as a data collector). I recall when classes at WPI resumed in the autumn, I had to do a lot of explaining to convince my colleagues that I was not responsible for it.

I did get an offer for full-time employment during my exit interview. However, after checking the location—Davenport, Iowa—and learning that the plant there used corn to make furfural and intermediate chemicals that were important, at least for DuPont, I thanked them for the offer and said I would let them know. I made a mental note to look elsewhere. Two close chemical engineer friends and fellow Skulls from WPI, David Gilbert and Walter Stewart, joined DuPont and stayed there for their entire working lives.

50

From Pen Pusher to Slide Rule Jockey

Sometime during the last year at university, one begins to realize but perhaps not accept the fact that one day soon the party will be over and one will actually have to get a job—work.

Having spent the previous summer working in a real live smelly chemical factory for E.I. du Pont, the last thing I wanted to do for the rest of my life was work in a noisy, smelly, corrosive panorama of pipes, motors, distillation columns, reactors, and hard-hatted engineers.

As I had been editor of the university newspaper and managing editor of the college yearbook, it was natural that my thoughts would turn to some sort of career in journalism. Mark seemed to be having a wonderful time as a foreign correspondent, first in Israel and then in Rome. So why not follow his example?

It was, therefore, not surprising that after a few interviews and a visit to their New York headquarters, McGraw-Hill Publishing thought it would be a good idea if I joined the staff of their weekly chemical industry news magazine, not surprisingly called *Chemical Week*. Amazingly, the magazine is still being published.

Having announced my intentions to my mentors and advisors one day, I was summoned for a "career talk" with Professors Kranich and Bob Wagner.

"Look, Hank," they announced, "we think you are probably making the biggest mistake in your life." Taking a job with McGraw-Hill hardly seemed to me like a life sentence, but they seemed to think it was. "You have almost finished four years of learning how to be a chemical engineer," they continued. "Give that up now to become a pen pusher and you will have wasted four years of your life. We urge you to try engineering. If you really dislike it, you can always go back to writing or something else, but you are unlikely to go from writing to engineering."

At first, I paid very little attention. Nevertheless I decided it might be worth a try, and so I had some campus interviews, filled in some job applications, and waited to see what would develop. A few weeks later, to my everlasting surprise, I received a letter of invitation to join Union Carbide in their division in Bound Brook, New Jersey. The salary was in line with the going rate and, most importantly, one of my best friends (and also a chemical engineer), Al Costantin, received a parallel offer. The only other offer I had was the one from DuPont to work in Davenport, Iowa, a city which I imagined was only marginally civilized.

Bound Brook was close to home, Union Carbide was a fine, respected chemical company, and I would be working with my best college friend. Another "sign" was that a Belgian chemist, Dr. Leo Bakelite, had invented the product the plant was manufacturing. So off Al and I went to work in the booming New Jersey countryside at the attractive salary of $370 per month. Most of what was being produced in our new home was a "wonder" plastic material that went into the manufacture of the then familiar-looking black telephones.

Al and I were in a pool of four recent graduates with the impressive title of "senior development engineers." During the short time I was there, I cannot remember doing any significant work. It was clear that as a commissioned Army officer, my time in Bound Brook would be limited, and so it was. I was there for two or three months before leaving to join the Army. Al surprisingly stayed with Union Carbide for twenty years.

After only a week on the job, I found myself as the star witness in a highly contentious labor dispute that eventually ended up in front of a judge or a National Labor Relations Board tribunal. It seems that one day, while on a formal training course, my instructor and I discovered an apparently sleeping shift foreman, who had unfortunately allowed a large chemical reaction tank to "cook" for too long and an entire tank full of Bakelite product had solidified and totally stopped production in that part of the plant. The foreman was immediately dismissed. He appealed, saying, "I was not sleeping—I just had my eyes closed."

In court, after being duly rehearsed by the company's attorney, I took the stand and was asked to describe what I had seen, which I did as accurately as possible.

"Did you personally actually see the defendant sleeping?" the defense attorney asked me.

"Yes, sir, he was sleeping," I confidently responded.

"How do you know he was sleeping?" I was asked.

"His eyes were closed and he was not moving, sir," I replied. At which point the defense lawyer went to his chair, leaned back, and closed his eyes.

"Was I sleeping?" he queried.

"I suspect not," I said.

"Then," came the response, "I suspect the defendant that you said you saw sleeping was also very much awake."

The defendant was back at work the following week.

Al and I decided to share an apartment near the plant. What we found was not an apartment but a small cottage in the back of the Old Heidelberg Restaurant. It suited us very well, except what we did not know when we made the arrangements was that our cottage served as an overflow bar after the main restaurant closed.

This meant that our living room became very popular.

The arrangement did not last long because, as expected, after several months I was called to active duty in the U.S. Army Chemical Corps. The plant manager gave me a rousing send-off, a lunch, and a promise that my job would be waiting for me when I came back from Korea.

Al and I remained close friends until his premature death in 2002.

PART VI

THIS IS THE ARMY, MR. JONES

Who, me?

Introduction
Your Country Needs You

A one-armed soldier, to his surprise, was drafted into the Army. He was sure it was a mistake. He complained to his sergeant, "You see I only have one arm. I'm useless in the Army."

"No, you're not, son," came the brisk reply. "See that man over there at the water pump filling up those buckets? Well, go over and tell him when the bucket is full. You see, he's blind."

After a less than brilliant career in the Reserve Officers' Training Corps in university, I was not exactly looking forward to two years on active duty. As things turned out, I have to admit that I not only enjoyed my military service but learned some new skills, traveled around a bit, almost got an advanced degree, and developed a new perspective on the role of the military. In fact, when it came time to be "de-mobbed" (demobilized), I seriously considered an attractive offer to stay in the Army and become a career officer.

One great perk of being a Regular Army officer during the Korean War was the most generous GI Bill, which paid for all of my post-graduate education for the next five years.

First day on active duty—well, active training, actually!

51

How I Almost Started the Second American Civil War

What does the Chemical Corps actually do?

The Corps was created during World War I to help American troops defend against German poison gas attacks. It subsequently was assigned a host of missions that used a variety of so-called weapons "systems," including the 4.2 chemical mortar grenade launcher, smoke generators, and flame throwers, as well as the operation of the unfortunately named "impregnation units," whose name was changed after a congressman complained that his niece had written to him from the front lines during World War II explaining that she had been assigned to the 115th Impregnating Company. After that, it was just called "processing unit." Its mission was to prepare uniforms impregnated with special chemicals that protected the wearer from chemical gas attacks.

The epicenter of the Chemical Corps training facility was in Fort McClellan, in Anniston, Alabama, and that is where I had to report for Basic Officer Training Course (BOTC) in the summer of 1954. Jim Fisher was in the class preceding mine that year.

When you drove into the city, you were greeted with a large billboard that proudly announced that you were entering THE CAPITAL OF THE WORLD'S SEWER PIPE INDUSTRY. It was an apt description.

In the training center, an equal amount of time was spent in the classroom and on field exercises or maneuvers. These exercises consisted of simulated combat conditions to test how future officers might react under fire. Typically they were unscheduled and unannounced, so preparation was not possible.

One of the Chemical Corps' most important battlefield activities was to create smoke screens. A typical smoke screen mission might include screening troop maneuvers, concealing breaching operations, conducting deception operations, screening avenues of approach for helicopters, or hiding a moving target, such as a column of tanks—this was much more dangerous than it seemed because typically the smoke generators had to be deployed ahead of the line of fire.

Smoke was made either by a motorized generator attached to a two-and-a-half ton truck or by portable machines called, not surprisingly, Portable Ground Emplaced Smoke Generators, on an M36 or something similar. This generator, which was essentially a big motor, took several soldiers to shlep and was attached in the field to a string of fifty-five-gallon drums filled with heavy lube oil mixed with aluminum oxide.

Despite technical advances in military systems, the production of smoke hasn't changed since it was first used by the Greeks in the Peloponnesian Wars (431–404 BCE).

Late one summer evening, a surprise field exercise was announced over the camp's public address (PA) system. As we climbed into our friendly two-and-a-half ton truck and drove out of the camp to an unknown destination, the consensus was that this evening's exercise would very likely involve making smoke since we had been studying about it for the whole week in the classroom.

What is so complicated about making smoke, you may ask?

Everything about the actual process depended on conditions that are uncertain, variable, and completely outside your control. It was critical to know the precise weather conditions existing and any likely changes before you turned on the generators. The temperature, humidity, and wind conditions are crucial. It was also vital to know and understand the terrain in which the operations would take place. Obviously, level ground with no trees needs different treatment than do heavily wooded valleys. Unquestionably, the single most significant variable was the exact placement of the smoke generators themselves. Since these smoke-making monsters were totally mobile, one had total freedom with respect to their actual placement.

To replicate real conditions, the exercise instructor would usually wait until we had reached our destination and then announce the objective for the evening and the command staff assignments.

"Men," he announced, "this evening down in the valley in front of you is one of our key strategic simulated airfields, which has been designated as the landing strip for a battalion of the 101st Airborne Company on a vital mission in this campaign. They will land at zero six hundred hours. They must be protected at all cost. We will unload, and Major Strage, this evening you will be in charge of the battalion. You have three platoons under your command in support. Lieutenant Bridges will be your weather officer. At sunrise, I want to see that airfield disappear. The lives of those paratroopers are in your hands. It is now exactly zero two hundred hours. You have four hours."

The honor of leading a major field exercise at Fort McClellan was typically a perk awarded to a student at the top of the class, the student who paid attention in class, took notes, asked intelligent questions, seemed interested, and relished leading. I fulfilled none of these specifications and, in fact, was tied with three others at the bottom end of the class. You can imagine my shock and horror when my name was announced as being in charge of the whole exercise.

It was late on a moonless summer night, somewhere in the depths of Alabama, far from anything that looked remotely familiar, and where there was nobody to whom I could appeal for an immediate field demotion. I even considered desertion. I checked to make sure it was Strage that was being anointed and not Strong, who was just behind me in alphabetical order in class. There was no mistake. I was petrified and tightened my belt.

"Major Strage?" shouted one of my classmates with unmitigated sarcasm in his voice, since he knew I had no idea what to do next. "Where would you like to set up your command post?"

While I was busy trying to compose a plausible excuse for why I should not be field court-martialed, my second in command had already set up a command center and was busy studying topographical maps of the location and checking the inventory of generators that were already being unloaded from one of the trucks in our convoy.

There was frenetic activity all around me for the next hour. Every time someone called or shouted "Major Strage," I kept hoping the real Major Strage would appear and relieve me of my responsibilities.

Captain Watson, the officer in charge of the generators, reported next. "We need a line of M26 along this ridge about twenty feet apart," he stated with authority. "Would you agree, Major Strage?"

All those under my command interpreted my silence as agreement.

"We may have a little problem," reported the weather officer. "We have a twenty-knot easterly wind down in the valley and a little bit higher on the ridge here. It looks like it will increase by sun up, but I have no idea if the direction of the wind in the morning will be the same as now."

I understood that wind direction and wind strength were vital elements to the success of our operation but since it was pitch black at that point, I had no idea where this imaginary airstrip was. In addition, I had no idea where my troops were or what they were doing and, worse still, what they should be doing. I was about to have a panic attack.

I did vaguely recall from class lectures that at this point one had to mark on the map the precise location of every generator available and, most importantly, in which direction they should be pointing. Crayon in hand, I approached the map table and began to make little numbered arrows to indicate where each of our generators should go. Everyone must have assumed I knew exactly what I was doing because as I started to draw, all grew silent. When the maps were finished, each platoon lieutenant quickly took his corresponding map and disappeared into the night to deploy his generators in the locations I had designated on the field maps.

About an hour or so later, I heard someone shout in a most authoritative commanding voice, "All locations at the ready to make smoke on your command, Major."

For a moment, I thought of all the disastrous officers' commands that had changed the course of history. "Charge!"—which had practically obliterated the entire Royal First Cavalry Light Brigade in the Crimean War—first came to mind. Then General Custer's last words as he was wiped out at the legendary Battle of Little Big Horn: "There are too damn many Indians." And General McAuliffe's response to the German suggestion that he surrender the Third Army at the Bastogne was, "Nuts!"

Then without hesitation, I confidently commanded in a most authoritative military voice the designated command, "Make smoke!" Suddenly what seemed like hundreds of automobile engines began to purr in the night and thin white plumes of petrol-smelling smoke began to fill the evening sky for as far as the eye could see. The mission had begun.

That morning, most of the 60,000 residents of Anniston, Alabama awoke as usual and began their well-rehearsed morning rituals—shower, shave, brush teeth, start the coffee maker, collect the morning paper from the front doorstep. It was at this point in the routine morning ritual that they discovered that this day would be very different from most other days. As they opened the door and bent over to collect their newspapers, they saw nothing. A thick cloud of dense, dirty white, misty smoke covered everything in sight.

On the same morning, on a hill a few miles from the center of town, as I looked out expecting to see our target "airfield" completely gone, what I saw instead was the morning sunshine bathing our objective, clear for anyone miles away to see. In the other direction, to my horror, the whole of the western side of the city of Anniston had virtually disappeared.

I had obviously miscalculated the direction and wind speed that evening, and placed and pointed the bloody generators in the wrong place.

What would I choose? Hanging, a lethal injection, electrocution, life imprisonment, a dishonorable discharge, or to join an infantry platoon in Korea?

52

Korea, Here I Come

On January 14, 1955, I was officially designated a Second Lieutenant in the United States Army Chemical Corps. Although in Korea active combat ceased in July1953, American military presence was only gradually reduced during the next ten years. Even as late as 2010, there were 28,500 U.S. Army troops on active duty in South Korea.

Newly commissioned Army officers statistically stood a good chance of being sent to "front line" units in Korea. Those of us in Officers Training Schools had no idea what the criteria were for being assigned to active duty in Korea. But you did not have to be a brain surgeon to figure out that you would be better off being in the top half of your graduating class rather than the bottom. Thus being forty-eighth out of a class of fifty-one was not a very good omen for me.

My class grades were far from brilliant, and my marks for field exercise and maneuvers were hardly more impressive. My disastrous

THE CHEMICAL CORPS SCHOOL
CHEMICAL CORPS TRAINING COMMAND
FORT McCLELLAN, ALABAMA

CMLTC-S-11   14 January 1955

SUBJECT: Academic Standing

TO: 2d Lt Henry M. Strage
           Co "A" CCTSC
           Fort McClellan, Alabama

1. In accordance with SR 605-85-10, 21 August 1954, paragraph 2b, you are advised that your class standing in the Tenth Chemical Officer Basic Course is number 48 in a class of 51.

2. Grades received on each subject are as indicated below:

SUBJECT	GRADE
Biological Warfare	92
Personnel and Administration	78
Intelligence	90
Map Reading	91
Intelligence	89
Plans	79
Operations	76
Training	73
Logistics	74
Atomic Warfare	86
Chemical Warfare	89
Materiel	76
Protection	76
FINAL AVERAGE	79.25

BY ORDER OF COLONEL VAN KEUREN:

ROBERT C. AYERS
2d Lt, Cml C
Asst Secretary

Being forty-eighth out of a class of fifty-one was not a particularly impressive record on which to request a special privileged assignment.

performance on the big smoke generator exercise was indelibly etched into Fort McClellan folklore.

My "silverware" collection added to my unmilitary performance.

One of the first lessons one learned in Officer Candidate School (OCS) was that in any difficult situation, or when you actually had to make a decision, rely entirely on your master sergeant.

Sergeant Casey only got me into trouble once, big time.

Part of our OCS training involved being in command of a platoon of new draftees. The platoon was the basic fighting unit in the U.S. Army and usually consisted of thirty to forty men. When you take command of a platoon, you take over responsibilities not only for the men but also for all of the supporting equipment, from weapons and bedding to anything that could be moved

I didn't pay much attention to exactly what I was signing for until one day, Casey pointed out that we were very short of the platoon silverware.

"Don't worry, sir," he said. "We can make up the shortfall." As the platoon signed out for the weekend, Casey told the whole platoon that the "admission" charge for signing back in Sunday night was a few pieces of silverware. When the men returned from their weekend and got ready to sign back in, they found that Casey had placed a large wooden crate to collect the replacement silverware. You will be surprised how much silver forty-five men can collect in one weekend. But the battalion commander was not amused, and I took the rap.

At the graduation ceremony, after the commanding officer pinned your gold bar on your uniform and gave you any special medals you had merited, he handed you a manila envelope that contained your orders, which detailed your next assignment and how you were expected to get there. I was prepared for the worse. By some miraculous and mysterious intervention, my travel orders were not to fly off to Korea, as I feared, but rather to take the train to Washington, D.C. That was better than I could have hoped for. Even my classmate Dave Gilbert, who was the battalion "valedictorian," ended up in Dugway Proving Ground, in Utah, in a town with a population of 2,000 in the middle of a treeless desert.

How did a newly commissioned officer who finished at the bottom of his class end up with a plum assignment and a great MOS (Military Occupational Specialty)?

Shortly after I had arrived in Alabama, my brother had written and told me about a young lady he had met in New York who was coming to stay with her father at Fort McClellan to recuperate from a bout of mononucleosis. Her name was Carol James. The only military family permanently stationed at the base called "James" was the much-feared commanding officer, but after checking, I discovered that no one knew anything about a Carol James, and I dismissed my brother's recommendation to telephone her as some plot of his creative mind to get me in some trouble.

Several weeks later, while passing away the evening at the BOQ (Bachelor Officers' Quarter) at the base, one of my mates answered the phone and said there was a call for me. It was the first call I had received in four weeks, and I wondered if it might be bad news about my family, since they were the only ones who knew my number.

I picked up the phone and a young lady with a clear New York accent said, "Henry, where have you been? You were supposed to call me weeks ago!" We finally met and spent some time together until I graduated.

Without going into details, I confess that, considering my dreadful class standing, my extraordinary assignment upon graduation could perhaps in part be attributed to Carol.

Thank you, Carol.

As I was the only one in my class to be sent to Washington, D.C., my assignment was either an administrative snafu, a sinister plot based on my reported exaggerated language skills, or divine intervention.

434

53

Ready, Aim, Fire

"She is going to be your best friend, I promise you that. You will soon get to know her inside and out. She will become your constant companion night and day, and she will always be by your side through thick or thin. Treat her well and she will never let you down. You will soon learn what makes her tick and how to keep her in tip-top condition and you will learn when she needs to have special attention. There will even be times when you will sleep with her and be happy you did."

The sergeant was not talking about Mary Lou or Belinda. He was describing my M1 rifle.

Of all field exercises at Officer Candidate School, the ones that were taken most seriously, and for good reason, were the trips to the firing range. Everyone meticulously observed the rules on the firing range. The initial and immediate penalty for any rule infraction was typically pushups. For example, pointing a weapon loaded or not at anyone meant "kissing Alabama for fifty." After that, infractions could mean the end of your career.

Once you became an officer, you were expected to be familiar with several different weapons, any one of which might be used should your unit find itself in a combat situation. The basic Army weapon in 1954 was the M1 semi-automatic carbine. It was crucially important that your rifle was always scrupulously clean, well oiled, and in perfect working condition. This meant that you had to be able to strip it into it its major components and, of course, be able to assemble it again. Tough guys would have races to see who could strip his rifle the quickest. The macho guys could do it blindfolded, just in case it was called for on a moonless night or perhaps during a massive electric power failure.

The other weapons we were expected to be familiar with were the standard M1, BAR (Browning Automatic Rifle), and the basic chemical corps weapon at the time, the field-mounted 4.2 mortar. All, of course, are useful lifetime skills.

There were three firing positions and a variety of different targets that everyone was expected to know. There were absolute minimum scores every officer was expected to reach.

I was not a very good shot. The root causes, I convinced myself, were that I wore glasses, had unsteady hands, and was, in general,

Every regular Army officer was expected to reach marksman level in at least one weapon in three positions.

nervous about using real bullets. So I knew something was "wrong" on the day we were shown how to use the Browning Automatic Rifle. Unlike a rifle, it fired rounds at some awesome speed, so it was imperative to press the trigger lightly. On this day, the target was a large square raised off the ground by two wooden posts, each perhaps one by two inches thick. I took careful aim as instructed, squeezed the trigger for the shortest possible time. To my everlasting amazement, I had pulverized both posts, and I watched with horror as the target fell to the ground.

One's scores on the firing range were never posted or generally reported unless you did so badly you were required to go back and have a second chance. Day after day, I was most surprised when my name was not called for a second try.

To my everlasting surprise, on graduation day, I received a marksman medal and the prime assignment to Washington, D.C.

Months later, I discovered that my award was not an administrative mistake. My range scores were indeed high enough to merit special awards. Apparently (but I will never know for sure) what happened, however, was that next to me on the range was a soldier called George Strong. In all activities, we were arranged alphabetically, so George and I became good friends. George had one problem, which he never spoke about, but it became obvious when one day we were on the field obstacle course. No matter how hard he tried, he was unable to walk on a wooden log across a little gorge. Poor George was slightly cross-eyed. But his father had some influence in Washington, the precise nature of which I cannot recall.

On the firing range, he apparently fired all of his rounds into my target.

Thank you, George. If it were not for you, I might have ended up on the 38th Parallel in Panmunjom.

54

Bacillus, Baseball, and Beyond

My military orders were to report for active duty to the Chemical Corps Center in Gravely Point, Washington, D.C. I had been assigned to the Biological Warfare Division, which was headquartered in Fort Detrick in Frederick, Maryland. This was the only information I was given about what I would be doing for the next two years.

Everything about the Biological Warfare (BW) Division was considered super top-secret, and I learned at Gravely Point that I had been granted the highest possible security clearance, which was essential for what I would be doing. For the next few days, about four of us who had reported at the same time were given extensive briefing about biological warfare, but as we were made clearly aware, we were told only what we specifically needed to know in order to do our respective jobs. This was called "security on a need-to-know basis."

Just in case any of us might have had the slightest moral reservations about working in BW, we were shown a realistic display of the precise damage done by various military weapons, from normal rifles to flame throwers, phosphorus grenades to different mortars, and howitzers to 200mm artillery pieces. The grisly damage that those weapons inflicted on people was to convince us that, by contrast, biological agents were rather tame and almost humane. People would get sick, very sick, but property was usually not damaged and a large percent of those afflicted would not die and, in fact, would get better, usually after vomiting nonstop for two weeks. It was a convincing performance and I, for one, never had any moral qualms about serving in the BWD.

For about the next thirty years, I never mentioned to any living person anything about what I did at Fort Detrick or other places I visited in connection with my work. In fact, I had to sign a release before I started my assignment that should anything happen to me, my remains would not be available to my family. The idea was that should an accident happen, and I succumbed to some secret agent with which I was working, the identity of the agent that killed me would be buried with me in a specially prescribed government-issued, lead-lined coffin.

The crack in my self-imposed silence was broken by seeing Dustin Hoffman in the role of a BW medical officer in a movie called *Outbreak*. There, in front of a movie theater full of potential security risks and likely NKVD operatives, I watched with amazement and horror as a large range of ultra-secret matters unraveled, in glorious Technicolor, in an all-too-real drama about a biological outbreak on an unprepared and unsuspecting population. After seeing that movie, in the infrequent situation when people inquired about what I actually did during my Army career, I told them to go and see the film. If *Outbreak* were not showing, they could find out even more about what I was doing by watching Jude Law and Kate Winslet in *Contagion*.

My initial assignment was in an equipment design center in Detrick, helping to create more efficient machinery for the bulk manufacture of toxic agents. Our job was to make the move from Petri dish to bulk manufacture as simple and safe as possible. I actually was involved in the invention of several patented innovations in biotechnical fermentation.

It was at this point that I was sent to take extension courses in pathogenic bacteriology at the University of Maryland. Then someone discovered that I had (rather sheepishly) listed French and Russian as my native language skills, and I was transferred to the Information and Analysis Branch at the base. This was as close as I came to being a counter-intelligence officer. I was not a spy.

Detrick was not all work, however. One day I was summoned to the Commanding Officers' headquarters. What had I done now, I wondered?

"Lieutenant," announced my CO. "I see here you played baseball in college. Do I have that correct?"

"Yes, sir, but very badly I'm afraid, and at the intramural level only," I replied.

"Good. You've just been promoted to be player manager of our baseball team with immediate effect. Good luck! I'll see you at our season's opener."

To describe my baseball prowess as marginal would be a gross overstatement. I played second base because that was the shortest distance one had to throw the baseball to reach first base. I could reach first base from third base but only on a bounce. I especially dreaded having to try to tag a runner trying to steal second. Imagine 200 pounds of human flesh hurling at you at ninety miles per hour, with

The camp commander at Fort Detrick in Frederick, Maryland threw out the first baseball in what turned out to be a completely winless season.

cleated feet high, trying to reach a fifteen-inch square canvas bag you were ordered to protect at all cost. It was a certain recipe for disaster. But it was even worse when I had to bat. I would take my stance at the extreme edge of the batter's box and hope to be walked. The few times I ever actually hit the ball were usually, I am certain, with my eyes shut. But by far my biggest problem was when the pitcher threw a curve ball. I was pathetically petrified that the ball, which was coming straight for me, would fail to curve at the last moment, and so I hardly ever waited to find out.

Fortunately I did not have to play very often, only when we had eight players show up for the game. I believe we never won a single game. Fort Detrick was a tiny base with a handful of soldiers. Our score lines resembled football scores more than baseball. But we had all the trappings—our own bus and uniforms, and a schedule that never seemed to end.

I never understood why I was not awarded the Fort Detrick Distinguished Baseball Service Medal.

I was assigned to a top-secret biological warfare division, Fort Detrick.

55

Another Chance to Serve?

My official full-time active duty in the U.S. Army ended in September 1956, exactly two years after I started.

Despite some attractive inducements to stay in the Regular Army on active duty, I decided to take the alternative route to be de-mobbed (demobilized) and remain on active reserve for six years, as I had agreed by written contract when I joined the Reserve Officers' Training Corps.

The definition of "active reserve" was never clearly spelled out, as it depended on your actual MOS (Military Occupational Specialty classification), location, and physical condition. If I lived in New York City, my commitment was a one day per month education and drill session plus as much as two weeks per year on active field duty— anywhere in the world.

As I was waiting in line to complete my discharge papers, the officer in front of me bragged that he was not going to get involved in any useless Reserve training and would refuse to give them his official home address or a forwarding address. When my turn for the exit interview came up, I took a far less aggressive approach and simply said I was unsure of what my forwarding address might be at this time.

Somehow, as a result, I never served any time in the active Reserve, never attended a monthly training session as far as I can recall, and never went for two weeks of active Reserve field training.

To my surprise, in about 1961, when my designated six years of active Reserve duty were almost completed, I received, by special delivery post, an information letter from First Army Headquarters inviting me to join a Special Forces Reserve Airborne Detachment unit that was being imminently activated in the New York metropolitan area. Newly married with one young son, slightly overweight and with poor eyesight, and having allowed my alleged language qualifications to atrophy, I politely declined the offer by not responding. I honestly thought that would be the end of story.

Then, in 1964, the United States became involved in the Vietnam War. By then, as I was living and working in London and had fulfilled my Reserve duty obligation, I never even considered the possibility of being recalled to active duty. It seems that the Secretary of Army had different plans for me. An official Army cable signed by Robert McNamara requested that I arrange my personal, professional, and

HEADQUARTERS FIRST ARMY
Governors Island, New York 4, N. Y.

AHFKC(13) 350

SUBJECT: Information Letter

TO: 1st Lt Henry M. Strage
        131 Riverside Drive
        New York, New York

1. The purpose of this letter is to apprise you of the imminent activation of a Special Forces Reserve Detachment (Airborne) in the NYC or Newark, NJ metropolitan areas. This organization will consist of one each AA (Administrative) and FB (Operational) and ten (10) FA (Operational) Teams organized under T O&E 33-510R, 25 April 1955. All Teams will be activated full strength officer (1 Maj, 1 Capt, & 4 Lts, per FB; 1 Capt & 1 Lt per FA Team & 1 WO in the AA) and reduced strength enlisted (10 EM per FB; 8 per FA; & 9 in the AA). For those desiring further information on the breakdown of team rank and MOS structure it is recommended you consult your military district headquarters.

2. A study of the records at this headquarters reveals that you are currently carried on the rolls of the Reserve Control Group and possess one or both of the following desired prerequisites for assignment to Special Forces training.

    a. Airborne trained and qualified prefix or suffix (whichever is applicable) "7" to your primary MOS.

    b. Non-airborne trained but possessing desired language qualifications.

3. Inasmuch as the records disclose you are not assigned to a specific reserve unit, the attached questionnaire is being furnished you in order to ascertain your desires for transfer from your present status to the new Reserve SF organization in question. Said questionnaire does not represent a formal application for parachute and/or Special Forces operations and training. Should you desire to apply please complete the attached inclosure together with any other information you desire and mail to CG, First Army, Governors Island, NY, Attn: ACofS G-3, Reserve SF Advisor.

(over)

What appeared at first to be a prank was unfortunately very real.

commercial affairs in such a way as to be ready to join my designated Special Forces unit within forty-eight hours in Fort Benning, Georgia.

Alberta was sure this was a practical joke by some of my old school buddies. It unfortunately was not.

By some stroke of luck, however, it turned out I was not needed at all.

I feel certain that the outcome of that war was not seriously affected by my absence.

PART VII
A REAL JOB

No more long beach holidays with Stanley

Introduction
Home from the Front Lines

My return home to New York in 1956, officially as a war veteran, did not include a ticker-tape parade down West End Avenue or a gala homecoming ball at the Waldorf Astoria. What I did have was a small bank account, a GI Bill educational grant that would cover all financial costs for education, and free medical care for the rest of my life through the Veterans Administration hospital network around the country. When I arrived back, most of my friends were either still in the armed forces or in law school.

While the prospect of taking the next few years "off" and going back to school full-time to earn a graduate degree was very appealing, having been away from home for the best part of the last six years, I decided whatever I was going to do, I should be based at home. New York had a wide variety of educational institutions from which to choose and most had very extensive schedules of part-time classes.

I decided on balance that the best first step for my postgraduate training would be an MBA, Master of Business Administration. Both Columbia and New York University had excellent programs. I chose to enroll in Columbia's business school, which had an outstanding faculty and was closer to 131 Riverside Drive.

The choice of full-time employment was marginally more complicated, with more variables, a great variety of opportunities, and many attractive learning challenges.

And so it was in September 1956, by an unscientific but pragmatic process of elimination, I joined a small chemical engineering partnership called Singmaster & Breyer. Having been briefly exposed to the character and lifestyle of large multinational chemical companies, I had concluded that this was not a way of life that would suit me. While I qualified via a nationwide examination for a Foreign Services appointment, the prospect of hanging coats and stamping official papers in some far-off embassy for a few years did not fill me with great confidence that by doing so, someday I might be the U.S. representative to the United Nations.

Joining an engineering company that was involved in the design and construction of chemical plants around the world provided an excellent chance to learn and develop a variety of skills in many challenging disciplines. Small teams of engineers executed most of the work, which provided an ideal learning environment. And I had a lot to learn.

56

Chlorine, Newark, Terrorism, and Me

Chlorine is a yellow-green gas with a strong smell of bleach, which most of us know is a part of common salt. It is abundant in nature and is critical to most forms of life, including human life. It combines with almost all elements to produce chlorides, of which NaCl and HCl are the most commonly known. Our bodies produce HCl in our stomachs and, if not controlled, it can produce ulcers and heartburn. Chlorine was one of the first known weapons of mass destruction extensively used by the Germans in World War I.

Newark is the largest city in New Jersey and the sixty-fifth largest city in the United States.

Terrorism is the calculated use of violence or the threat of violence to obtain goals that are religious, political, or economic.

The process for producing chlorine that was invented in 1904 and is still used today involves the electrolysis of brine, or sodium chloride. Electricity introduced into the brine liberates free chlorine at the negative carbon anode, produces sodium at the positive pole, and reacts with water, producing sodium hydroxide and hydrogen. The entire process is carried out in what has come to be known as a "Hooker cell."

In 1957 much of the nation's manufacture of chlorine was produced in Hooker-type vertical diaphragm cells.

Standard practice and contractual obligation require the design and construction firm to test the installation before turning it over to the owners, running it at rated capacity for a prearranged period of time, usually three weeks.

Chlorine plants are run 24/7 and so it was necessary for Singmaster & Breyer to arrange for round-the-clock staffing that could operate the newly constructed plant at its agreed capacity before handing it over and, importantly, being paid for its work.

Being a registered PE (Professional Engineer), single, and involved in the actual design of the plant, I was an obvious choice for running the testing during the grave shift, which was from midnight to noon the next day.

The plant was relatively simple to operate, consisting of about fifty huge Hooker-type cells. Brine was pumped into each cell automatically. Both carbon cathodes were lowered into the brine as they were consumed. Chlorine gas was collected from each cell and stored in gas containers, and the sodium hydroxide flowed out of the cells as it was produced.

Each of the cells was topped by a heavy concrete cover, sometimes called a "hat," that sat on the cell and was not attached, in case the pressure in the cell increased. If the pressure began to climb, the heavy cover would "pop" up, giving an early warning that something was wrong. As the cover by design was not airtight, it was not uncommon for tiny, usually undetectable, quantities of chlorine gas to escape into the atmosphere. These so-called "sniff gases" were sucked up into a plant-wide vacuum system and eventually passed into a massive tank containing a bed of sodium hydroxide, where the stray chlorine gas would be absorbed and neutralized.

One weekend evening during the test period, when I was the designated plant manager, the unmistakable smell of chlorine gas became unexpectedly strong. One of the operators came over to me and calmly suggested I might want to check the green gas that was conspicuously collecting above the plant.

A quick check of the instrumentation that I had designed suggested that everything was normal. Nevertheless, as the smell of chlorine gas became stronger and stronger, I reached the self-evident conclusion that something was seriously amiss. The small quantities of gas escaping from the cell were not, in fact, being vacuumed up by the sniff gas collection system and were not being neutralized in the sodium hydroxide tank.

As the poisonous green cloud of chlorine over the factory grew larger, I had visions of being charged with the murder of almost a million people in Newark. I only had two options.

First, I could shut down the plant completely and incur the lifelong wrath of my employer, who would be forced to restart the trial period and no doubt suggest that I should go back to delivering flowers.

The second option was to keep the plant operating at rated capacity, and hope and pray that the ever-increasing green cloud of poisonous chlorine gas currently on its way to downtown Newark would somehow be dispersed in the wind and somehow the ill-smelling green wind would change direction.

A third option was to hope that the malfunctioning sniff gas system would fix itself and begin doing its specified job. Since at that point, I had no idea why it was not working, fixing it did not seem like a viable option.

As I was trying quickly to think of what to do, for one whimsical minute I was actually hoping that most of the Newark population had their own personal gas masks.

I shut the plant down.

The entire plant was fully automated with the exception of the sniff gas tank. Someone had forgotten to tell me this significant fact.

At noon, our next operating shift arrived to continue the three-week test run.

"Who shut down this plant?" demanded the incredulous project manager.

"Me," I responded.

"Do you realize what you've done to our hand-over schedule? What were you thinking, Henry?" Elliot demanded.

"I had to shut it down to avoid gassing a million or so people living downwind from the plant," I explained. "It wasn't a tough decision."

No one was poisoned that fateful night at the plant or in Newark.

I did not lose my job. The problem was that the gas collection tank had to be periodically replenished manually with sodium hydroxide. The following day an emergency automatic replenishment pump was installed next to the sniff tank so that there would always be the correct amount of sodium hydroxide in the tank to absorb all of the chlorine gas that escaped from the cells.

I do not remember ever being asked to serve as plant manger on a start-up again.

One year later I was transferred to the S&B marketing department.

Footnote to history, from the *Wall Street Journal,* 21 May 2003:

> The nation's leaders considered drastic measures to combat industrial terrorism. High on their list of most likely targets for terrorist attacks were one hundred chemical industry factories producing toxic chemicals that could release poisonous clouds that could kill or sicken a million people. The senate unanimously passed a tough bill in 2002.

57

Insider Trading, Mea Culpa

As we recently watched the movie *Wall Street*, my mind drifted back to that era, when I was a newly hired chemical engineer at Singmaster & Breyer and had my first taste of the games people play to get rich. I found myself, one day, assigned to special short projects, where it was assumed I could do little harm and learn something useful. My simple assignments seemed to be just a step above fetching coffee for the boss but, in fact, one such simple project made financial headlines.

It was all about the manufacturing of USP grade citric acid. Because of its extensive use of citric acid in the food industry, the FDA and other government agencies were keen to ensure that purity standards were meticulously adhered to. A single company, Pfizer Chemical, had a virtual monopoly on the production of citric acid in the United States. In the late fifties, a small, little known specialty company called Kolker Chemical announced to the industry's surprise that it had built a plant in southern New Jersey that was capable of manufacturing USP grade citric acid, using its own proprietary process, and would soon be going into direct competition with Pfizer. The mark-up on citric acid was exceptionally high and represented an important source of profits for whoever was able to produce it to the demanding standards required for human consumption. Kolker Chemical, although a listed New York Stock Exchange company, was an exceptionally marginal player in the chemical industry, and its announcement that it would be able to produce citric acid using its own proprietary process and know-how became a significant business item and caused a major stir in the financial markets.

Because of the almost unanimous skepticism about Kolker's announcement, it was decided that an independent chemical laboratory should be hired to test the veracity of its claim. Singmaster & Breyer was hired to visit the plant and take samples for analysis by a recognized independent laboratory.

I was assigned the task of calling on the factory, collecting the samples, and delivering them to the designated laboratory, where the purity of the product would be checked. In order to ensure fair play, the date and time of the visit would not be announced beforehand.

Armed with a current flow sheet and map of the Kolker plant, I proceeded to study the flow of the product through the maze of vessels, heat exchangers, pipes, and holding tanks in the entire plant and mark out where I would take the designated twelve samples. Roy Sweet, my first boss and mentor, confirmed my decisions and together we selected a day and time the following week for the visit. All I had to do was find out how to get to and from the plant, collect and label the sampling bottles beforehand, and decide what to wear on my first solo assignment.

Kolker Chemical at 80 Lister Avenue, on the Passaic River, was a multi-product chemical site, primarily a producer of pesticides and herbicides. I found it without problems and was warmly greeted by both the plant manager and the chief chemist. In the factory conference room, I spread out my marked-up flow sheet and showed them exactly where I proposed to take my samples. After a short discussion, I turned down the offer of refreshments and went out to the factory floor with the plant manager as my guide.

For most people, a chemical plant appears as a veritable cats-cradle of pipes, curiously shaped vessels, tanks, storage containers, motors, pumps, instruments, and gauges of every possible description. All of this is in addition to a mixture of unpleasant smells, viscous fluids flowing in often open trenches along the "road" within the plant, curious noises emanating from foreign-looking contraptions, and an army of men wearing hard hats and dressed in overalls and white coats, all moving around in silence, carrying out carefully prescribed tasks. That was exactly what I found, but having worked in such surroundings before, I knew exactly what to expect.

My sampling process was uneventful. I followed my roadmap

precisely, and all the locations of the valves from which I was to take samples were exactly in the places specified in the flow sheet. After collecting the samples, I passed on a luncheon invitation and drove directly to the testing laboratory site to deliver my tray of samples as planned. Job done. It all seemed like a pleasant way to spend an afternoon. Did I have to spend four years in engineering school for this?

Of course, the financial press was made aware of this independent testing process and dutifully waited for the results to be published. I am sure the Kolker brothers and other investors were eager to know the results. Myself, I was anxious to get to my next assignment and do some real engineering problem solving.

The results were made public about a week later and were much better than anticipated. Kolker was producing 99.9 percent pure citric acid. As a result, the Kolker share price skyrocketed. I do not recall by how much, as I was already busy on another project and had little interest in the assay results or their financial consequences, as I certainly would not have dreamed of either buying or selling Kolker shares.

I happily deposited my bimonthly check and never even thought about how rich I could have been.

Fifteen years later, at a conference in 1971 where I was part of panel of "experts," someone approached me and introduced himself. I was certain that I had never met him before. He introduced himself as Dr. Bajer and said he was at one time chief chemist at Kolker Chemical works, and he reminded me that he had accompanied me when I went to the plant to take samples of citric acid.

"I can tell you now," he explained with a wry smile on his face, "that we played a little trick on you. Sorry. Before you came, we filled every vessel, pipe, and heat exchanger in the plant with USP citric acid that we had purchased from Pfizer. Since we did not know exactly when you were coming we just kept recycling Pfizer's material through the whole plant until you arrived. So all the samples you so carefully and professionally collected were actually not our material but Pfizer's."

I do not recall what my response was. By that time, the company had ceased to exist. In any case, I was certain nobody would be particularly interested. More than ten years later, in August 1983, several lawsuits were filed against the owners of the Lister Avenue plant for contravention of the hazardous waste laws by dumping dioxin and other wastes directly into the Passaic River.

58

The Advantages of Having
a Big Nose

1958 was a good year to be a bachelor in New York. Peace finally broke out in Korea. A gallon of gas cost twenty-four cents. The New York Yankees won the World Series—again. The U.S. launched its first satellite—Explorer. And if you were a freshman at Harvard, it would only cost $1,250 tuition for the year.

Everyone in my gang was in his mid-twenties, had completed his military service, and was starting his career. Maury Allen was a baseball reporter for the *New York Post*. Gerard Smetana was just beginning his legal career. Marty Hanfling was on a relatively low rung of the corporate ladder in a major U.S. utilities company. I was at Singmaster & Breyer, helping to build chemical plants wherever clients would pay us to build them.

Saturday was our night for going out on the town. Usually this meant a play or concert followed by dinner, which often ended up in Greenwich Village, where all the action seemed to be.

As I was getting ready to go out and pick up my date one evening, the phone rang rather impatiently.

BOB:	Hi, Hank! This is Bob Klied. Remember me from WPI? We were in the same fraternity a few years back.
HENRY:	Hello, Bob. What a nice surprise to hear from you! Are you still living in Connecticut? What are you up to these days?
BOB:	Hank, I need some advice.
HENRY:	How can I help?
BOB:	Well, you see, my mother was talking to her friend in Boston and they decided that I should meet this girl from New Jersey who was living in New York, who was very attractive, single, and really smart. The girl was my mother's friend's niece and they agreed this would be a nice arrangement.
HENRY:	Good for you, Bob. So what is the problem?
BOB:	Well, I don't know New York very well and I thought you might have some suggestions for what we could do this evening. I have picked up my date and am calling from her apartment in midtown Manhattan.
HENRY:	It is Saturday night. You have left it rather late, old buddy. It is after seven already.

BOB: Yes, I know, but have you any suggestions?

HENRY: Look, Bob. A couple of us are going down to Greenwich Village to hear Woody Allen play some jazz and have dinner afterwards. You are welcome to come along.

Well, Bob was delighted that he now had a plan for his blind date, and we arranged to meet in one of our favorite haunts for dinner, 17 Barrow Street. Bob arrived early and was taken to our usual table next to a large window facing the street. He told his date to "watch out for Hank Strage. He should be coming along shortly."

"I have no idea what he looks like," his date responded. "How I am supposed to look out for him?"

Bob's response will live on in infamy. "You can't miss Hank. He has a big nose."

Soon everyone arrived and introductions were made. When Bob introduced his date, I remember thinking how odd to name a child after a province in Canada. As the meal progressed, I made a mental note to myself. This Canadian province lady was a lot more attractive than *my* date, and certainly smarter and a lot more interesting. One of these days, I thought to myself, I must ask Bob if he would mind sharing her telephone number with me. As the evening wore on, all of my extensive high-secret military intelligence background kicked in, and when this Canadian lady told us that she worked in publishing for Alfred Knopf, I immediately deduced that I could reach her by telephone in her office on Monday. No sense wasting time, I thought.

Being shy by nature and temperament, I finally gathered up enough courage to call late in the afternoon on Monday. I would

*Alberta Gotthardt, 1958—the lowest paid
college graduate in New York City*

have asked Bob if it were OK with him if I tried to see his blind date, but, like Cyrano, I was not amused by the way he suggested I could be identified. Fortunately, Alberta seemed to remember me, and to my everlasting surprise and unbelievable good fortune, she seemed happy to meet for dinner later that week.

Our first date came dangerously close to being our last. I chose a tiny, romantic French bistro called Les Deux Lapins. How was I to know that Alberta had never eaten rabbit? In fact, she did that first day we met, and I am certain she has never touched rabbit since then. To

No competition for Cyrano de Bergerac in the nose department here.

add to the possible disaster, my after-dinner entertainment idea was to go to the Barnum and Bailey Circus. What could be more exciting than seeing close-up the world's greatest circus, not in one but in three rings? Alberta was politely unimpressed. I don't know which was the bigger disappointment for Alberta, the rabbit or the circus.

If she thought I was some sort of mad eccentric, she certainly didn't show it. In fact, we had two more rendezvous that first week, *sans* rabbit or circus. Dinners, movies, concerts followed in the next few weeks. It was soon obvious to me that this was rapidly becoming a serious romantic encounter.

Our whirlwind romance almost came to a screeching halt after several weeks of high-intensity encounters. I had arranged to lead a busload of spring skiers to Tuckerman's Ravine. It was obvious to me that this would be a wonderful opportunity to spend more time with Alberta, despite the fact that she had never skied before. In fact, she had made a prior engagement for that weekend, in Washington. The prospect of not seeing her for a whole weekend was emotionally unbearable to me. How could she do this to us? Would this signal the end of a glorious romance?

Absence certainly makes the heart grow fonder, and when we saw each other again after going our separate ways that fateful weekend, I had decided that I had fallen insanely in love and couldn't possibly live for the rest of my life without her at my side. My dilemma was, how was I going to tell her about my decision?

It was at about this time, a few weeks after we first met, that I realized that I had kept my newly found treasure and future life partner all to myself. It was about time that I had her meet the family so that she could have a preview into what she might be getting herself.

I found the perfect occasion—my mother's birthday party. As there would be a lot of people around, Alberta would not feel as if she were "on display" and could blend in with the crowd. Of course, guests would know something was up, as this would be the first time I would bring a date to a strictly family event. For some reason, rather than the usual home venue for family events, it was decided to hire a private room in a restaurant for the party. The place selected was a Russian bistro called Balalaika, in midtown Manhattan.

As I hoped and suspected, Alberta blended painlessly and quickly into the crowd and her name, at least for that evening, was changed from Alberta to Dorogayoalbertushka or Mayozolotse Albertushka. Neither of these terms of endearment registered with Alberta, and it would be years later until she realized people were actually talking to or about her.

470

As the evening rolled on amidst much merriment, songs, and toasts mostly in Russian, Alberta became more relaxed and began to participate in the spirit of the celebration. All was going well until someone noticed that she was the only one not drinking. Russians typically do not drink vodka. They swallow it, usually in one gulp, which is thrown from the glass as far back in one's mouth as possible, passing painlessly past ones tonsils and sliding effortlessly in one's stomach. Rather than a thimble-sized shot glass, vodka at parties was customarily drunk out of tumblers that could be as much as the equivalent of four or five shot glasses.

Alberta managed to avoid drinking any vodka until my mother came to our table. It was customary for the one being celebrated to stop by each table and be honored with a special toast and by everyone at the table. The entire table was expected to participate. For the toast, Alberta was handed a glass of vodka, which she politely drank at the appropriate time. This was her first taste, and she described it later as drinking liquefied glass slivers. I am sure she must have thought, what kind of a vodka-guzzling, decadent Russian family is this? *My* thoughts were, am I witnessing the final stages of a glorious romance?

Somehow the evening passed and Alberta's performance was unanimously awarded an alpha plus. A bit later, I finally summoned sufficient courage to ask her to spend the rest of our lives together. And to my constant amazement, she accepted. We were married a few months later and there was no vodka at the wedding. There was wine instead.

The rest—well, almost the rest—is history.

... and the happy ending. October 12, 1958.

59

How Warren Buffet Paid for Our Honeymoon

When I was transferred to the Singmaster & Breyer marketing department there were only two people in the department. That explains why I started my new career in chemical plant construction sales as director of international marketing. In addition, there was a rumor that I spoke three languages. My boss, Jim Roy, was a very kindly, soft-spoken engineer, who welcomed me into the department and promised me that I was about to embark on a long, lucrative, and challenging career.

After a few weeks in my new position, I concluded that the

majority of our efforts were responding to inquiries rather than trying to develop new business. In fact, most of my duties in those first few months were playing host to potential overseas clients and very often their wives. In the main, most of the visitors had already made some commitment and their visits were more ceremonial than strictly commercial. I saw the Empire State Building, the Statue of Liberty, and the Metropolitan Museum of Art so often that the guards began greeting me by my first name. If I were honest, I should have put "International Nanny" rather than "Director of International Marketing" on my visiting card.

One of these ceremonial visits, however, led eventually to a small but important order to construct a chemical plant in India. Gopalkrishna Singhania, of J.K. Industries in India, was a charming and sophisticated international industrialist whom I was instructed to host while he was in the United States. I had no significant input to the technical or commercial aspects of the final deal, but Gopal and I quickly established a close, and eventually long-lasting relationship that I am certain helped seal the arrangement. I could now use my business card. (Long after I had left S&B, Alberta and I had a delightful visit with Gopal and his family in India.)

S&B chemical plant construction activities were well respected internationally but limited to a few established market niches. At a high-level strategic planning meeting of the marketing department, Roy and I concluded that we should try to acquire the rights, or at least a license, to some proprietary chemical industry processes that we could market and hopefully sell alongside our traditional products.

It was at about this time, during the autumn of 1958, that Alberta and I, having already decided to marry, began to consider some options for a honeymoon. Ironically, some of the corporations that had licenses we might be interested in were in Europe, one of the honeymoon destinations we were considering. The Eureka moment came when I put the two challenges together. Why not combine a honeymoon to Europe with a marketing trip to explore license arrangements? This certainly was practical, although perhaps not very romantic.

It did not take long to find three likely commercial targets, Montecatini in Italy, Rhone Poulenc in France, and I.G. Farben in Germany. Jim approved the plan in principle. I sealed the deal with the news that since this was highly speculative and I was planning to go to Europe in any case, I offered to pay all my travel expenses if I could combine my commercial objectives with my honeymoon plans and receive my salary while traveling. It was an offer he could not, or at least did not refuse. At this point, there was no discussion of how long the trip might be. There was one major bottleneck in this otherwise imaginative scheme. On a salary of $11,000 a year ($82,500 in 2012 currency), it would be difficult to travel very far, especially after paying taxes.

While working for S&B during the day, most of my weekday evenings were spent at Columbia Business School, where one of the most popular courses was on investment management, taught by the legendary Benjamin Graham and David Dodd. The "Oracle of Omaha," Warren Buffet, often spoke of their principles as the basis for all of his investment success.

The night version of the course, while not taught by either Graham or Dodd, was nevertheless extremely popular, as it was liberally infested by visiting Wall Street gurus. They frequently turned up in the evening class as visiting experts to reveal all of their secrets, especially as they related to the concept of value investment, now frequently cited by Buffet.

Unlike Buffet, when I was ten years old I did not want to become a stockbroker. However, investing was a very tempting occupation as one sat in class and listened to the heroic tales of how the uninitiated students were making fortunes. I decided to develop my own risk-free interpretation of the value-added investment laws that Warren Buffet loved so much.

One route to owning equities was and still is buying options on a specific equity rather than the share itself. Options allow you the chance to make money, whether the stock market goes up or down, at some predetermined time in the future. These options are known as "puts" or "calls." Calls increase in value when the underlying stock is going up. Puts increase in value when the stock drops.

At the time, the stock market was rocketing. Hence I concluded that calls were a better bet. Which ones to bet on? My concept was to buy three options each in very different industrial sectors. To make a handsome profit, only one of the sectors had to go up beyond the so-called "strike price." Since one did not exercise options that were not "in the money" (by letting them lapse), the only amount you lost was the price of the original option, not the cost of the drop in value of the underlying stock, thus limiting your losses.

The three sectors and stocks I chose were electronics (GE), transportation (American Airlines), and pharmaceuticals (Johnson and Johnson). To my everlasting amazement, on this particular occasion all three equities boomed and their corresponding options became very valuable, which is why I still remember which they were. I made a small fortune, or at least enough to make a three-month European honeymoon practical and a so-called business trip a reality.

Thank you, Warren!

Returning to the site of our honeymoon at Port Soller in Majorca twenty years later. The city had changed a lot. We stayed the same.

I did not start out with the objective of washing the whole apartment.

478

60

The Cleanest Apartment in New York City

You might be forgiven for thinking that the photo is an advertisement for a Whirlpool dishwasher. In fact, it is the beginning of a drama that in the end created the cleanest apartment in New York City.

Alberta and I flew in separate planes until our youngest child, Jennifer, was twenty-five years old. This was to prevent the catastrophe of having our children grow up as orphans, while we enjoyed the pleasures of traveling to exotic—and not so exotic—destinations. Usually we were able to book planes that departed within an hour or so of each other. On this occasion, the two planes we booked after a stay in New York were a few hours apart. I let Alberta take the earlier plane and I was left to "straighten" out our friend Reiko Ohye's apartment, where we had been staying.

"All you need to do is put the dirty dishes in the dishwasher, add some soap, and push a button. No problem," explained my normally didactic wife.

After putting the dishes in their appointed racks, adding soap, and pushing the button, I proceeded to put my things in my suitcase and got ready to go to the airport. While I seldom was early for a flight, I also never missed a flight.

I noticed on my way out through the kitchen that the dishwasher was leaking. I stopped the machine and opened the door to see if perhaps something was blocking the overflow opening. This diagnosis was based on my four years of engineering education. All I found inside were soap suds, which seemed odd, but perhaps this machine operated differently from ours in London.

When the leaking got worse and started to take up most of the kitchen floor, I was getting worried about how I could leave the apartment with this apparently rogue dishwasher spewing soap suds out into the kitchen. I concluded that I had too much soap in the machine and it needed to be rinsed away. No problem.

I confidently turned the knob to the "rinse" mark and went to collect my coat and bag. But just to be on the safe side, before I rang for the lift, I decided to check on the dishwasher. To my horror, when I crept back to the kitchen, I found a few inches of glistening white soap suds on the floor. I would just use a sponge and get these off the floor. With the aid of a sponge and dust bin, I began to feel like Mickey Mouse in "The Sorcerer's Apprentice" (*Fantasia*), trying to sweep the water away.

The next step was my biggest mistake! While it was still on "rinse," I opened the door to the machine. A virtual avalanche of suds cascaded out and eventually found their way into most of the remaining areas of the apartment. With a vision of the whole apartment house being soon enveloped in the bubbling soap suds, I decided to make a hasty retreat and read about the resulting storm in the next day's newspaper.

Why didn't someone tell me there is a difference between soap for dishes and soap especially prepared for automatic dishwashers?

61

Career Crossroads, Mark III

One of the requirements for becoming a licensed Professional Engineer in the State of New York is to achieve a score of 82 percent on an eight-hour examination on the fundamentals, principles, and practices of civil, electrical, mechanical, and chemical engineering. After almost three years of working at Singmaster & Breyer, my colleagues had embarrassed me into trying to pass the examination, an incredibly detailed examination of one's knowledge of a broad range of engineering problems in twenty-one subject areas. In fact, there were bets made as to how low my score would be. The most common preparation was to take a review course that highlighted the major subjects on the exam, but this was not a trivial commitment of time and effort, as it required forty-five hours of weekday evening and Saturday morning class time plus, of course, homework.

You were required to know everything from how to build a bridge to the details of designing a modern hydroelectric power station or a drainage system for a large modern city. As a chemical engineer, I might as well have been learning Greek philosophy. On the positive side, to replicate real life conditions, all parts of the exam were "open book." Depending on how big a suitcase you could carry into the exam hall, there were no restrictions on what books you could use during the test. The skill was not how many books you could carry but rather how quickly you could search for the right page in the right book to help you respond to the question. As this was 1959 B.C.C. (before computers and calculators), preparation for the test included fine tuning your manual search skills in real books.

By some miraculous stroke of good luck, I passed the exam the first time and proudly hung my official license on the wall behind my desk and ordered my own personalized embossing seal. I was now qualified to design six-lane highways, build suspension bridges, or develop modern municipal power stations, all undoubtedly very useful skills, and received a modest salary increase. I happily settled down to what I fully expected would be a long, fulfilling career as a chemical engineer consultant.

Fate stepped in and altered my course. A celebrated West Coast engineering firm, Fluor, advised by a respected management consulting firm, concluded that it should establish an East Coast presence by acquiring and integrating a small, well-regarded engineering practice in New York. Singmaster & Breyer was identified and in the early part of 1959 became the East Coast office of Fluor International.

This acquisition had only a minimal impact on any of the S&B employees except me. Somehow I was identified by Cy Fluor, the chairman, as an ideal candidate for transfer to Los Angeles to join the international marketing department there. An increase in salary, all moving expenses paid, a generous settling-in allowance, and an exciting career-challenging opportunity were all tantalizingly dangled before my eyes. In addition, a suitably appropriate title, "Vice President, International Project Development," was suggested.

Changing jobs is always a traumatic experience. When such a change also involves a major physical relocation to a completely new environment three thousand miles away, non-career related factors also have to be considered. Three factors helped me to decide. First, Alberta and I were both attending Columbia University graduate schools part-time, studying for advanced degrees. That would have to be postponed or abandoned. Second, New York was very much the epicenter of our social universe. Our family, friends, and most social activities were all concentrated in the New York area. Finally, the position as it was described to me would involve a glamorous global travel agenda—a chance to see the world—and spend a significant amount of time away from home. I reluctantly declined Cy's attractive offer.

Having turned down a big promotion from the chairman of the company, it seemed clear that the continuation of my career would require a major adjustment. I was fortunate to have developed close personal ties with a thoughtful and wise professor at Columbia Business School, Charles (Charlie) Summers, with whom I had taken several courses. He was, next to Alberta, the closest thing I had to a personal mentor, and I felt at ease exploring such serious matters as changing careers.

"Well," Charlie inquired, "what would you like to do with the rest of your life?"

Instead of asking him, "What are my options?" I told him that my course work at Columbia had opened my eyes to a variety of worlds about which I had previously known little. I indicated three broad possible career areas I would like to explore. First, a public sector appointment, perhaps in the U.S. diplomatic corps; second, something in the financial sector close to venture capital or private investment banking; and third, management consulting, a field about which I knew the least but was mesmerized by, having taken a one-semester course with Bernard J. Muller-Tyne, a part-time adjunct professor whose day job was with a management consulting firm.

I was somewhat surprised at Charlie's responses.

"Diplomatic corps…do you really want to hang coats at formal receptions, approve an endless flow of visa applications, and have to learn how to speak some obscure foreign language in some remote country for the next five years?" He suggested, in any case, that I take the FO (Foreign Office) examination if that turned out to be my only option.

"Banking," my mentor said, "might be more interesting but after a few years of evaluating industries, and poring over annual reports and balance sheets, you'll get really bored and look for something new."

Finally, in respect to my third option, Charlie confided, "I do have some experience with management consulting. It is a challenging and continually varying profession. However," he said, looking straight into my eyes, in his most earnest voice, "I really don't think you have the temperament, patience, and leadership required to succeed in this highly competitive profession." He quickly followed with, "Why don't you join the faculty here at the business school? You'd be a great addition to our staff."

Several months after my chat with Charlie my career scoreboard was:

I had taken and barely passed the Foreign Service Examination.

I had an offer to join a small boutique, family-owned, venture capital firm called Payson Trask.

I postponed joining the business school faculty for at least the next thirty years.

I had an offer to join McKinsey & Company, a management consulting firm, in their New York office.

Despite Charlie's advice, I decided to join McKinsey. Ironically, the firm that had advised Fluor to acquire an East Coast engineering company was McKinsey & Company.

I maintained contact with Charlie, and he followed my career with much disbelief for many years.

Years later, I learned that the management consulting firm Bernard

J. Muller-Tyne worked for while teaching at Columbia at night was McKinsey & Company, although his career there was rather brief.

I proudly displayed my PE license when I joined McKinsey, just in case. It still hangs in my office at home today.

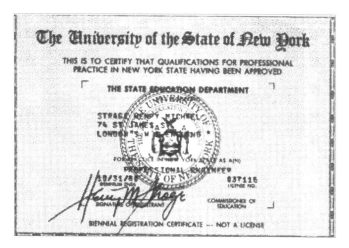

The much-coveted New York State Professional Engineering license gave me the right to design and construct roads, bridges, tunnels, and power stations. Anyone interested?

PART VIII

FISH AND CHIPS

For an American, merging seamlessly into the English establishment was not too difficult as long as you did not have to speak too often or for too long.

Introduction
"When a man is tired of London, he is tired of life…"

Our decision to come to London in 1962 was a no-brainer. It took about ten minutes to decide.

In the spring of 1962, the McKinsey & Company London office was hired by the then largest company in the United Kingdom, Imperial Chemical Industries (ICI), to help its newly appointed chairman, Sir Paul Chambers, review the organization and structure of his top management. This was an enormous coup for the Firm. When the largest company in the UK and the then second-largest chemical company in the world asks a relatively unknown American consulting company for help, people take notice. In addition, in 1962 management consulting in the UK was hardly a household term. Most people thought it was the result of an amalgamation of an accounting firm and time-and-motion experts. I recall one potential client prepared for our first meeting by arranging for us to have a list of all the typewriters, desks, and Gestetner machines in his various offices around the world.

The proposed assignment was going to be for a specifically limited time—six months was suggested.

62

Welcome to London

The surprise of McKinsey being hired by ICI was compounded by the fact that Sir Paul Chambers was the first chairman to be appointed by the board from outside the company. In addition, having been for most of his life in the insurance industry, he had no previous experience in chemical manufacturing.

To guarantee a successful outcome, McKinsey marshaled a top-heavy team of directors. This was a once-in-a-lifetime opportunity and would, if successful, clear our path for future professional activity at the highest level in the UK, the Commonwealth, and most likely for other industrially mature countries around the world. Our total London office at the time consisted of less than a dozen consultants.

The initial star-studded team consisted of Marvin Bower, Hugh Parker, Carl Hoffman, Gil Clee, and John McDonald, and when they discovered that hardly any of them had any understanding of the chemical industry, Gil Clee, with whom I had been working at Celanese Chemical Company in New York, asked if he could persuade Alberta and me to transfer to London for a limited six-month assignment to provide industry expertise to the team.

The cable in 1962 from Hugh Parker, the London office manager, changed our lives.

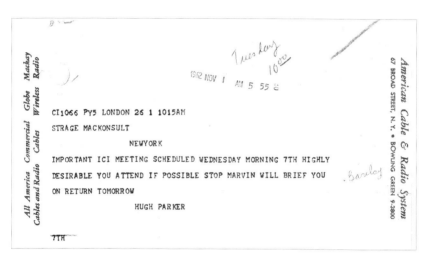

Marching orders from Hugh Parker, London office manager, was a dream come true.

Our first son, David, left, with his cousin Michael, my brother's first son, just before leaving for a temporary assignment to London.

We did not need much persuasion. On November 6, 1962, Alberta, our almost-three-year-old-son, David, and I found ourselves on a plane to London, economy class.

Our stay started inauspiciously when we arrived at Heathrow airport twelve hours later and were greeted by Jack Preschlack. Sending someone to the airport to welcome new London office staff was a lovely practice that, unfortunately, did not continue for long. Jack bundled David, a slightly pregnant Alberta, and me, with all of our luggage, onto a double-decker London airport public bus, and we majestically proceeded towards London to start an adventure that lasted for more than fifty years. Jack assured us this was the very best way to get from the airport to the city. The cost, he promised us, had no role in his decision.

The following day, with little fanfare and even less background information, I was ushered, under the watchful eye of officer manager Hugh Parker, into the ICI board lunchroom to be introduced to some members of the board. It was like a scene from a Thomas Hardy novel. The setting was more like a museum than a corporate dining room, and it was a surreal introduction to British boardroom practice.

We were escorted to lunch by the company secretary, Donald Heffendon. That was my first surprise since I soon learned that in the United Kingdom, the company secretary was a key member of the top management team and not a typist or file clerk. Then we were all offered pink gin. A basic rule in McKinsey was no drinks at lunchtime. When I politely refused, I was given the alternative standard fare, a tumbler of Scotch whiskey. Fortunately, I did not ask for ice (on the rocks). It would have been considered a great insult to poison ten-year-old, aged-in-the-barrel Scotch with ice. I thought I would just hold the glass and slowly drink it, until I saw Hugh sipping his pink gin.

Pre-lunch drinks served two purposes. First, it allowed latecomers to arrive and not have to be seated after everyone had begun the meal. Second, it was a chance to relax after a trying morning making momentous decisions. I soon concluded that it was best to schedule appointments with top management in the morning if at all possible.

Once we were seated, the first course arrived. In a rather small, two-handled soup dish, a clear soup was silently placed in front of me. I was immediately faced with the first of many stressful decisions. There was so much hardware before me that I was totally confused as to which was the correct weapon with which to attack the soup. There were at least three choices. No one had told me the difference between a dessert spoon, a soup spoon, and a coffee spoon, and I recall that on that day there were two spoons that might have been officially designated as soup spoons. Having made almost a classic blunder about the pre-dinner drinks, I decided I would watch carefully what others did and follow. As the soup course wound down, I noticed some of those around the table picked up the soup dish by each handle and slurped what was otherwise unavailable by spoon directly. I passed on this gesture, just to be on the safe side.

I was hoping the next course would be less traumatic for me. What appeared next, however, was something I had never seen before. In a small circular glass dish was a handful of shrimp (I later learned it was proper to call them "prawns"), on top of which was about half an inch of solid yellow butter. I discovered, by referring to the printed menu card proudly held upright in front of me in a silver place holder, that I had been served "potted shrimps." Apparently, before the advent of refrigeration, freshly caught tiny brown shrimp were simmered and preserved in small glass dishes under a blanket of butter, which could be stored in one's larder for long periods of time without spoiling. At least that is the story they told me.

While certainly familiar with shrimp, I was at a loss as to how to eat this obvious staple delicacy. Does one eat the butter first to gain access to the shrimp? Tip the whole glass dish upside down on your plate and then free the shrimps from their preservative? What about using the butter as a sauce? My concerns were somewhat abated when I saw that almost everyone had their own unique way of attacking this dish. Toasted triangles (browned, crust-free bread) were distributed and I resisted asking for cocktail sauce.

I was sure the main course would cause me no problems. Dover sole, new potatoes, and peas had to be straightforward. When the sole arrived, however, I became petrified. What arrived were not boneless sole filets but rather the whole fish—skin, head, body, fins, and tail altogether. Americans do not eat fish with bones. My own experience with fish turned out to be limited. I could easily handle gefilte fish, herring in various guises, including chopped herring, and even white fish in tomato sauce. While in the course of time, I learned that waiters would ask if you wanted the fish "on or off the bone," no such choice was provided in the ICI dining room. Deboning fish was considered an art form, and having some third party do the deboning was considered an unmanly act.

By this time, we had already been offered three different types of white wine to go with the fish, in addition to the pre-luncheon drinks.

Once again, I decided to watch exactly how the other guests were dealing with the whole fish. Unfortunately, my observations were not very helpful as, everyone seemed to have his own approach to this dish, too, but the individualism encouraged me to try. I felt similar to a surgeon on his first day in the operating theater. Had this been a hospital, I am sure the patient would have died on the operating table. My method was not a success. The plate resembled a miniature

Gettysburg battlefield scene.

Nevertheless, I was sure I would do better with the peas. I confidently picked up my fork and was about to shovel some peas onto it when I realized that everyone else had the tines of their forks pointing down, exactly the opposite from how I was holding my fork. Stabbing each pea separately seemed to be a wholly inefficient and time-consuming occupation. Instead, what was happening was that the peas were being energetically crushed onto forks with the prongs pointing down, using the knife as one would a snow shovel. This move was made more difficult for me because my fork and knife were in the wrong hands.

Having failed both the fish and pea-eating examination, I settled back comfortably and waited for the dessert course. At this point, I asked one of the waitresses if I could have some coffee please. "Sir," she responded, "unless you need to catch an early afternoon train, we customarily serve coffee after the sweet, savory, and cheese. Would that be satisfactory?" I could hardly imagine having to go through three more courses. In fact, fortuitously, I was given a choice.

I studied the menu card for guidance and watched what others were doing. The listed savories were not only bewildering but unintelligible. I could have Scotch woodcock, Welsh rabbit, or Angels on horseback. I concluded that dessert would be a fail-safe choice but on offer for sweet that first lunch was syllabub, gooseberry fool, or Roly Poly pudding.

As discretion is the better part of valor, I asked for cheese.

I later learned that the savory is the last course, following the sweet pudding or dessert course. It is designed to clear the palate before the port is served. Scotch woodcock is not an edible fowl but rather consists of scrambled egg on toast. Welsh rabbit is not a meat dish but melted cheese served on hot toast spread with Gentlemen's relish. Angels on horseback are usually oysters wrapped in fried bacon.

One of the early consequences of my less than brilliant luncheon performance came a few days later when, to the whole office's surprise, a call from ICI requesting my presence at a luncheon with the Company Secretary. After it was confirmed that the lunch was for me only, I wondered if I should call Alberta and tell her not to unpack.

In fact, Donald Heffendon's objective was far less sinister. At lunch, he kindly explained that he had observed me struggling while trying to operate on the sole the other day.

"Henry, my dear boy," Donald declared, "after this meal, I promise you will be awarded the silver fish knife medal as recognition for your skills in deboning and filleting any variety of edible fish served in the United Kingdom."

With this introduction, he proceeded with extreme kindness and exceptional skill to take me step by step through the acknowledged Royal procedure of eating fish in public places. This was one of the many lessons in my career as a management consultant that I learned from my clients.

Somehow I managed for the rest of my thirty years in McKinsey never to reveal the objectives of this luncheon appointment.

63

Never Talk to Strangers

The diminutive, smartly dressed lady carefully slid the train compartment door open and in a sweet, soft voice asked, "Is there a seat free in this compartment?"

"Yes, ma'am," Jack replied, "and may I help you with your case?"

"That is very kind of you. Yes, please."

Jack Preschlack and I were on our way home to London on the 18:35 train from Welwyn Garden City, after a long day at the ICI headquarters of the plastics division. It was in the early phases of our overall review, and each of us had just completed a full day of interviewing key executives. We planned to compare notes and decide on the next day's schedule during the hour-long ride. The division chairman, John Sissons, was keen that we meet separately with each member of his management team, in order to have a comprehensive view of the complexities of his division's operations and so better understand the myriad of strategic issues he was facing.

As both Jack and I had recently joined McKinsey, certain fundamental, absolutely immutable rules of professional behavior had been indelibly engraved in our brains. Treating all client information as totally confidential was near the top of the list of rules. That meant never talking about or even mentioning your client's name in any public place, especially trains or planes.

To avoid being overheard, Jack and I had diligently searched for an empty compartment, where we could talk and work confidentially and uninterrupted. So it was that we were both perturbed on this evening that our private compartment was being invaded, albeit by what seemed to be an absolutely harmless Miss Marples look-a-like.

As the train left the station, Jack and I exchanged knowing glances and silently agreed that under the circumstances our compartment partner was neither a client, competitor, or media representative and would have absolutely no interest in our detailed review of our day's conversations and conclusions. To confirm our decision, Jack scribbled a note to me on his yellow pad, "Our new compartment passenger looks totally disinterested in what we are doing. Let's start our review, Henry."

For about the next hour, Jack and I exchanged information about our day's interviews, reviewed our study issue maps, and summarized which areas we needed to collect additional information about the next day. We discussed our understanding of the division's strategy, management style, staff capabilities, systems facilities, skill inventory, shared values, and overall structure.

As the train approached our final stop, Paddington Station, we began to collect our papers and bundle them into our bulging attaché cases. As it slowed and pulled into the station, our compartment guest, to whom we had not spoken a word during the entire trip, also prepared to detrain.

"Would one of you boys," she asked, "help me with my case, please?"

"We would be delighted to help, ma'am." I responded and proceeded to lift her case from the overhead rack and offer to carry it to the street-end of the station platform where, she explained, she would be met by her son. When the train finally stopped, I dutifully followed our fellow traveler past a handful of people who were waiting to greet incoming passengers.

"Just a bit farther," I was told. "Thank you so much. Oh, there he is, just to the left, waiting for me."

"Hello, Mother," said the man.

As I handed the bag over, my whole body froze in fear with the sudden realization that I knew this person. It was John Sissons, the infamous chairman of the ICI Plastics Division, and our current client.

"Hello, Henry. Hello, Jack," said Mr. Sissons.

"Do you know these boys, John?" asked the kindly Mrs. Sissons.

"Yes, Mother. They are both working for me," explained John

Sissons.

"Well, John, you should be very proud to have these lovely young boys working for you. Not only were they so helpful to me on the train, but from the time the train left Welwyn until it arrived here, these boys worked the entire time, discussing your business problems and how your staff is getting on."

As the full horror of our unprofessional conduct suddenly dawned on us, I began rewriting my C.V.

64

Welcome to Our Guest House

"They've stolen all my clothes!" shouted my American colleague Don McVay, as he charged into my room at ICI's Widnes guesthouse.

"Calm down, Don, no one's taken your clothes. There must be some mistake," I responded.

"My suitcase is empty, Henry. While we were having cocktails downstairs, someone came into my room, opened my case, and took everything!"

"Perhaps your baggage got mixed up and you have someone else's bag?"

"Look," he said as he dragged me across the hall into his room to see the empty suitcase for myself. "See those initials, DMcV—Don

McVay. That is my bag and it's empty!"

"Perhaps you forgot to pack it this morning."

"I don't travel with an empty suitcase, Henry!"

At that moment, a tall, smartly dressed man appeared in the doorway. "May I be of service?" he asked. This, I later learned, was Clarence, the butler.

"All my clothes," Don began, "are gone!"

"I beg your pardon, Sir," Clarence responded in a clipped English accent. "I took the liberty of unpacking your bag, Sir, and I have asked housekeeping to iron your suit. You will find all of your belongings in the bureau. I trust you will find everything in order. And I took the liberty of leaving in your wardrobe a dinner suit and evening shirt. The chairman prefers to dress for dinner."

When Clarence left, Don, in a state of intense skepticism, went over to the bureau and opened the top drawer, I suspect to do a quick count of his underwear, shirts, and socks.

This was my introduction to business travel in the UK on assignment to ICI.

The company guesthouse in Widnes was a historic Elizabethan mansion, Winnington Hall, built in the sixteenth century in a combination Tudor and Georgian style. Each division in ICI had its own guesthouse, where guests of the divisional top management were entertained. Meals were impeccably prepared, stunningly served, and brilliantly supported from an almost unbelievable wine cellar. In fact, Widnes, which was the home of the alkali division, was lovingly referred to by insiders as "the alcohol division." The house had been purchased in 1872 by the original ICI founders, John Brunner and Ludwig Mond, primarily for the land associated with it. They had planned to build a chemical factory there after demolishing the house. In the end, they not only preserved the house but both families took up residence there. Widnes, sited on the country's largest concentration of salt and brine, was in 1933 the laboratory where polyethylene was discovered.

After a long, memorable, and very liquid-enhanced supper, our host brought out some ancient brandy and port. I concluded it was a special treat because when he announced the details of what we were about to drink, I could see a certain incredulous stare from some of the other divisional directors present. Obviously the choice of our after-dinner drink beverage raised our standing in the eyes of the other dinner guests. "Not just your ordinary run-of-the-mill Yanks," one muttered in a slightly noisy stage whisper.

After the statutory cigars and what seemed like an endless round of the port bottle being passed clockwise without ever touching the table, and not much of the brandy left, the chairman cheerfully inquired, "Do either of you lads play billiards or snooker?"

My own thoughts at that point were more along the lines of a comfortable bed and rest, not a long, cigar-supported, boozy evening playing billiards. "I am afraid," I responded as politely as I could, "that this is a skill we have heard about in the colonies but sadly I have had no practical experience."

"Good," the chairman gleefully replied. "We don't play either, but we have a unique alternative, played, as it happens, on a regular snooker table and played nowhere else in the world except in these hallowed halls. We call it, as you might have guessed, Winnington Fives." This was going to be a long evening.

The entire ensemble proceeded to follow the chairman through a mysterious maze of corridors and staircases until we finally emerged into the windowless Winnington Fives room. The only furniture in the room was a full-sized snooker table, lit by what I later learned was a fairly traditional green-shaded battery of lights. There were no cue racks in sight nor was there a snooker score keeper.

The chairman proceeded to explain the finer points of the game to the novitiates. "We like this game because it requires no special skills, no expensive equipment, has a very short learning curve, and since everyone wins there can never be any sore losers or hard feelings."

Why, I wondered, if this is such a great game, can this really be the only place in the world where it is played? Should I ask the editors of *Hoyles* to include it in their next edition?

The chairman continued his explanation as all the rest of the dinner guests began to take off their dinner jackets and carefully roll up their sleeves. "This is the opposite of snooker. The idea is to pot the cue ball. That's the white ball at the end of the table. Each player selects a colored ball as his unique weapon. Instead of using cues, each player can roll, hurl, throw, pitch, fling, or just bowl his ball, trying to pot the cue ball. Alternatively, he can throw his ball at another person's colored ball to foil his position. That's it! Get it?"

Let the games begin, I thought to myself, grabbing an orange ball, one of the only two colored balls left at that point. I had heard all the rules but was totally unclear about such basic things as scoring, turns, penalties, and other details, which I am sure existed when the game was invented but which, over the decades, had been lost in the heat of the actual ensuing competition. In addition, I suspected that each generation invented new rules and regulations without recording them for the next generation of players.

"Don't worry, Henry," the chairman confided. "You'll get the hang of it soon enough."

I began to worry, since this was the first time that I had been called anything but "lad" or "Yank."

At that point, I was astonished to see the condition of the walls. It looked very much like the whole room had been the site for a re-enactment of the battle of Anzio. As soon as several players had taken their turns at hurling their own ball, I began to realize why jackets had been removed and sleeves rolled up. Unlike normal snooker or billiards or even the American pool, there was no time to study the positions of the balls or even contemplate some sort of overall game strategy. There was a premium, obviously, to being able to get to your ball quickly and that usually meant running around the table to reach your weapon. You were able to take your turn while some of the balls were still in motion from the previous turn. The only time I knew it was my turn to play was when I heard, "You're up, Yank."

The explanation for the mortar shell scars on the wall took longer for me to understand. After a while, the notion of just rolling your ball at your competitor or directly at the cue ball was replaced by the much more effective strategy of actually throwing it in the general direction you wanted it to go. A thrown billiard ball landing on a felt-covered granite table made a perfect situation for an imitation of the Barnes Wallis World War II bouncing bomb.

It was a long evening and I ended up with some unexplained black-and-blue marks, a nearly sprained ankle, and a desperate need for fresh air and sleep. The reason I cannot be any clearer on the precise rules of the game is because there weren't any, or perhaps I hadn't been cleared for such highly secret corporate intelligence.

Winnington Fives survived many decades because it was seen as a form of corporate bonding for the divisional board. It obviously outlived its usefulness, however, since there is today no longer an alkali division, ICI has virtually disappeared, and Winnington Hall has been converted by a service company into forty offices for rental. Pity!

65

Where Is Tanzania, Anyway?

"Henry," George declared, "I'm told you're an expert in financial management and control."

As someone who can hardly balance his own checkbook, I found this characterization wildly overstated.

"Not exactly," I responded carefully.

"Well, you've written an excellent chapter on the subject in a book that has been highly recommended to me," he retorted with a twinkle in his eye.

That was how it all began in my office in London on a spring day in 1966.

At the time, George Kahama was the Tanzanian ambassador to

the European Economic Council (EEC), living in Brussels. After three years there, he had just learned that he was to be sent back home to become the managing director of the Tanzanian National Development Corporation or NDC, an industrial conglomerate holding company with over thirty different enterprises in its portfolio, ranging from a diamond mine to an orange juice squeezing factory. George confided to me that he had absolutely no experience in commerce and was terrified at the thought of running such an important conglomerate.

"So, Henry," he exclaimed triumphantly, "you see why I need your help."

My silence prompted him to try another tact. "At least come down and visit for a few days."

I confessed to George that I, frankly, was not sure where Tanzania was but I would be happy to put him in touch with some African experts in financial matters.

George's response was characteristic of his nimble brain. "Henry, Tanzania does not want an African solution. We need to install the best, latest, and most comprehensive financial control system available in the world today. Tanzania has no time for experimenting."

Now it was *my* time to think outside the box. "George, I'm flattered and would dearly love to take up your offer for a visit, but I'm off to Australia next Monday for a client."

"Excellent!" he replied. "Tanzania is practically on your route home."

Since I had already confessed that I did not know where Tanzania was, I was in no position to disagree with him.

"There's a plane from Perth in Australia to Mauritius every week and a direct connection from there to Dar," George proudly announced. And he had in his brief case an East African flight schedule, just in case I might disagree with him.

Before he left, he gave me some NDC papers, a book by President Julius Nyerere, and instructions on how to contact him when I had firmed up my plans.

Immediately, I began thinking how to explain this "side trip" to my office manager, Hugh Parker, and, of course, how to break the news to Alberta that I was going to Africa without her, as she desperately wanted to visit East Africa.

Hugh did not seem very upset. "If you want to waste your time in a country where most people can't even read yet, that's up to you."

Then I spoke to Alberta. I assured her that I had absolutely no intentions of working in Africa and this was just an opportunity to look around.

"I know your look-around missions," Alberta retorted. "You'll be there for at least six months."

I told her that since McKinsey had never worked in a less-developed country and had no experience with economic development institutions, there was no chance that my visit could be converted to a study, even a short one.

She was almost right. Actually, this exploratory visit turned out to be the beginning of a more than six-year involvement, twenty different

What started as a modest organization study for a parastatal entity in Tanzania, in time turned out to be a comprehensive review of the government structure, using over one hundred consultants.

assignments for the president, and the direct involvement of almost one hundred McKinsey consultants from around the world.

Taking an assignment in Tanzania was a high-risk professional decision. It would be the first study McKinsey did in an underdeveloped economy. There was no certainty that I could attract consultants to work in this environment; that we could have any impact; that we would be paid; and that we would have the skill set to understand the complex interplay between the social, economic, and political forces at work in a nation with a per capita income of less than $100 per person but one of the highest literacy rates of any country in Africa.

We must have done some things right. In a picture of the Dar es Salaam office three years after we began, note the standard footwear—bare feet—as well as the efficient transport and all of the happy faces.

It is interesting to note that I had checked the actual air distance between London and Sydney, and Sydney–Dar–London, and to my amazement found there was not much difference. George was right, as usual.

Today, forty-eight years later, George is Sir George, retired in 1995 from the Tanzanian Cabinet after forty years of government service. Today McKinsey & Company has more than thirty offices, employing several thousand consultants, in countries that in 1967 were considered "developing," including five offices in Africa.

While I was working closely with George, our children became very friendly with his family.

66

Paradise Lost

Just two miles from the Tanzanian mainland lay an uninhabited, almost prehistoric-like island paradise called Bongoyo Island. Spectacularly clear water gently washed the almost perfect white sandy beaches that surround it. In the late 1960s, Bongoyo was usually deserted and ideally suited for shelling. Not just any old shell, but cowry shelling.

Cowry, sometimes spelled "cowrie," is the common name for a group of sea snails, marine gastropod mollusks in the family Cypraeidae. The word "cowry" is also used to refer to the shells of these snails, which are often shaped more or less like an egg, except that they are rather flat on the underside.

Many people throughout history have found the rounded, shiny ceramic-like shells of cowries pleasing to look at and handle. Indeed, the term "porcelain" derives from the old Italian term for the cowrie shell (porcellana), due to their similarly translucent appearances. Shells of certain species of cowry have historically been used as currency in several parts of the world and are still used extensively in jewelry and for other decorative and ceremonial purposes.

It was reliably rumored that there were forty-eight different types of cowry shells in the waters around Tanzania. People collected as many species as they could find and displayed them appropriately in

Apparently, 250 species of cowries have been catalogued. Although everyone collected cowry shells, no one had found more than two dozen varieties.

hand-carved wooden cases sold in local shops expressly for display purposes. Our four children had found only about six varieties and we promised one day to take them on a boat ride to search in a secret place for more cowries for their collection.

When Charles Shelton, an associate working with us in Tanzania who had rented a small motorized fishing boat for a few months, heard that we were keen to go to Bongoyo, he offered us his boat for a day trip. I could not refuse this offer, and arranged for our island adventure without thinking much about either the seaworthiness of the boat or my lack of experience in "boatmanship." Had I done so, I would have found that among other things, the boat had no radio, insufficient life preservers, no navigational instruments, and a rather indifferent superstructure. As I had no experience in handling a boat in the Indian Ocean, or in any ocean for that matter, I never bothered to check on the state of either the engine or the hull.

So on a beautiful, clear, calm Sunday, Alberta and I, along with our four children, piled into Charlie's boat, which was conveniently docked at the modest local Dar Yacht Club. A rather weather-beaten blackboard on the dock served as a check-out station, and we all proudly signed our names, together with our destination and expected time of return. Our baggage consisted of lunch, a change of clothing, some simple diving masks and snorkels, and, of course, our cameras to record the historic occasion.

Daniella was an eighteen-foot, locally built wooden-hull motorboat with plenty of room for all of us. Charlie had explained the simple controls. "Turn the key, shift the throttle forward, and steer eastward. You can't miss the island. It's the only one around here and about one hour away. Have a great day!"

He was right.

The one-hour ride to the island was idyllic. Flat sea, no wind, brilliant sunshine, and no other boat traffic.

As the island was deserted, there was no place to berth the boat. "No problem," Charlie had told us. "Just run it up on to the beach." That sounded fine and we did as we were told.

As we jumped off the boat, we were careful to avoid stepping on the colorful coral reef, and the children quickly found a shaded spot under a palm tree for lunch. Searching for cowry shells was the next activity on the agenda and everyone scampered to the edge of the sea, put on their snorkeling equipment, and started to hunt for any of the thirty or so cowry shells that were missing from our collection. In her eagerness to find some new shells, our daughter Susy accidently stepped on a sea urchin. These animals have razor-sharp spikes, some a foot long, to protect them and compensate for their slow movement. In some species, the spikes are also poisonous. Fortunately, none of the ones that broke off in Susy's foot contained the poisonous venom. But in several places, the skin was broken and tiny droplets of blood soon appeared. We all agreed it was time to go home.

Getting back into the boat was not a problem, but we noticed that in the outdoor cabin a small pool of water had accumulated. As I went to start the boat, I felt it would be a good idea to bail out some of the water, which would make the trip back more comfortable for everyone. Alberta tried to use a plastic dish left over from lunch, but it was obvious she was not getting very far. One piece of equipment that *Daniella* was equipped with was a hand-held bailing or bilge pump, which looks very much like a bicycle pump. Alberta tried that next, but it did not make much of a dent either. I suggested that perhaps she was using the bailing pump upside down. That did not seem to be the problem.

As we continued on our way back to the mainland, the water level inside *Daniella* continued to rise quickly. What I did not know then was that in the process of beaching the boat, one of the hull planks had come in contact with some coral and had come loose. That was the reason water was slowly leaking in.

By the time we were several hundred yards out to sea, it was clear that the water would not stop coming into the boat and we feared that in a very short time the boat would sink. It did not take long to make the decision to abandon ship, even with four children aged thirteen, ten, seven, and five. Returning to the island by boat was not a viable option, as we were already very far out to sea. The water in the sea was still flat and seasonably warm, so it was not hard to at least get into it. While there were no life preservers as such, the two seat pads, each about the size of a small cushion, were made of material that floated and seemed designed to be used as floats in case of an emergency. The two little girls had their own floatable armbands. We divided the children. I swam with the boys; Alberta was with the girls. We started to swim for shore, the children clutching their cushions with one arm and swimming with the other arm. I suspect they regarded it as a big adventure, not realizing the serious position we were really in. The decision to abandon boat turned out to be a terrible, almost fatal mistake. Every boat safety instruction manual will tell you to stay with the boat, as they do in movies.

I then made the second big mistake. I decided to swim back to the boat to collect my Nikon camera, leaving Alberta in the water with the four children. People do strange things in emergencies.

I do not think we actually thought we would have to swim all the way to the mainland, which we could see in the distance, perhaps a mile away. Hopefully, someone from the club would notice we were missing, as it was past the time we had said we would return, and they would come out and rescue us. Failing that, a passing boat would see us, find us, haul us on board, and return us to land.

After a while, I made my next big mistake. I yelled over to Alberta that my arms were getting tired. Alberta had been encouraging all of the children to be calm and cheerful, and promising that after this adventure they would no longer have to do any homework for the remainder of the summer. Now she began to wonder how she would cope if I stopped swimming. To add to the desperate situation, Susy's injured foot began to bleed. Fresh blood in shark-infested waters is not recommended.

What saved us was a local lady walking along the faraway shore who spotted us and called the club. At about the same time, a passing boat noticed us, pulled us out of the water, and brought us to shore. How long had we been swimming? Perhaps forty-five minutes—a most agonizing, frightening, horrifying forty-five minutes.

Onshore, a doctor whom we found looked at Susy's foot and

expressed surprise that, having been in shark-infested waters for so long with a bleeding sore, we hadn't attracted any sharks! Perhaps the sharks had already had their dinner.

As we gathered our things from the yacht club dock, the American ambassador of the day and his companion passed us and asked how we were. Alberta was brief but emotional as she described our trauma to the ambassador. "We thought we and all our children were going to drown."

He was preoccupied with his thoughts and only half-listened to our tale of woe, as he then remarked, "That's nice. Enjoy the rest of your day."

Our good friends Emilio, the resident Spanish diplomat, and his wife, Regina, happened to be in the club when we finally arrived there. They kindly invited us all to their home to unwind and relax. When Emilio noticed the Nikon around my neck, he suggested that we quickly get the saltwater out of it before the salt did irreparable damage. Good idea, I thought. But how do you get salt water out of a camera? "Simple!" he said. "First, wash out all the salt with fresh water. Then, let it dry." I didn't have the strength or energy to argue. After thoroughly washing the camera with fresh water, Emilio said it would be fine to "put the camera in the oven, at a low temperature of course, to dry out." If ever there was a half-baked idea, that was it.

In my camera cupboard upstairs, I have a slightly used, salt-encrusted, fully baked Nikon camera that, as you might expect, is way beyond repair. It stands as a reminder to make sure you get your priorities right. Maybe someone on eBay might want one. To compensate for my loss, Alberta later arranged for Emilio to buy a Hasselblad camera for me, as a present from her.

Meanwhile, the local houseboy and chef at Emilio's decided they would extract a few remaining bits of sea urchin spikes from Susy's foot. She vividly remembers walking around the house for the next few hours with a melon tied to her foot.

Later that day, the club called to say that "our" boat had just washed ashore about a mile north of the club, and when could we come and collect it?

"Anyone have Charlie's telephone number?" I asked.

Charlie's somewhat abbreviated career with McKinsey had nothing to do with this episode.

Later that summer, our dear friend and client Michel Romanciano, chief economist at the National Development Corporation, had another adventure in Bongoyo Island. Some friends dropped him on the island so that he could explore its extraordinary caves. Unfortunately, they forgot he was there and so he had to swim all the way back to the mainland.

67

Over and Out

In Tanzania in the early 1970s, one tried to avoid making long-distance trips except by air, unless it was absolutely necessary. The road network was primitive by modern standards. Petrol stations were scarce and often closed. And one was fortunate to average thirty miles per hour on a typical journey. The rail network was essentially turn-of-the-century and only connected two or three of the major population centers. But there existed by then a thriving business in small aircraft charter companies to ferry passengers from the capital, Dar es Salaam, to about a half a dozen towns around the country. Primitive unofficial runways began to spring up around the country, although they were often unusable because of wild animals grazing

By far the best way to explore East Africa was by air.

on them. In addition to the small commercial enterprises, there were a growing number of private planes for hire. Very limited service was also provided by the national carrier.

During our first few years there, most of our professional work was in Dar, so I had only a few opportunities to travel by air around the country.

By 1972, having been in Tanzania for about five years, Alberta had experienced the pleasure herself of being a passenger in some small aircraft in both Tanzania and Kenya. She was immediately hooked on flying. It was much less trouble to hop on a plane then to drive for many hours on dusty, second-class roads.

My own flying career was limited. In 1955, while in the Army, stationed in Frederick, several of us had chipped in and bought a single engine, slightly used plane, an Aeronca Champion, and created the Frederick Flying Club. I am certain that this group has long since been disbanded, but I still have my original share ownership certificate—just in case.

The 1946 Aeronca Champion 7AC ("Champ") was a tail wheel airplane, also known as "conventional gear." It had room only for two seats, in a tandem (fore and aft) configuration. It used a center stick instead of a yoke, and was unique, a Sport Pilot-qualified airplane. This meant that it was legal to fly it with only a Sport Pilot certificate. Since it had no electrical system, one had to start it by hand propping. As far as I can remember, it looked as if it were made with toothpicks, held together with Super Glue and covered with tissue paper.

I never really enjoyed flying and so it was not surprising that I dismissed Alberta's interest as a Walter Mitty moment that would soon go away. But one day, after flying to the Ifakara Tropical Research Center and back with Sam Koechlin in a Piper Cherokee, her passion for flying was rekindled.

Shortly after that, Alberta mentioned to our guests at a dinner party that I was being unreasonable, in this day and age of women's rights, by preventing her from learning to fly. "If Alberta wants to take flying lessons," our guests agreed, "you must allow her to do so."

I replied, "I don't want to stifle her urge to learn new skills, but learning to fly here strikes me as a high-risk activity. And I am afraid she will kill herself."

I don't recall formally changing my mind but before we had even finished dinner, Alberta excused herself from the table, contacted our friendly pilot, Chick Ehrhorn, and arranged to have her first lesson. She was desperately keen to get started right away.

Chick explained that the next day was impossible, but he could arrange for a one-hour lesson the day after.

Chick never made the appointment.

On August 25, 1972, Chick's Cherokee with seven people on board crashed. All eight people were killed. Chick, a qualified DC 8 pilot with thousands of flying hours, knew very well that the Cherokee was designed for only six people.

When the news reached Alberta, her knees turned to jelly. She never again raised the question of flying lessons, and began looking for less risky forms of entertainment. Bridge, anyone?

THE WRECKAGE of the aircraft after it crashed at Mkamba.

4 crash victims to be cremated

Bodies of the four West Germans of the seven tourists killed in a plane crash on Wednesday at Mkamba, some 120 kilometres from Dar es Salaam, will be cremated this morning in the capital.

The body of the pilot, Mr. Charles "Chick" Ehrhorn, an American was cremated in the city yesterday evening.

An official of the French Embassy said yesterday that they were still contacting relatives of their two nationals in Nairobi and France to give a word concerning the burial.

An official of the Federal Republic of Germany Embassy confirmed yesterday that the bodies were identified as those of Mr. and Mrs. Molpe, Mr. Schmidt and Mr. Meyer.

The bodies of Mr. and Mrs. Toussaint, all French were still lying at Muhimbili mortuary yesterday.

A full report is to be submitted soon by the Directorate of Civil Aviation's accident investigator, Mr. K.R.Grant, who visited the scene of the accident yesterday morning.

"Chick", who had 2,000 flying hours' experience, was employed by Ker, Downey and Selby Safari Ltd, a Nairobi based hunting company, a month ago.

Alberta's flight instructor's untimely death (the day before she was scheduled to have her first lesson) was big news in Dar es Salaam.

529

68

Snake Eyes

Tanzania in the late 1960s proved to be a great place for partying and entertainment, albeit not in the same way we celebrated in London. Gather a few friends, go down to the beach, buy some freshly caught lobster or crab from a local dhow fisherman, order some strips of filet mignon (which was cheaper than chicken), fire up the "barbie," usually just a drum cut in half, with some holes in it, throw the lobster and meat on the fire, add freshly picked corn and unpeeled potatoes, and enjoy the glorious African sun shining over the Indian Ocean.

On special occasions or for overseas visitors, we would arrange some local entertainment. One could have local steel drum bands,

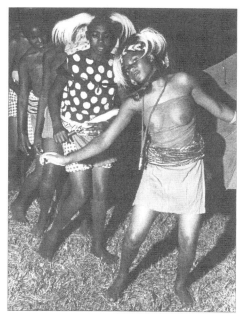

Tanzanians really know how to throw a birthday party.

native dancers, flame eaters, acrobats, or various combinations of the above. For our four seasoned "African hands," the food became the secondary attraction to the fascinating entertainment.

We did not need a special occasion to have a big celebration bash. In addition to all our friends, colleagues, clients, foreign ambassadors, and members of the government, the children were allowed to invite some of their friends. We usually bribed the children by hinting that in addition to great food, music, and dancing, we were planning some surprises.

On one occasion, I remember very well the surprise was on me. It was not my birthday in August, but I think that is the way the party was billed. I was working late that afternoon and it was only after David Reid came into my office and in a most sincere voice told me, "Henry, you better get home right away!" His voice had a distinct quiver and I deduced that whatever it was, it was serious.

Alberta had bought some recently imported Chinese lanterns and at one end of the garden friends had improvised a very amateurish platform that would, after dinner, double as a stage. Our neighbors had provided extra picnic tables and benches, and other friends had contributed a supply of iron tubs full of drinks to suit everyone's taste.

I was truly surprised when I arrived home to find a garden full of thirsty guests waiting to toast me and make me feel at home. As the dress code in Dar was almost always casual, I was appropriately

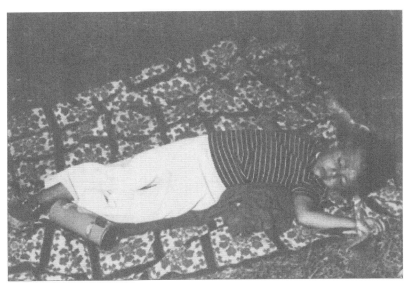

Jennifer had to take a little rest before the snake charmers arrived.

dressed when I arrived and ready to party.

After the feast, we all settled down to watch the entertainment. Well, most of us did. I suspect Jennifer had had too much Ribena or apple juice, and dropped off for a rest saying, "Could you wake me up when the surprise comes?"

We had fire-eaters, dancers, and drummers, all passionately doing their enchanting original routines. And as we had promised, we woke Jennifer before the snake charmers appeared. The group from a nearby village brought their own snakes in straw baskets (the baskets also served as laundry hampers). They briefly described each snake, pointing out that they were all deadly and we should not come too close or try to touch them. I have a vivid memory of one enormous python, as fat as a rubber tire, that required several bearers for its "performance." It was a real spectacle and lived up to our billing it as a special treat—especially when they fed him live rodents, and we all watched with amazement as they disappeared in a single swallow.

As the evening ended, the entertainers gathered up their props, coaxed their long friends back into their baskets, and drove off home.

Several hours later, one of their leaders returned, looking worried.

"Is there something wrong?" I asked.

"Well," he sheepishly replied, somewhat embarrassed, "there might be. You see, Bwana Nkubwa, we seem to be missing three snakes."

What followed was an extraordinary flashlight-assisted hunt for the ectothermic, amniote vertebrates, aka snakes, covering every inch of our garden and the ground floor of our house. When none were found, it was suggested that they must not have counted very well. The search party was over, but our concern and fear was not.

Two days later, as I was about to fill the trunk of the car with groceries, we found our three slightly bewildered and traumatized snakes. All were well and soon reunited with their masters.

As far as I can recall, that was the first and last entertainment at our home with snakes.

Our years in Africa from 1967 to 1974 were a great, memorable adventure for the whole family. Left to right, Susy, Juma, Jennifer, Geoffrey, *and* David, *in front.*

PART IX
I ALMOST FORGOT TO
TELL YOU

Afterthoughts

Introduction
When Is Enough, Enough?

In *The Agony and Ecstasy*, Pope Julian is concerned about how long Michelangelo is taking to complete the Sistine Chapel. He asks, "When will it be done?"

Charlton Heston boldly replies, "It will be finished when it is finished."

After several years, I was encouraged to finish my literary effort, even though there is much more to write. These stories didn't fit neatly into the other vignettes, so I decided to include them in their own bespoke niche.

It was less expensive to stay on our honeymoon in Europe than come back to New York and face the real world.

69

The Mail Must Go Through
... even on a honeymoon!

It was Richard Brilliant, my brother's close friend and a professor emeritus of ancient history at Columbia University, who first mentioned to me the tranquility, beauty, and serenity of Puerto de Soller, on the northern shore of the island of Majorca. At the time, while still very unattached and with no particular prospects in sight, I remember thinking it sounded like a perfect place for a honeymoon.

After Alberta and I were married in 1958, our first two nights together (we were rather old-fashioned) were spent at the Playhouse Inn in New Hope, Pennsylvania, where we had the most expensive room in the house—imagine, $12.50 per night. Outrageous!

I am certain that Richard would have been very surprised to learn we actually did go to Majorca. With the exception of Majorca, Copenhagen, and London, we had no fixed plans for our honeymoon, which in the end lasted for three months. "We will just have a general look around," I explained to Alberta, "and stop whenever there is something worthwhile or interesting to do or see."

In fact, we have been doing that for more than fifty-five years wherever we go!

The family was not particularly pleased to have us away for so long without knowing where we were or how to get in touch with us. Remember this was 1958—the Dark Ages as far as communications were concerned. We found a solution—Poste Restante—public mailboxes where people could pick up their mail while on the road. Through its worldwide network of offices, American Express used to store and hold mail addressed to members and marked, "HOLD FOR ARRIVAL." In fact, this service is still available today. We found the American Express public mailboxes a perfect solution, except we had no idea which cities we would be in on any date.

After a two-week rest at the Hotel Esplendido in Puerto de Soller, we decided we had better get a start on our unplanned European odyssey. Our first stop was Barcelona. It was a little bit of a shock to find ourselves in a busy metropolis after vegetating in the serenity of Puerto de Soller. But it was fascinating to play tourist for a while and discover marvelous world-class museums, spectacular unfinished churches, and Miro sculptures all over the beautiful parks.

After a few days of visiting the prescribed sights, I suggested we might check at the American Express office to see if we had any mail. As the likelihood of anyone actually bothering to write to us was slim, we put off checking for a few days. Then, by complete chance—well, almost chance—we found ourselves in front of the main American Express office in Barcelona one afternoon.

"Perhaps," I suggested, "we should just check and see if we have any mail waiting for us." Although she was positive there would be no mail for us, to humor me, Alberta agreed to inquire.

When the clerk behind the counter handed Alberta a letter, addressed to her with an American stamp on it, she was understandably astonished. Astonishment turned to utter disbelief when she thought she recognized the handwriting—mine.

It was not difficult for me to plead total ignorance.

It did not take long for Alberta to open the letter and indeed discover that it was in my handwriting. Unfortunately, the contents were private and romantic and so must remain confidential. Needless to say, besides welcoming my new bride to Barcelona, I recall a few words reminding her of my everlasting love and unequivocal devotion, and looking forward to a passionate and eventful life together, full of adventure, challenges, and lots of children.

After Barcelona, the ritual of visiting the American Express offices to check the mail became almost the first thing we did when we arrived in a new city. I can specifically recall that the offices in Milan, Paris, Geneva, London, and Copenhagen all had letters waiting for Alberta. I did promise *some* day to explain how I was able to pull off this magic.

On second thought, perhaps I will wait for a few more years. There are still lots of American Express Poste Restante in Europe to which we have not yet been and that Alberta needs to check out.

I am sure there are still a few more letters waiting for Alberta at various American Express offices in Europe, since I had not provided a return address.

70

The Day I Nearly Gave Up Skiing

It was Sam Koechlin's idea. "You've been skiing on the same slopes in Wengen for years," he told me one day. "Why don't you try something different? Ski touring. It's a thrill you'll never forget." I did not.

At the time, I had only a vague idea of what ski touring was. Since the Internet had not yet been invented, I did not have access to Wikipedia to check on what I was agreeing to do. How would I have reacted if I could have read the Wikipedia description, "Ski touring requires cardiovascular fitness, mental toughness, and a firm understanding of mountain craft"?

Since I would not have had any of what seem to be the basic

requirements, I suspect I would have given the whole idea a "miss" at the outset. If I had felt it would be a worthwhile challenge, the next paragraph would have certainly put me off it: "Touring involves navigating and route-finding through potential avalanche terrain, and often requires familiarity with meteorology along with skiing skills. For advocates who possess the skills to enter safely the backcountry in the winter, the rewards of touring can be exceptional."

When I discovered that our trusty local Swiss School in Wengen ran occasional day ski-touring excursions from the Jungfrau for intermediate skiers, I decided for once not to be a wimp and to sign up. When I was given the list of equipment suggested for the trip, perhaps I should have reconsidered. First, you needed "skins" to attach to the bottom of your skis while walking uphill. "What is this 'walking uphill'?" I thought. I assumed we were going *down* from the Jungfrau, not up. Skins on your skis are meant to keep you from slipping downhill as you are going uphill. While you could use your own skis, you needed special bindings that allowed you to lift your heels while walking—again, that "walking" term.

The rest of the kit was more straightforward. Sunscreen, special for Alpine conditions—number 75 was suggested or absolutely necessary if you didn't want to get fourth degree burns; light, warm, windproof clothing—a somewhat ominous combination; dark Alpine sunglasses—the ones that look like swimming goggles were suggested; extra warm clothing in case the weather changes; and, of course, a suitable lightweight rucksack; and plenty of water, lip wax, silk inner gloves, hand warmers, and a compass.

If all that did not put me off, the planned schedule should have. The meeting time for the group was at the Wengen railroad station at 6:30 a.m., ready to board the first train for the almost two-hour trip to the top of the Jungfrau.

And the instructions concluded that we should plan to be home before 6:30 p.m.

The next sign, which I did not read or interpret correctly, was the list of people who had signed up for the trip. Besides the guide and me, there was only one other entry, SCDO—Ski Club Darmstadt Odenwald. It turned out there were seventeen of them, all of whom I am sure got to the station at six just so that they would not miss the train. The other ominous sign was that the whole group looked like Olympic triathlon stars, even in their ski-touring outfits. They all wore their club jackets, liberally sprinkled with badges of their various previous hiking and skiing conquests.

After about thirty-five minutes, we arrived at Kleine Scheidegg and were greeted by a beautiful sunrise and a cloudless sky—both good omens—finally. Then we took a second train for the hour-long journey to Jungfraujoch. On the way up, Hans (all Swiss mountain guides are called "Hans") gave us our first briefing. His message of welcome was short and to the point. First, he explained, it would be a glorious trip and the weather was perfect—sunny, not too hot, and windless. Second, his plan was that after a short rest at the Jungfrau we would get started right away so that we could reach Concordia Platz in time for lunch. Each of the group was then issued a small parcel that contained a specially prepared extra-light, high-altitude, high-energy lunch. From Concordia Platz, rather than staying overnight at the well-frequented, highly popular Alpine hut, we would descend for 38 kilometers down to Goppenstein, from which we would take the train back to Wengen. The way down was, he explained, essentially an intermediate run except for two or three slopes, which were a bit more challenging.

Soon we were all at the starting point getting our equipment, rucksacks, and courage together. In front of us was a pure white carpet of virgin snow nestled between two glorious mountain peaks and stretching as far as the eye could see—perhaps as far as Geneva. The oddest part about the vista was that it seemed practically flat but with a clearly noticeable downhill gradient. So much for the walking, I thought. This vision was confirmed when Hans said there was no need to put on our skins at this point.

My German colleagues were anxious to get started, so there were only a few minutes for taking in the beauty of the view and snapping a few photos. This "anxiousness" seemed to be a characteristic of the whole group—almost as if they had to catch a plane to get home.

At about 8:30, beneath a cloudless sky and a temperature of -5 Centigrade, we began our journey. I was pleasantly surprised to find the snow perfect and the piste ever so slightly downhill. The next moments turned out to be the best part of the trip. I was immediately struck with the breathtaking beauty of being in this valley between two rocky peaks and the total absence of any sound—almost as if one were in a vacuum. I later figured out that one reason for being breath-taking was that we were at 3,454 meters above sea level (11,716 feet).

Not wanting to interfere with any club rules, I dutifully took up my position at the rear of the line of German skiers—a sort of unofficial sweeper-upper. After about a half-hour, Hans instructed the group to take a break and put on their skins.

As I looked ahead, I was certain there was some mistake because there was absolutely no indication of any uphill. In fact, the reverse was true. It seem that the gentle descent would continue until we got to Spitz.

It is hard to be clear at what happened next except that the group, in much the same line-up as before, began to move ahead. It became clear after a few minutes that this part of the trip was not going to be as easy as the first half-hour or so. To my everlasting surprise and despair, the apparent downhill slope turned out to be an optical illusion. In fact, I was later told by a reliable source that the slope is between 4 and 6 percent for the entire route up to the Concordia Platz. That does not sound much, but a combination of the altitude, being out of shape, and not expecting to do such hard work melded together into a potential nightmare. Climbing uphill on skis is a unique experience. The only way you know you have, in fact, been going uphill at all is when you are certain that if you take one more step your lungs will either explode or completely deflate. While I was moving, slowly but steadily, my German colleagues must have been going at twice my speed, and as a result they soon became a thin line so far ahead of me that it was clear I would never catch up with them—and I didn't.

Soon Hans was by my side encouraging me not to rush. I was hardly rushing, more like surviving, and he assured me it was all right to stop and take a rest. Well, I rested then and I think every twenty minutes or so thereafter. Hans explained that I should just follow the tracks until I got to the Platz, where the rest of the group would be waiting to have lunch.

By the time I got to our rendezvous, my colleagues had already finished eating and were waiting anxiously for me to gobble down my high-energy lunch so that we could get to the piece de resistance—the 38-kilometer, totally off-piste downhill ski run.

Then the absolutely unexpected happened. While up to now the sky had been cloudless, from nowhere, or so it seemed, dark clouds began to gather (why do clouds always "gather"?) and there was a hardly perceptible but extremely light snow shower. Hans took this opportunity to explain that high up in the mountains, it was not unusual for the weather to change quickly and dramatically. This was going to be one of those not-unusual occasions.

"We need to ski down the mountain together very carefully," Hans explained. "While the terrain is not difficult, from now on the light will get much worse and I will ask you all to follow me as close as possible so that no one gets lost in the snow, fog, or poor light." Yes, sir, I responded silently. Hans was then on the phone checking the weather conditions, and we could tell from his expressions that there was no good news.

The descent from Lotschen Pass—a total of 8,500 feet—should have taken no more than two hours. As the storm began to get worse, I think everyone's concern was just to get down safely irrespective of the clock.

As we began our trip down, it was clear to me that something was up with my colleagues. Apparently a number of the macho club members took a dim view of skiing downhill carefully behind an uber-concerned Swiss mountain guide on what was one of the greatest pistes in Switzerland. No way were they just going to follow Hans. They would find their own way down. After all, they had not come a long way for this trip just to crawl down the mountain. And besides, the visibility was not that bad. This was more a drizzle than a blizzard. So, as Hans led the group down to the village of Brig in an ever-so-slow descent, a number of the German club members decided to make their own trail down the deep powder snow. After a while, perhaps thirty minutes, those of us behind Hans froze in our tracks as a blood-curdling scream broke the otherwise perfect silence.

One of the non-conformists who had decided to go on his own way had disappeared from view. We were soon relieved when our worst fear, that he had gone over a cliff, proved wrong. Instead of a cliff, our daring club member had fallen into what seemed like a deep crevasse and was screaming for help. These crevasses were, in fact, huge cracks in the ice and snow.

I never saw exactly how big—wide or deep—the crevasse was, but Hans knew exactly where it was and what to do. First, he made sure that the rest of us were well away from the edge. Than he unpacked his rucksack and pulled out a lot of rope, to which was attached some gadget—a sort of sky hook—that would catch the victim or his clothing and pull him out. While the snow continued to fall and the sky darkened, Hans and a handful of us pulled out the terrified

Crevasse hazards and dangerous turns are not marked on alpine ski trails.

skier, Fritz. Miraculously he had survived the plunge by landing on his skis on a plateau. Hans phoned a helicopter to come and take him down the mountain but, unfortunately, the weather had grounded all aircraft and so Fritz would have to ski down like the rest of us.

It was after two o'clock by the time we got on our way again, and the weather was getting worse. Once again, Hans led the way, pleading with everyone to stay in line and follow him. There was no question that without Hans leading, we would not get off the mountain.

The second "Fritz" was not as lucky as the first. He did not fall into a crevasse. His accident occurred when, instead of following our single line, he decided to take a parallel track perhaps twenty feet to one side of us. He unfortunately hit some ice that he could not have seen because of the new-fallen snow. He had a bad fall through the ice and his leg was twisted badly; we soon discovered that he had broken it in several places. He was in terrible pain.

Our options at this point were limited and none of them were particularly appealing. We soon discounted the obvious one of leaving poor Fritz alone and let him either roll or crawl down to Brig, some 30-odd kilometers away. That was only marginally better than letting him lie in snow and freeze to death. I was sure the club would have been delighted in time to erect a statue in his memory to mark the spot.

While the idea of each of us taking turns carrying Fritz on our backs seemed more creative, it was realistically impossible despite what one may have seen in the movies. Apart from the fact that Fritz was a hefty chap, it was folly to think any of us could navigate the trail in these conditions carrying him on his back.

What happened next can only be called a miracle.

Hans, as if he had been in this situation many times, once again undid his rucksack and this time took out two stretcher aluminum braces. Each brace was then neatly attached to the front and back of Fritz's skis with a heavy-duty thumbscrew. Over this rectangular frame, Hans stretched what looked like a rubberized envelope. Hans had created a stretcher. In a flash, we moved Fritz onto the stretcher, pumped some brandy and schnapps into him, and found various clothes to cover him so that he would not freeze. I think Hans also administered some pain-killing drugs, either orally or via an injection.

I was still not clear what would happen next. The patient was out of the snow, feeling no pain, and was protected from the elements. While I did not notice it then, I later saw that Hans had also created a temporary splint and bound Fritz's leg to stop movement. What now? Do we just aim the newly created sled down the hill, give him a gentle push and hope that Fritz on his new sled follows the fall line directly to the Bahnhof at the bottom of the mountain? The thought of a man with a broken leg hurtling down a Cresta-like run at 90 kilometers per hour with no brakes on his stretcher, or sled, was too awful to contemplate.

If it were not for our mountain guide's quick thinking and experience, Hans would never have made it to the bottom of the mountain.

As we all were thinking what next, speedy Hans had attached four ropes to each of the four corners of the sled and began to explain the next step in the rescue process. Indeed, the sled would be used to transport Fritz to Brig, but he would need our help. Hans chose those he decided were the strongest and best skiers, and explained what we had to do.

He created four teams of two each. Each of the first two teams would take a rope, attached to the fronts of the skis, and steer the sled down the hill. The other two teams would be at the rear of the sled, basically slowing or braking the sled down the hill. I do not know why I was chosen for one of these braking assignments. Perhaps because he saw how well I was able to snowplow.

Slowing down a makeshift sled with a 200-pound patient on a slope that may have been twenty degrees, even for four able-bodied men, seemed a totally unachievable task. But the alternatives were certainly unthinkable.

There was little time for trying to find an excuse to be declared unfit for duty. The obvious excuses—it's too cold, my goggles are fogging up, my toes are frost-bitten, I have a bad shoulder—I knew would not work. So, with little ceremony, off we went.

The next four hours, as Churchill once said, "will live in infamy." Four hours of snowplowing in a blinding storm, down an unknown off-piste trail, in failing, flat light, and at the same time holding back (braking) deadweight of perhaps 100 kilos can hardly be defined as a pleasant winter sport.

For the non-skier readers, let me explain something about the snowplow position, which the International Ski Association should outlaw. Your skis form an inverted "V," which you hold by pushing the skis and snow away from you, instantly causing extreme pain to your knees and thighs. In the kids' ski school this is called the "pizza position." The orthopedic surgeons must love it.

With eight people involved, the only time one could stop to rest was when Hans felt some pity for those of us at the rear. Unfortunately this was not often enough.

We did make it to our final destination, the Bahnhof in Blatten. Fritz had his leg looked after and is now probably an Olympic pole-vault champion. As we waited to board the train, several of the SCDO Club members came up to me and graciously offered their sincere thanks for my help. There was no talk of building an appropriate monument for the overweight American who helped save their buddy. When they suggested that they would make me an honorary member of the club and send me a complimentary club jacket, I said thank you very much but it would never match my ski trousers.

I was hoping that when I finally got to Wengen, I would find someone who would buy my skis and poles for ten dollars.

It seems a shame to give up after trying to learn for sixty-five years.

71

Wrapping It Up

Producing this volume has been a challenging, totally absorbing, riveting task. What started as a final examination paper for an Open University TV course in "How To Write a Family History" has, in fact, become a family history. In almost 100,000 words and about 150 photographs, I have tried to stitch together the complex, often tragic mosaic of some of the most memorable events in my family's past. The resulting product is a selected collection of family legends, reminiscences, and adventures over several decades and spanning three continents.

I am certain that all writers of autobiographies regard their finished product as "work in progress" and so do I. As I look back on the period I have written about, I realize that by starting with individual segments or events and then trying to piece them together, many gaps in the story will have to be patched together by means of the imagination of the reader.

Most perceptive readers will quickly see that I have barely touched on events during the past fifty years. Alberta, the children, and grandchildren are hardly mentioned. This is not an omission by mistake; it is rather a conscious decision to leave something for a second volume. Perhaps for this effort, Alberta will join me as a co-author!

ACKNOWLEDGEMENTS

Two Ceramic Horses on a Cracked Base began as a personal collection of anecdotes based on randomly selected family photographs. Friends and relatives to whom I sent some of these "mini-sagas" suggested that I collect them and publish them as a "surrogate" family history.

Once I started to stitch together the stories I had written, I discovered enormous gaps not only in reliable accounts of our family history but in my own personal memories. I contacted some existing family members to begin to fill in the many holes in our family history. Some were filled but most remained blank or at best fit a category I would call "legends." If a legend about a particular event or fact was repeated more than once with essentially the same details, I concluded that it was accurate. If I received conflicting or disparate inputs, I made a calculated choice based on the likelihood of the event happening. I thank all those who contributed to my journey of discovery. I am certain that after reading my interpretations, many will send me their own versions of people and events. My immediate family was not shy in correcting my recollections of family events, even though in some cases they were not directly involved or even born.

Without the help of Meliza Amity, the history of the paternal side of my family would have remained essentially blank. Meliza has undertaken a massive effort to catalogue, trace, document, and assemble the history of most of the original Jewish families in Finland. She has woven these stories together and created a remarkable user-friendly web site with superb photos, fascinating references, and remarkable summaries. As a result of her work, I discovered about 400 relatives about whose existence I was totally unaware.

I decided once I had started that I needed professional advice with my efforts. I found Kitty Axelson-Berry and Alison de Groot, my editors not in New York or London but rather in a modest office on Main Street in Amherst, Massachusetts. Needless to say, their help was essential to the preparation of this book. They were patient, understanding, and knowledgeable about the whole process of moving from idea to final publication. In addition, they were extremely understanding of my obvious literary limitations, which include being dyslexic, an inveterate dreadful speller, and speaking English only as my third language.

Of course my biggest supporter, helper, and advisor was Alberta. As a former professional editor, she took me under her wing and rescued me from dangling participles, split infinitives, and the devilish subjunctive contrary to fact phrases. She discovered many mistakes, found gaps in my memory of some events, and raised questions I never would have thought of on my own. She read numerous drafts so often that I suspect she could recite some of them from memory. But she did much more. While others hinted that I should write my family story, Alberta was the driving force behind my actually undertaking this in the first place—and ensuring that I stuck with it to the bitter end.

Anyone trying to write about historical events needs a reliable historian to call upon to confirm, correct, or adjust factual data and provide necessary background information. I had three main sources upon whom to draw. Our own religious leader, Rabbi Thomas Salamon, made certain my Jewish history, culture, and traditional practices were accurate. Professor Xu Xin from Nanjing University in China filled in some gaps in my story of Jewish life in China. And Professor David Ben Canaan at Heilonjiang University in Harbin helped me understand better the reality underlying the exodus of the Jewish population from Harbin after almost thirty years of peaceful coexistence with the native population.

I felt it was important to make extensive use of photographic and other documentary evidence. Since it was not the custom in most families to annotate photographs with either dates or names, I was forced to make some educated guesses about the identities of people in several photos, some over 110 years old, in my archives. While one would hope for accuracy in original documents, often, especially during periods of extreme political and economic upheaval, this was not the case.

For the historic photos of Jewish Helsinki I am deeply indebted to the Jewish Archives of the National Archives of Finland, which gave me permission to use photos from its collection. These pictures, I believe, provide an important dimension to our history as it unfolded.

I, of course, take personal responsibility for the contents of my narrative. I already had a complaint regarding one event that I wrote about and in which I was personally involved. The complainer in this case remembers the details completely differently from what I clearly recall. In this case we can only agree to differ. If I have misrepresented some person or persons, or inaccurately interpreted some events, I apologize unreservedly, and hope not to have done anyone an injustice or to have caused any unnecessary anguish.

•